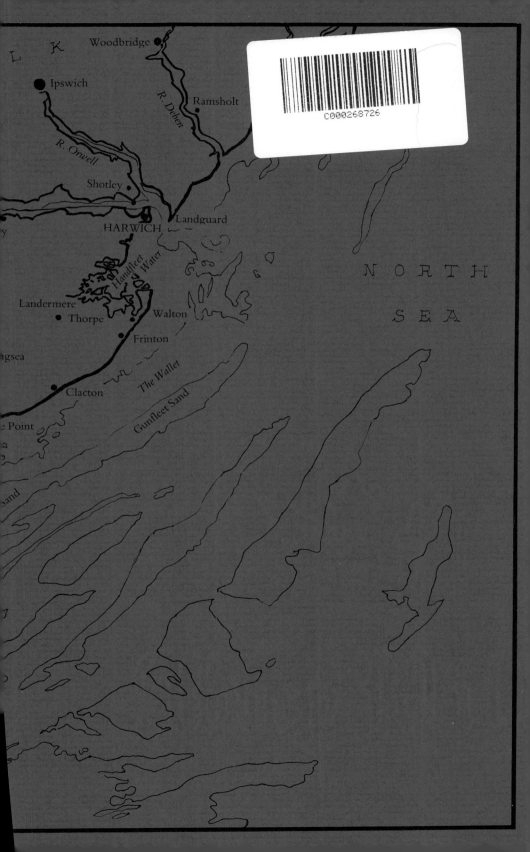

THE SMUGGLERS' CENTURY

A late eighteenth century Revenue cutter.

THE SMUGGLERS' CENTURY

The story of smuggling
on the Essex coast, 1730 - 1830

HERVEY BENHAM

ESSEX RECORD OFFICE · CHELMSFORD

OTHER BOOKS BY HERVEY BENHAM.

Last Stronghold of Sail (Harrap 1947, reprint 1981).
  Stories of the Colne and Blackwater.

Down Tops'l (Harrap 1951, reprint 1971).
  The story of the East Coast sailing barges.

Once Upon a Tide (Harrap 1955, reprint 1971).
  East Coast Shipping in the 18th and 19th centuries.

Two Cheers for the Town Hall (Hutchinson 1964).
  A Study of the structure of local public affairs before re-organisation, based on Colchester.

Some Essex Water Mills (Essex County Newspapers 1976; second edition 1983, Mersea Bookshop).
  The mills of the Colne, Chelmer and Blackwater, and the coastal tide mills.

The Stowboaters (Essex County Newspapers 1977).
  The story of the Thames Estuary sprat and whitebait fishermen.

The Codbangers (Essex County Newspapers 1979).
  The story of the Icelandic and North Sea Cod Fishermen in the days of sail.

The Salvagers (Essex County Newspapers 1980).
  The story of wreck and rescue on the Essex coast.

The Big Barges (with Roger Finch; Harrap 1983).
  The story of the 'boomies', schooners, ketches and square rigged barges.

Essex County Newspapers titles are now distributed by Boydell Press Ltd., P.O. Box 9, Woodbridge, Suffolk.

First published by Essex Record Office, County Hall, Chelmsford, CM1 1LX.
© Hervey Benham, 1986.
Essex Record Office Publication No. 94

Reprinted 1987

I.S.B.N. 0 900360 67 4

Printed by Anchor Brendon Ltd., Tiptree, Essex.

Contents

MoDE of Carrying Tubs

Tubs were roped in pairs for slinging across a horse, and also across a carrier's shoulders.

Illustrations by Roger Finch

Other illustrations

Decorative illustrations on other pages are from *Smuggling Days and Smuggling Ways*, 1892. (See Preface.)

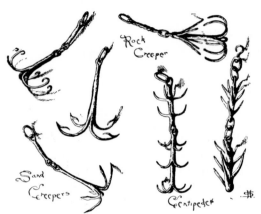

Grapnels, or creepers, for recovering sunken contraband, were made to various patterns.

Preface

THE primary sources for the study of smuggling are the Customs' Letterbooks containing the correspondence between the Board and its outports, and the Treasury Papers, both housed in the Public Record Office at Kew. The former are dealt with in detail in the Introduction. The latter are easier of access, being calendared and indexed, and so have been more often used, but their evidence is fragmentary. Their Lordships at Treasury Chambers exercised such a tight control over the Customs that they saw fit to issue a warrant every time one boatman replaced another in some obscure outport. These voluminous records are therefore peppered with such trivia, incongruously interspersed among affairs of State, but few items of importance were discussed and minuted. The *Victoria History of Essex* (vol 2) used this source for its inevitably scrappy reference to smuggling, including a quite fallacious assumption that a Revenue cutter transferred from Aldeburgh to the Essex coast in 1730 was the first of her kind in the county. The Treasury Papers have, however, revealed one or two items (including the kidnapping of Lisle, the Colchester Riding Officer, which does not seem to be mentioned in the Customs' Letterbooks.) Those disposed to hunt about in this bran tub may discover other titbits.

These sources have been supplemented by references to local papers – chiefly the *Ipswich Journal, Chelmsford Chronicle, Suffolk Chronicle, Colchester Gazette* and *Essex Standard*. The story of the smugglers as Crown debtors has drawn on the Quarter Sessions rolls at Essex Record Office, which has also provided the records of the Vice-Admiralty, the 168-year old note of the examination of Philip Sainty, and the original Letter of Marque and Muster Rolls of Captain Munnings' schooner *Courier*. As ever, Miss Nancy Briggs and her staff at the Record Office have been of unfailing assistance, as have Mr Philip Gifford and Miss Jane Dansie at Colchester Public Library, where a manuscript transcript of the memorials in St Nicholas Church, Harwich, has served to check and supplement many biographical details. Above all, however, I am grateful to Mr Graham Smith, librarian of the Customs & Excise, for much personal help and guidance, as well as for that contained in his own books referred to below, and to one of his predecessors in that office, the late Mr R C Jarvis, who apprenticed me to the whole subject over thirty years ago.

The only previous excursions into this particular aspect of smuggling

1

have been in my own *Once Upon a Tide*, and, to a less extent, *Last Stronghold of Sail*. I have as far as possible sought to avoid allowing material to make a second appearance, but I have had to repeat some of the fundamentals. For the general background I have relied chiefly on H N Shore; *Smuggling Days and Smuggling Ways* (1892 – and still the liveliest authoritative picture, though dealing only with the South Coast); Atton & Holland: *The King's Customs* (Murray 1905); Graham Smith: *Something to Declare* (Harrap 1980): and *King's Cutters* (Conway Maritime Press 1983); David Phillipson: *Smuggling: a History* 1700–1970 (David & Charles 1973); and Keble Chatterton: *King's Cutters and Smugglers* (Allen 1912). Readers interested in the constructional details of the Revenue cutters, the pay of their officers and the arguments with the Navy over the wearing of pennants will find these dealt with by Chatterton, who based his history on the orders from the Board of Customs, illustrating it with incidents from various outport records.

Graham Smith's similarly named *King's Cutters* provides a broader-based background to my localised account. To the extent that it covers the same ground (for example concerning the Revenue cutters *Repulse, Swift* and *Walpole*) some minor discrepancies will be found, which go to show the variations which may occur in the interpretation of material so rich and diffuse. The different views of the contract system do, however, deserve explanation. I have parted company with Mr Smith, and indeed with all those who have written on the subject, in my conclusion that the Revenue cutters were not owned by the contractors and leased to the Customs, but were owned by the Customs and operated on a 'management contract'. I base my theory on the fact that I find no references to the sale of cutters, or shares in them, when contracts changed hands, in whole or in part, nor when the contract system ended. Moreover, the cutters were not registered, as were the North Sea packets, which were indeed the property of their commanders who leased them to the Post Office, but this may be because the Registration Act was passed in 1786, only two years before the Customs ended the contract system.

Philip Benton's gorgeously gossipy *History of the Rochford Hundred* provides some background for that salty corner of the county, including the role of Thomas Howgego Bennewith, the informer at the seizure by the Foulness boatmen, as second to his brother Robert in the brutal prize-fights which were a feature of that island's life. Benton also quotes from the diary of John Loten, who died at Leigh in 1815, aged sixty-three, after serving for thirty-three years as Collector there. This suggests that Leigh had its own Collector and Comptroller in the eighteenth century, for Thomas Lee (who died in 1765, aged thirty), William King (who died in 1783, aged thirty-one) and William Henry King (who died in 1858, aged seventy) are all described on their tombstones as 'late Collector of HM Customs in this Port', while Thomas Simpson (who died in 1814, aged fifty-nine) was Comptroller. The contemporary record, however, reveals that William King was in 1776 actually appointed as Surveyor, and Collector and Receiver of Coal Duties. The latter was a very minor function, but was perhaps regarded as an excuse to claim the grander title.

In addition to published sources identified in footnotes, more details of eighteenth century Harwich as a corrupt 'pocket Borough' are in Lewis Namier's *Structure of British Politics* (Vol 2). 'The Vice Admirals of the Coast', an article by R G Marsden in *English Historical Review*, Vol 22 (1907) remains the best source for this still imperfectly understood subject. For the details of the Bridge family I am indebted to that indefatigable historian of Harwich, Mrs Winifred Cooper, and for Robert Martin to Mr J Bensusan-Butt, of Colchester. I have also consulted two unpublished theses – 'The Struggle against Smugglers in Eighteenth Century Essex' by Evelyn Haynes (1970, Customs & Excise library reference 31499A) and 'Smuggling on the East Coast in the 18th century' by Mrs Gillian Griffin (University of Essex 1981).

Local books dealing with other parts of the country include Leonard Thompson: *Smugglers of the Suffolk Coast* (1968); for the Isle of Wight, D Arnold-Foster: *At War with the Smugglers* (1936 and 1971), for the West Country, H N Shore: *Old Foye Days* (1907); and for the south coast G Morley: *Smuggling in Hampshire and Dorset 1700–1850* (1983) and Mary Waugh: *Smuggling in Kent and Sussex 1700–1840* (1984). The Rev James Woodforde's *Diary of a Country Parson* gives a glimpse of the smuggling role in Norfolk, and another clerical classic, Rev Richard Cobbold's *History of Margaret Catchpole*, gives an equally colourful but considerably less authentic picture of Suffolk, where Ernest Read Cooper's *Suffolk Coast Garland* and *Storm Warriors of the Suffolk Coast* have some more reliable references.

I am indebted to Roger Finch for the original drawings and the jacket, and also for advice on many points in the text. The local scenes are mostly by courtesy of the Essex Record Office. The little decorations (as well as the detail of the *Speedwell's* concealment) are reprinted from *Smuggling Days and Smuggling Ways*, by courtesy of Macmillan Publishing Company, New York. Though they derive from the South Coast, and some of the more elaborate contrivances shown may not have been known on the East Coast, they depict the sort of ingenuity which was probably fairly universal. The picture of Bradwell waterside is from Herbert Brown's *History of Bradwell on Sea* (1927); efforts to trace the original watercolour, then in the possession of Ald C. W. Parker, have been unsuccessful. Chelmsford Gaol is by courtesy of Chelmsford Public Library. For the watch vessels at Burnham and Stansgate I am indebted to Kevin Bruce, and for the *Boadicea* to Michael Frost. The endpaper map is by Jane Benham.

Finally this book has finished where it began, with Essex Record Office as its publisher as well as the source of much of its material. I am deeply grateful to Mr Vic Gray, the County Archivist, for his encouragement and advice, without which it would not have seen the light of day.

Hervey Benham,
'Feldy',
West Mersea.
1986

Introduction

THE correspondence between the Collectors and Comptrollers at the Custom Houses all round the country and their Board in London constitutes an attractive, important and neglected source of maritime history. Few if any records go back 250 years with such unbroken continuity and such a wealth of vivid detail, yet few are more neglected by local historians.

Day by day these worthies reported on their local shipping, principally its misfortunes and misdemeanours, but including many other aspects of maritime life, for they wore many hats, acting as Receivers of Wreck and Registrars of Shipping and Seamen on behalf of the Board of Trade, as well as levying import and export duties and making war on those who sought to evade them.

I have in this book concentrated on smuggling because it is a subject of universal fascination which has been romanticised out of all recognition, and deserves to be seen in its true perspective. The bare facts are quite sufficiently dramatic and colourful.

I have also been content to concentrate on my own local scene, the Essex coast, because I believe the frontiers of knowledge, over social history of every kind, are best explored and extended by close and detailed research.

And if the Essex story is less lurid and bloodthirsty than that of some other areas, there is the compensation that the rivers and creeks between Leigh and Harwich have not been changed out of all recognition by industrialisation and coastal development. Those seeking to re-awaken the ghosts of bygone times along most of the south coast find it a frustrating and depressing experience; in Essex the tides still ebb and flow among sandbanks and saltings which are basically unchanged, and lap the hards and quays of towns and villages which, while given over to yachts afloat and housing estates ashore, still retain their character and suggest their traditions. In these waters the weekend yachtsmen may still see the scenes I have described and identify with the characters who played their parts in them.

Even within my chosen geographical limitations I have also had to select a period, for the total available material is overwhelming. The Harwich Customs letter books alone run to over 200 massive volumes, starting in 1713; Maldon to ninety-five, starting from 1732; Colchester to 103, starting from 1835.

3.d August 1778

Hmble Sirs

    Inclosed We transmit Your Hon.rs a Letter from Capt.n Bridge Commander
of the Argus Cutter, craving a new Cable the Expence of which will be
according to the Estimate inclosed £ 39..9.9. We humbly refer to the
said Letter.
                              R.D. Davies.
                              Cole.

4.th August 1778

Honble Sirs

    Inclosed we return your Honors Capt.n Bridge's answer
to the charge we gave him, of neglecting his duty in not seizing the
Lark Cutter John Girland Master, as your Honors directed us on the
23: Ult.o   We humbly beg leave, upon this occasion, to
send your Honors a List of smugling Cutters who constantly run
their Goods upon the Coasts of York, Suffolk and Norfolk, your
Honors will observe, at one view, the impossibility of Capt.n Bridge's
ever being able, with the present weak complement of the Argus,
to bring in any one of them

Mas.rs Names	Tons	Guns	Men
Reynolds	134	12	45
Steph.n Cann	75	6	24
Steph.n Marsh	140	uncertain	34
John Cock	113	D.o	28
Wm. Marsh	120	D.o	30
James Cree	114	10	32
Baker	112	10	28
John Girland	110	4	24

    Capt.n Bridge has desired us to propose to your Honors, that, as
your Refusal to increase the Complement of the Cutter under his
command, is occasioned by your unwillingness to load the
Revenue with such an additional expence, that the charge of
ten additional mariners may be deducted out of the gross
amount of the Seizures made by the Argus.   We humbly
submit this to your Honors   And are
                           R.D. Davies
                           Ja.s Cole

A typical page from the Harwich Letterbooks. Capt. Bridge must obtain the Honorable Commissioners' approval to renew his anchor cable. He also has to suggest a means of supplementing his crew without any cost to the Treasury.

From this embarrassment of riches I have endeavoured to reconstruct the goings-on on the Essex coast in 'The Smugglers' Century', which conveniently divides into two half-centuries, the second half of the eighteenth and the first half of the nineteenth. The former saw the climax of the 'old style' smuggling – the running of cargoes on to open beaches into the hands of waiting horsemen in broad daylight; the latter the heyday of the 'new style' smuggling – the clandestine sinking of contraband in the creeks and estuaries – and the belated introduction of the Preventive measures (including the Coastguard) which at last wrested the initiative from the 'free traders'.

The temptation was, of course, to confine myself to the eighteenth century, full of deeds of derring-do, armed violence and incidents so bizarre as to bewilder the imagination. This has been the practice of most of those who have attempted local studies of smuggling. I have been no less interested in the nineteenth century, however, firstly because it has not hitherto been exposed even to the romantic and misleading light which has been cast on earlier days, and secondly because the contrast between the two periods seems to illustrate and illuminate the social and maritime history of a fascinating age of development.

To this end I have concentrated on the Harwich Letter Books for the eighteenth century and those of Maldon for the nineteenth. I have, of course, also studied the Colchester collection, in which however the Collector's letters previous to 1835 have not survived. For this reason I suspect I do less than justice to the activities of the Wivenhoe, Rowhedge and Brightlingsea smacks before, during and just after the Napoleonic Wars. Indeed, my whole basis of selection inevitably involves some imbalance and much exclusion, which it is up to others to repair, for a great deal still remains to be researched.

The authors of these letters were interesting people in their own right. Originally the Comptroller was the senior officer, with the Collector his subordinate, but over the centuries the order of precedence was reversed and the Collector became the chief official, with the Comptroller sharing his responsibilities and countersigning all the correspondence.

The Harwich Collectors were leading personalities in a town which was a remarkable example of civic power and privilege in the days of the unreformed Pocket Boroughs. Griffith Davies, who schemed against his rivals in the packet boat service, built the first public baths and was Mayor in 1743, and in alternate years from 1756 to 1776, so that for twenty years he bossed the town every other year. His son, John Pelham Davies, who succeeded him as Collector, was Mayor in

1780, two years before he died at the age of thirty-two, and the Collector who succeeded him, William Crowder, in 1783 and 1792. Many other Customs officers and Revenue cutter Commanders were also members of that closed civic circle, the Corporation. Influence was probably required to secure a job with prospects in the Customs, but both Griffith Davies and his predecessor David Rushton (whom he succeeded in 1731) were previously Tide Surveyors. Most of the cutter Commanders also worked up to that position.

In the nineteenth century the Maldon letters have proved of particular value for three main reasons.

Firstly, Maldon Custom House for some reason – presumably its geographical propinquity – dealt with the gaol at Chelmsford, where most of the smugglers were confined, as debtors up to 1833, and usually as convicts thereafter. Smuggling gangs of five or more, and specially those using firearms or disguises, were tried before juries. This, however, did not usually apply to the small–scale operations which were usual in ninetenth century Essex. They were punished by a fine, based on a financial bond, or on three times the value of the contraband. Failure to pay led to committal to the debtors' prison. To this day the Customs preserve the mitigated penalty as an alternative to prosecution.

Secondly, the port of Maldon then covered most of the Essex coast, from West Mersea to Gravesend, where it joined the Port of London at an imaginary line across the Thames between the Round Tree, just above the Gravesend lock gate, and the centre of Bilmery Creek at Tilbury. When during the cholera epidemic of 1832 orders were issued for precautionary quarantine for vessels 'from the River Thames' Maldon asked if this meant 'from above the Round Tree'.

Leigh, geographically remote, with its officers claiming the title of Collector and Comptroller, wrangled with Maldon, for one controlled the south bank of the Crouch and one the north, with predictable consequences. Communications within this area were also difficult, and much of the correspondence is concerned with complaints about having to travel to Maldon for clearances, or the Customs' own problems in reaching places such as the remote Tollesbury Old Hall landing (handling a vessel a fortnight in 1823) or sending money from Maldon via Leigh to Hole Haven, or Havenhole as it was then called.

Thirdly, the Maldon letters were consistently vivid, detailed and lively. From 1798 up to 1814 they were written by John Gurr as Collector and John Pond as Comptroller, but when on December 26, 1814, the King's Chest under the control of these worthies was opened the contents were found to be £830 short. Whether this was a case of embezzlement or of the virtual impossibility of coping with the notorious complications of the Department's financial arrangements is not clear, but both men were dismissed, an additional charge being that they had not known or had connived at some malpractices by their Burnham Tide Surveyor referred to in Chapter 21. Pond, a gamekeeper turned poacher, set up as a ship's agent and used his knowledge to represent owners' interests to his former employers. Gurr, who had previously been Comptroller, repaid the money but is not heard of again.

His successor, William Bugg, is probably an example of appointment by patronage. Aged sixty-two he had been for many years master of Maldon Grammar School. An alderman and magistrate, he had also served for twenty years as Clerk to the Magistrates. He was, in addition, Clerk to the Commissioners of Taxes. He died in harness in 1830.

The recipients of these letters were the Honourable Board of Customs, an assembly of Commissioners sitting lordly and aloof in Thames Street, receiving information and issuing circumlocutory instructions of all kinds on every subject that occurred to them, from the most urgent to the most trivial. As they received around three letters a week from each Customs House, and transmitted almost as many replies and orders, and as they were dealing with over one hundred Custom Houses, they must have employed a formidable bureaucracy. Incongruously they chose to subscribe their orders as from 'Your Loving Friends'.

Though they had to administer some impracticable and incomprehensible enactments, and often did so in a pedantic and pernickety fashion, the Honourable Commissioners generally showed a firm grasp of the situation. Just occasionally they asked for the impossible, as when in 1773 they told the Harwich Collector to 'obtain an account of all persons who take passage out of this Kingdom . . . their age, quality, occupation, employment and former residence . . . to what place they go and for what purpose'. This the Collector had no hesitation in replying was 'totally out of our power', referring his masters to the Agent for Packets, who doubtless gave a similar answer.

The rapidity of communication before the introduction of the penny post in 1840, let alone telegraphs and telephones, is also striking. Replies were received the day after questions were asked – even if sometimes their purpose was only to prevaricate. During one wartime emergency, on 2 September 1798, the Maldon Collector was in the office at 3am, passing on an order presumably just received. This was to forbid any vessel, British or neutral, including fishing boats and small craft, to sail for the next three days, probably to give the Press Gangs a chance to reap their human harvest. The Bradwell Riding Officer was told to pass it on to the gun brig *Acute*, and the Burnham Tide Surveyor was likewise to notify the gun brig in his river. This suggests the Navy had no local signalling as efficient as the Customs letter traffic.

This efficiency did not, however, extend into other aspects of the administration. The Essex ports had a small revenue from duties, so that their local cash flow was always in debit. The Harwich Collector explained in 1733, 'every quarter we are obliged to Crave an Imprest, generally granted by your Honours on Bristol. Through distance it is often a month after the quarter's end before the Bills are received, and then these Bills are of thirty days' date.' As a result, financial control was chaotic, and officers and tradesmen were kept waiting for months for their wages to be paid or their accounts met.

Transport of bulky goods was also primitive. A boat built at Harwich for Hull was passed from Revenue cutter to Revenue cutter down the coast, though probably a passage hoy would have taken it had the Customs not been too mean to pay.

Likewise when several members of a Revenue cutter's crew were required as witnesses at an Exchequer trial in London, it was thought cheapest to send the cutter, leaving her station unguarded for weeks. As for the sending of prisoners to gaol or to trial, this presented problems dealt with in a later chapter.

The Board expected to rule on the most trivial points, delegating scarcely the smallest authority. When the Harwich Revenue cutter *Argus* broke her bowsprit, the Board not only had to sanction a new one, but to decide whether it should be sent from London or made locally. On a more human level, when in 1816 a clerk named Egbert Busbridge was accused by the landlords of the White Horse and White Hart pubs of recommending the Ship, which he himself kept, the Board had to be solemnly informed. (Egbert was forgiven on that occasion, but some twenty years later, in 1837, having left the service and set up as a ship's agent, he was in trouble for forging the Collector's signature on a 'transire', or permit to sail, to enable the barge *Honest Miller* to get away on the tide. Prosecuted under a penalty of £200 he got a mitigated fine of £50, but being 'in distressed circumstances' could not pay and went to the Convict Gaol at Chelmsford.)

In 1820 when an officer named William Rubie was in some trouble or distress the Collector not only submitted a surgeon's report but included his own simpler diagnosis and prescription. He recommended that Rubie be transferred to another station, adding 'The like occurrence would very probably be preventable as the object of his Folly (Love) would then be removed.'

The whole correspondence is a reminder that top heavy centralised government is far from being a phenomenon of our times.

It was not a humane system. The benefit of the doubt was not given. As a result many a petty wrongdoer and perhaps a few innocent men who would have been let off with a caution by the Collector were flung into gaol. Tradesmen and contractors were treated with arrogant contempt; their accounts ignored or arbitrarily reduced (one wonders if they added a contingency figure to their estimates and bills against this prospect). There was perhaps an excessive bias towards 'respectability' which was enough to get a plea accepted, a sentence reduced, or a bill paid.

The reliance on small salaries supplemented by fees and rewards for seizures doubtless prompted keenness, and also perhaps provided a better remuneration than the parsimonious outlook of the day would otherwise have allowed, but it was also an incentive to make out a case at any cost, specially with the magistrates in a weak position to adjudicate. Extortion of information, both from suspects and convicted smugglers, as the price of freedom may also have been an essential means of detection, but it led to a continual betrayal of comrades which cannot be called attractive, even if one remembers they were also criminals.

The extent to which the Customs were prosecutors, judge and court of appeal in their own right may seem surprising, but this is one of the anomalies of a bygone age which survives today, for under a system of 'compounding', perpetuated in the Customs and Excise Management Act of 1979, one of the Great Train Robbers gaoled in 1963 was, in 1984, freed on a VAT conspiracy charge at the Central Criminal Court on payment of £400,000 to the Customs and Excise to avoid court proceedings.

Another comparison between those times and ours may be drawn from the re-appearance of the 'super-grass' as an unpleasant but indispensable agent in the prosecution of terrorists in Northern Ireland. The basic moral and legal issues remain unchanged, but one may note that today a safe refuge for the informer and his family is an essential part of the bargain. How did those turning King's evidence 200 years ago escape retribution? Perhaps that age was not after all so much more violent and vengeful than our own. But on several occasions an informer claimed a place in a Revenue cutter's crew, with the Board always telling the Commander to give him the next berth. Such men may perhaps have been seeking safety from former associates as well as a secure job.

In the end, with all its faults, and with exceptions discussed in several chapters, justice was probably done, even if it was the rough justice of a brutal age. And though the outlook and attitudes of the period often seem shocking today, at least the prevailing parsimony prevented public expenditure soaring out of the control of those responsible for it, and the tough administration of an accepted penal code did not fill the prisons with the percentage of the population sent there under the more liberal and enlightened conventions of today.

Local memory and family tradition have, on the whole, proved a disappointment. Surprisingly few of the names which feature in these tales are to be found in the same towns and villages today, and few of the families which remain prominent have any knowledge of their great-grandfathers.

There have, however, been exciting exceptions. Ever since I first heard the story of Philip Sainty, the noted Colneside shipbuilder, being released from gaol at the behest of the Marquis of Anglesey to build the famous yacht *Pearl*, I have wondered if it was too good to be true. And now here is the contemporary record of Sainty's smuggling career.

Similarly, having enjoyed many happy days sailing and trawling aboard that unique survival, the 170-year-old Mersea smack *Boadicea*, and having found equal pleasure in researching her history with her present owner, Mr Michael Frost of Colchester (as recounted in his book *Boadicea CK 213*) I had supposed we had closed the story. And now I have once again encountered John Pewter who bought her in 1825, and am able to recount his misdeeds and misfortunes and the way they have been improved out of roguery into respectability in their transmission from generation to generation of his family.

Many of the characters who feature in the little dramas that follow deserve to be rescued from oblivion. Daniel Sutton, Colchester's ne'er-do-well Town Clerk, was certainly one of the town's characters. And how one would like to meet his redoubtable antagonist, Captain George Munnings, Revenue cutter commander and privateer, whose peppery behaviour so closely presages the similar disposition of a later member of the family, Sir Alfred Munnings, PRA. Another Revenue cutter commander, Cyprian Bridge, was the forebear of a family which has attained high distinction in the Navy, the Army, the Church and the Law.

Even some who only play walk-on roles were part of the local history of their communities. In 1769 one meets Golding Constable, father of the artist, anxious about some iron bars from Gothenburg, seized aboard the *Suffolk* through being improperly entered, and needed no doubt for work on his Flatford Mill, for the heyday of the smugglers chanced to coincide with the busiest years of mill-building in the Eastern Counties. Here too is Richard Rigby, developer of Mistley, insisting in 1772 that some hampers of wine be shipped at his new quay aboard the *Thorn* for London, and getting the local Waiter-and-Searcher into trouble as a result, for all dutiable goods (including even coal) had to be loaded and unloaded at legal quays, leaving the common quays available for little besides grain and timber.

Here are the antecedents of two important nineteenth century Burnham merchant families, the Richmonds and the Smiths. Peter Richmond, who had a bit of trouble over silk handkerchiefs in his oyster smack, was father of the builder of the beautiful schooner barge *Lucy Richmond*. John Smith is mentioned in passing as builder of the Tillingham coastguard cottages in the 1820s. The full saga of that contract may be told another day; sufficient here to say that he played ducks and drakes with his specification, was patiently advised and supervised by John Sadd, himself a forebear of the important Maldon timber merchants (now part of the Boulton and Paul group) and ultimately confronted the usual reluctance of the Honourable Board of Customs to pay their bills. It was customary on these occasions to petition in terms of obsequious humility, but Smith displayed some of the truculent character that later gave his firm, Smith Brothers, barge-owners and proprietors of the Crouch Oyster Company, a reputation for being tough people to deal with. 'You are the hardest hearted men I ever did business with' he informed their Honours. Then, after threatening legal proceedings, he had a better idea. 'The *Maria* [Revenue] cutter is now undergoing repairs at my wharf. I shall detain her till my account is settled' he wrote.

Here too are the Lewises, most famous of all the Harwich salvaging families, loading half-anker tubs in Flushing a few years before turning to the more heroic trade of wreck and rescue. Even the millers, whom I met in another field of research, make their appearance on this scene, with the story of Henry Ward's fight with the Customs in building up the great Beeleigh watermill, which fascinated me as the most splendid of all these fascinating enterprises.

Ships as well as their seamen assume their own personality as one meets them over and over again. In writing *The Salvagers* I was curious about the existence among the cutter-rigged smacks of a converted three-masted lugger, Edward Bacon's *Aid* of Brightlingsea. What on earth was the appearance of such a strange hybrid? Now, suspecting her of smuggling, the Maldon Collector gives this description: 'Formerly a lugger. All black, Clench. Large square stern (no tuck) and has been raised aloft' (meaning presumably built up to give added freeboard).

To those who object that such people and such matters are far from the main stream of local history I reply that they are just as much a part of it as the economic statistics and political niceties which obsess today's sociologists – and a great deal less tedious. They will also serve, I hope, to replace the tales of secret passages and of boats' crews of Revenue men found with their throats cut, with which the romantic wafflers have so gaudily decorated the story of smuggling.

The Respectable Roguery

*Eighteenth century Bravado and nineteenth century Cunning: The
Entrepreneurs: Favoured Cargoes: Coastal Duties: Policing the Salvagers.*

WITH the possible exception of original sin, regarded as regrettable
but inevitable for an even longer period, smuggling occupies a unique
position among human activities and codes of conduct.

Anti-social in time of peace, when it defied the law and undermined
the national economy, treasonable in time of war, when it provided
direct assistance to the enemy, it was an illegal way of life tolerated,
accepted and even practised by respectable and generally law-abiding
citizens of all creeds and classes.

Such apparently amoral attitudes would seem today almost incomprehensible if there had not been a comparatively recent reminder of
the extent to which propriety will adjust and react when subjected to
excessively repressive pressures. The welcome given to the bootleggers
during the American experiment with Prohibition in the 1920s showed
that if people want a drink they will find a way to get it, and not be
too particular about it. So it was when, in default of such later and
more refined forms of financial extortion as income tax and VAT, the
Government sought to load the burden of national expenditure on to
the cost of gin and brandy, tea, silk and tobacco and ultimately any
sort of commodity which seemed capable of bearing a duty.

Certainly little stigma attached to the way of life of those who
sought to circumvent such charges. John Wesley spoke up against 'the
detestable practice of cheating the King', but there were few who took
such sentiments seriously. Lord Holland was nearer the spirit of the
age when he opposed a Bill to suppress smuggling in the Channel
Islands in 1805: 'My Lords, I call it a mischief, for though I am aware
I cannot speak of smuggling as a fair trade, yet, if it is the necessary
consequence of high duties that smuggling should be carried on more
or less, it is better it should be carried on by subjects than by
foreigners.'

Even the Customs service fought its unending war not so much
with a view to achieving outright victory as with a policy of containing
and keeping down to acceptable proportions something that was a
recognised fact of life – though in this they may also have been
influenced by the law of the survival of species; never completely
eliminate the prey on which you depend. Only so long as they could
show evidence of some smuggling in their areas could the Collectors

'crave' the funds and resources they sought, or the Honourable Commissioners obtain them from a tight-fisted Treasury.

To fishermen it must have seemed a necessary source of income. The Essex fisheries have always been seasonal; only the oyster trade and the Harwich cod fishery with its three seasons provided an all-the-year-round living. Smuggling must have made up a livelihood, just as salvaging and the crewing of yachts went on to do – and as some reliance on unemployment benefit has to do to-day.

Nor was any cloak of secrecy found necessary. One example will serve to illustrate the astonishing acceptance of smuggling among recognised trades and livelihoods.

Richard Chaplin, a victualler of Ardleigh, a village between Colchester and Harwich, was tried before the Lord Chief Baron in Westminster Hall in 1779 for running goods to the value of no less than £26,000. About seven years later, having moved to Suffolk, he inserted this remarkable advertisement in the *Ipswich Journal*[1]:

'Richard Chaplin of Sudbourn, Suffolk, near Orford, begs leave to acquaint his friends and the public in general that he has sometime back declined the branch of smuggling and returns thanks for all their past favours. Also to be sold on Monday August 8th, 1785, at the dwelling-house of Samuel Bathers of Sudbourn, the property of Richard Chaplin aforesaid, a very useful cart fit for a malster, ashman or smuggler. It will carry eighty half-ankers or tubs. One small ditto that will carry forty tubs, also two very good loaden saddles, three pads, straps, bridles, girths, horse cloths, corn bin, a very good vault and many articles that are useful to a smuggler.'

This book reconstructs some of the smuggling scenes on the Essex, and to some extent Suffolk, coast during the second half of the eighteenth century and the first half of the nineteenth.

The eighteenth century was the age of brash bravado, of cargoes openly run ashore by armed cutters and luggers into the custody of organised bands of horsemen in defiance of Revenue cutters at sea and of Riding Officers, Tide Waiters and Dragoons ashore. The periods of greatest activity, reflecting duties imposed usually for the needs of war, were from 1720 to 1750 and from 1770 to 1790, but these were peaks in a century of continuous smuggling rather than outbreaks between peaceful interludes.

The first half of the nineteenth century was, by contrast, the age of subterfuge, of the clandestine avoidance of greatly improved Preventive forces. In practice this largely meant surreptitious sinking of contraband for later recovery at an opportune moment rather than the earlier bold runs on to open beaches. In the eighteenth century tubs were slung in pairs for the riders; in the nineteenth in 'trots' or skeins for later grappling.

While the growing dislike of protective duties and more effective counter-measures spelled the beginning of the end of smuggling in the 1830s, spasmodic operations continued throughout the 1850s. The decline since then could be the subject of another story. A few cargoes still came ashore 'over the wall' (as the saying goes in marshland estuaries) down to recent years; maybe some still do, but in general the tradition has now been reduced to the occasional folly of an over-enthusiastic yachtsman, or the more serious and unpleasant traffic in drugs, chiefly through the Continental car and lorry ferries.

Smuggling never attained quite the social and economic importance on the East Coast that it did on the South. 'There was scarcely a fishing village along the South Coast which did not own a vessel, often several, whose sole and peculiar employment was the importation of contraband articles for the use of the adjacent populace' declared Lieut

Armed three-masted lugger, from J. Rogers' Celebrated Sailing Vessels, *1825. As well as topsails on all three masts, she sets a large jib topsail and a main topmast staysail. The rig required a large and well-trained crew, as the lugsails had to be lowered and dipped round to leeward of the masts when the vessel tacked, but it gave great speed, due to the huge area of such powerful sails. It was also effective to windward in the days of hand-made flax sails, because these set baggily on a cutter's spars, but could be strained flatter by the bowlines on the luffs of lugsails. This craft even has bowlines on the luff of her mizzen topsail.*

17

Shore in *Smuggling Days and Smuggling Ways*. A nineteenth century historian of Guernsey (Tupper, 1840) could recall admiring in his boyhood 'the smugglers with their athletic crews, who looked and lived like gentlemen'. The trade never attracted such pride and dignity on the East Coast – but equally it never descended to the murderous butchery which stained the coasts of Sussex and Kent. There was brutality, and lives were lost, but nothing to compare with the ruffianly cruelty of the well-publicised Hawkhurst gang or 'Ruxley's crew' at Hastings.

Even by East Coast standards, Suffolk was better provided with open landing places for the eighteenth century 'runs', and almost certainly bred more whole-time smugglers and mariners primarily concerned in smuggling than Essex, where such regular operators as the Dowsetts of Paglesham were the exception rather than the rule. 'A great many of the inhabitants of Ipswich and places adjacent are smugglers' warned the Harwich Collector in 1746, when he considered the gaol there insufficiently secure to house a prisoner, and recommended his removal to the Fleet 'very privately or with a strong guard'. And of all the East Anglian smuggling groups, 'the Hadleigh gang' was the most notorious. Between May and December 1745 no fewer than fifty-six major runs on the Suffolk coast were officially recorded,[2] each involving from twenty to 100 horse loads, this being the official reckoning. The total of horse loads landed was put at over 4,000, and as it was reckoned that a horse could carry 1½ cwts of tea and twenty-one gallons of brandy, the loss to the Exchequer was considered to exceed £100,000.

With the nineteenth century change to clandestine smuggling and the intensive blockade of the Kent and Sussex shores, however, the Essex creeks and estuaries came into high favour for the sinking of tubs, and the coast was probably as busy as any in the 1820s and 1830s. But most of these tubs were still the responsibility of outside enterprise, with Essex smacksmen only involved in their landing and disposal, as an occasional way of supplementing their earnings from fishing or freighting. The *Speedwell* of Brightlingsea was fitted with an ingenious and elaborate false lining to her foc'sle, as described in Chapter Twelve, but this was as unusual in Essex as it was common on the South Coast, where, to quote a few examples, the Portsmouth smacks *Fox* and *Lively Lass* were found to have false bottoms, the *Flower* and *Providence* of Rye, the *Mary* of Plymouth and the *Plough* of Hastings had false bows, and the *Lavant* of Chichester had a two-foot cavity between her lining and the bottom of her hold. (Customs officers were warned to take a measurement down the pump to check against the depth of the hold).

18

Most of the geneva which features so freely in these chapters originated at Schiedam, where in 1779 the distilleries were producing nearly four million gallons a year, mostly for smuggling into England. It was shipped largely at Flushing, where many English emigrés settled. Following a quarrel in 1824 between various interests there, one concern, Truman & Co, moved to Ostend, where they erected several tobacco presses and commissioned two large luggers. Another concern, Phillipson & Co, established itself with three luggers. Additional tobacco presses were also erected at Ghent, their product being exported in the local fishing 'doggers' to be exchanged for fish or money with Harwich and other smacks at sea. It was probably firms such as these that commissioned the cutter *Jane* of London (203 tons, forty men, expected to run to Berwick), the cutter *Earl of Spencer* of Dover (142 tons, thirty men, working Norfolk and Yorkshire), the cutter *Idas* of London (141 tons, thirty men, working Yorkshire and Scotland), the lugger *Folkestone* of Folkestone (130 tons, thirty men, Norfolk and Yorkshire), the cutter *Avis* of London (ninety-two tons, twenty men, Berwick and Scotland) and an unnamed cutter (seventy tons, fifteen men) for Yorkshire. All these were reported fitting out in Holland in 1816, with the additional comment 'NB. The largest will be armed'. Three years later, in 1819, another warning from Flushing again referred to the *Jane* and the *Folkestone*, adding the 200-ton lugger *Vlunix* and mentioning *Idas I* (157 tons) and *Idas III* (180 tons).

Craft such as these loaded gin from the Schiedam distilleries in tubs already roped in pairs, and the trade attracted a colony of English outlaws, such as the notorious John Pixley, mentioned in Chapter 3.

Few others attained such celebrity, but when the lugger *Fox* of Southwold (George Debenham, master) was seized off Flushing with 158 casks aboard in 1815, the Customs' belief was that the spirits belonged to an Englishman named Weeks living there. (Her defence was the oft-used claim that she was bound for Bergen, but the officer concerned observed that with only one day's provisions on board she was 'not for Norway'.) And when in 1801 a Woodham Walter farm labourer was 'induced to be concerned in illicit transactions with a view to getting a few shillings for his family's support in the late dear times' he mentioned a supplier in Flushing going under the name of Sparrow.

Dunkirk, where an Essex JP's dinner with the Paglesham smugglers is described in Chapter 2, was another principal entrepot. Napoleon allotted a large part of the town to the English smugglers on whom he relied for information and for gold, but, in his own words[3], 'as they latterly went out of their limits, committed riots and insulted everybody, I ordered Gravelines to be prepared for their reception, where they had a little camp for their accommodation. At one time there were upwards of 500 of them in Dunkirk.'

All along the Channel coast, from Prussia to Britanny, the smugglers plied their trade, with the East Coast naturally served chiefly from the Low Countries and the Eastern French ports, and the West Country largely from Roscoff, a little Britanny village developed into a smugglers' entrepot after some restraint was put on the Channel Islands, whose main staple had been the smuggling trade. But the import of Channel Islands oysters into Essex involved one exception to this rule.

One of the biggest operators on the Essex coast was a Dutchman named William Sextroh, 'the most notorious smuggler we have ever known' according to the Harwich Customs (though these superlatives were fairly freely used). He sailed from Dunkirk in the twenty-ton *Three Brothers* in 1765 with a cargo of tubs brazenly marked with his initial – BS for his brandy and GS for his geneva. He went to a fleet of light ships lying in Aldeburgh Bay, where he was spotted by the Harwich Revenue cutter *Walpole*, which sent a boat to board the *Three Brothers*. Getting a hostile reception the boat returned to the *Walpole* which set off in chase. The *Three Brothers* threw overboard thirty half-ankers, which were picked up and brought into Harwich by a smack owned by one Farley Spratlin (who appears often in Chapter 3), but though the *Walpole* fired on her 'near twenty times' she could not be overhauled till she carried away her 'topgallant' mast. (As she was only a twenty-tonner this was probably her topmast.) She was then carried into Harwich – 'the third vessel of which Sextroh was either master or mate legally condemned.' Inexplicably, like so many others at this time, Sextroh went free to make another run next year at Frinton. This led to the arrest of twenty-year-old John Howard, who had brought three horses to carry away 150 half-ankers and some sacks of tea. He had 'on several occasions assisted in landings chiefly from the vessels of George Murphy and William Sextroh.' His grandfather had to pay £50 for his release. Then in 1782 Sextroh achieved his most spectacular coup by capturing at sea one of the Harwich mail packets – an event depicted in a Dutch engraving.[4]

Sextroh's associates included Thomas Cross, who in 1766 was in prison for running several cargoes, 'having first drawn in labouring persons to increase his fortune and is now laying information against them'. His plea of poverty from the Fleet Prison in 1767 was answered by the Harwich Collector's comment that he must be worth £700 or £800.

Strange as it may seem, the branding of contraband with a smuggler's name was not confined to Sextroh, for the same practice was the undoing of Daniel Sutton, who combined smuggling with his duties as Town Clerk of Colchester, as recounted in Chapter 9.

A more lurid notoriety was enjoyed by John Skinner, sentenced to death at Chelmsford Assizes in 1746 for murdering his servant, Daniell Brett, two years before, and described as 'late a great Oilman and Dry Salter just without Aldgate' who had 'come into Essex to take possession of an estate' (evidently Brightlingsea Hall Farm, where he is recorded as living in 1788). According to a contemporary pamphlet[5] he was known among the smugglers of Boulogne as Saucy Jack or Colchester Jack. His Essex bride's £5,000 fortune soon went in gaming and whoring, and he was bankrupt for £10,000. He paid 15s in the £, in the opinion of the pamphleteer 'a very handsome composition for a man who had so little interest in his affairs', but instead of resuming his trade he took the King's Head inn at Romford, which was supplied by smugglers. This was his introduction to the trade, though as a decoy he kept two farms at Old Heath, Colchester, the Tan Office and Cox's. After falling out with Brett over a smuggling deal and shooting him on the nearby Donyland Heath, he lay low for a while but then rashly emerged to claim an estate of £15 per annum at Brightlingsea Copyhold Court. He was recognised, arrested and condemned. He had plenty of money and 'behaved with modesty and decency' till his end, which was unpleasant, for he tried to kill himself with a knife in his cell, but was patched up and dragged half-conscious to the scaffold.

But despite these colourful characters and picturesque goings-on, most of the East Coast smuggling was of a petty nature, promoted by petty tradesmen, with a high proportion of publicans among the sinners. 'The Colchester Gang' made a run at Thorpe in 1729, leaving tea, brandy and geneva in a barn belonging to Jeremiah Warren (who was not thought to be involved) but the only man arrested was a hired horseman – a common experience – and no more is known of these desperadoes.

Brandy and gin (generally referred to as geneva, a name having no connection with the Swiss city, but deriving from the Dutch name of juniper, used in its manufacture) were always the chief imports, due to the convenient access for Continental distilleries. Nutmegs and pepper were common in the 1720s. Tea and tobacco feature to some extent in the eighteenth century but are mentioned only infrequently after the French wars. Silk, being easily concealed, was often a temptation. The story of John Skinner, already quoted, observes that 'more duties are lost by lace smugglers than by all the smugglers in the

Kingdom besides . . . more French laces are annually worn than paid duty in ten years.' But as duties were levied on one commodity after another, all kinds of articles were found worth smuggling, with glass remarkably popular after import duties were raised in 1787 and 1818.

The smuggling war was also sometimes waged against exports as well as imports. The earliest of all Preventive measures had been enacted – at Bradwell and Goldhanger as long ago as 1361[6] – against the 'owlers' smuggling wool out of the country, and this was still a matter of concern at the end of the eighteenth century, for in 1786 the Collector at Leigh, John Loten, recorded in his diary that ten vessels, from thirteen to thirty tons, were making large fortunes in this trade, and in 1784 forty-eight bags of new wool were auctioned by the Customs at Mistley.

A leading operator was Isaac Fitch who in 1784 shipped at Maldon ninety-eight cloths for Wakefield, to be landed at Hull. They did not arrive, and it was suspected they had gone to France. When a warrant was issued for his arrest it was found he was already detained as a bankrupt in Chelmsford gaol. He was, however, at it again five years later for in 1789 he once more found himself in Chelmsford gaol for a breach of his licence to carry wool coastwise. He had smuggled it for John Sellers (who had signed the licence bond), 'now of Dunkirk and in low circumstances', William Limmy, keeper of a public house in Calais, and Adam Smith of no fixed abode, already previously convicted for wool smuggling 'which crime appears to be done away with by the late Wool Act'. Despite this, in 1797 two cutters were specially fitted out to prevent the export of wool from Essex, Kent and Sussex, John Sharpe of Dover being appointed to command this force.

Every stage in the movement of wool was scrutinised. In 1799 the Chelmer Canal Company petitioned that Heybridge Basin was 'a very proper place for the reception of wool'. In 1812 the Maldon Collector reported the seizure of a horse and cart because the sacks it was carrying were not clearly labelled Wool, and two years later Thomas Green of Purleigh sent three parcels into Maldon to a buyer, only six days after it had been sheared. He then set off to the Custom House for a licence, only to find on arrival that his cart had been seized. The year after this the chairman of Colchester Wool Fair, Edward Wakefield of Burnham Wycke, asked that the Dengie Hundred farmers should be allowed to get the permits for their samples at Burnham instead of having to travel to Maldon for them. (The Collector appended a note recalling that in 1785 the Burnham Landing Waiter, Jasper Robbins, had been dismissed for issuing blank permits.)

A wartime clamp-down on the export of corn also caused much

confusion. A warning in 1789 that it was being smuggled to France in fishing boats, and an order to watch all small vessels, brought a despairing protest from Maldon in 1790. 'We have twentytwo vessels clearing with corn to London at nineteen different places – eleven vessels at Maldon at six places, three vessels at Tollesbury at three places, five at Burnham at six places, and three at Bradwell, all sailing at spring tides so they cannot wait on each other or on our officer.' As a result John Lewis of Old Hall, Tollesbury, was given powers as temporary Coast Waiter to deal with shipments there – 'specially the *General Elliott, Sally* and *Jeremiah* barges.' Tollesbury Creek still meanders through the saltings up to this old landing, but today carries no traffic heavier than the occasional sailing dinghy making a high water voyage of exploration. A house which in busier times was a pub still stands there, but there is little trace of whatever quay or dock John Lewis presided over.

In addition to foreign traffic, coastal freights, subjected to duties in the scramble to raise revenue from any possible source, also presented problems.

Oyster imports from the Channel Islands proved particularly contentious, since this was in fact a home trade but for all practical purposes a foreign one. Coal from the North of England ports had to be unloaded through regular bushels, paying a duty of 9d per chaldron (thirty-six bushels) – an impost thought worth evading. Both these subjects are dealt with in later chapters. Some slate and marble were made liable to coastal duties in 1795 but it did not seem clear whether this was intended to apply to ragstone for seawalls. Sixty tons brought from Kent in 1815 had to pay £5, but the Customs then consented to a remission for Canvey and Foulness islands. This brought a petition from the Dengie Hundred in 1817, saying they had paid no duty up to the past two years, since when they had been charged £26 8s per cent.

Duties on coastwise traffic meant that even the humble local hoy barge had to carry a cargo manifest and be cleared. This led to some quaint little complications, of which one local example may be quoted.

James Parker cleared from London for Bradwell in 1821. When he arrived home he was found to have a half-chest of oranges, bought for £1 7s 6d from a merchant in Lower Thames Street, and though he declared they were for his own use they were seized. Three years later the corn hoy *Albion Mill* was in trouble at the same place for carrying two half-chests of oranges not on her cargo list. This suggests that the sterner tasks of Revenue protection were perhaps enlivened by local controversies between residents and a possibly officious Tide Waiter.

When Smugglers Fought Their Way

The Thin Line of Defence: The Dowsetts of Paglesham: Swipes' 200-tonner:
Stories from Holland Gap: Patrolling Handfleet Water.

THE forces of the Customs throughout the eighteenth century were modest.

In 1715 there were no officers between Harwich and Colchester, with the exception of two boatmen at Brightlingsea. Two Riding Officers at Walton were then suggested, to assist the officer at Manningtree, David Rushton, who soon afterwards was promoted Collector at Harwich. In the end a Riding Officer named Hugh Doyley was appointed at Kirby in 1721 to patrol the long stretch of coast. 'He frequently meets with smugglers who ride with Goods in great Partys, consisting of twenty, thirty (or sometimes more) in a body well armed whom he finds it impossible to encounter with alone, but believes if he had the assistance of but one able-bodied person it might conduce to a more effective service.' He had in fact an assistant, John Eslin, but the Collector suspected 'he hath too much understanding with one Mr Mason, a glazier at Colchester, Mr George Gooding of Clacton and Mr Bushell of Gt Holland, all three notorious smugglers.'

There were only two boatmen at Ipswich, and if they were boarded in foreign craft no-one was left to attend to the growing fleet of colliers. The proposal here in 1732 was to move the men from a boat at Levington, down the river, and to appoint a Riding Officer to patrol to Stratford St Mary, on the Stour, and thence to Shotley, meeting once a week with the Riding Officers at Woodbridge and Walton. Riding Officers were certainly required to ride! In this year also a guard boat was established at Bawdsey, to watch the mouth of the busy Deben river.

By 1760 a slightly stronger presence was established.

At Maldon the Collector (Charles Malden) had two boatmen at his disposal. He was also responsible for Burnham, with a Waiter-and-Searcher and two boatmen; Leigh, with a Surveyor and two boatmen, and North Shoebury with a Waiter-and-Searcher.

At Colchester the Collector (John Kirby) had a Surveyor, a Land Waiter, a Waiter-and-Searcher and two Tidesmen-Boatmen. He was also responsible for Brightlingsea, with two boatmen, and for Mersea Island with two boatmen.

At Harwich the Collector (Griffith Davies) had a Surveyor, a Waiter, and an Inspector of Waterguard controlling a Tide Surveyor and six Tidesmen-Boatmen. He was also responsible for Manningtree with a Waiter-Searcher.

At sea Colchester had the sloop *Princess Mary* and Harwich the *Walpole* (both referred to in Chapter 3), while inland there were supervisors of Riding Officers at Colchester and at Witham (the latter controlled by Maldon).

But even this was a thin line of defence against the formidable gangs engaged in the smuggling exploits of this time.

A report by the Maldon Collector in 1783 clearly explains the old, eighteenth century smuggling style. 'The practice has been and is to carry greater numbers of hands in their cutters than our officers dare attack . . . and when they land their goods they will guard them by night to their destined places to lodge them and be defiant to any officers who may oppose.' This is in marked contrast to the accounts of the concealment of contraband forty years later.

The hottest parts of Essex at this time seem to have been the Crouch and Roach, the Clacton beach at Holland-on-Sea and the Walton Backwaters, or Handfleet Water as it was then known. It seems surprising that the Crouch was preferred to the Blackwater, for its narrow entrance would have been easy to blockade, but presumably before the time of permanent watch vessels a Revenue cruiser could not be continually on this station, and while the cat was away the mice could play. The Colne may well have been equally busy, but since the early Colchester Letter Books are lost there is little evidence of this.

The same Maldon report goes on to list at Burnham 'a cutter supposed to belong to William Dowsett at Paglesham, which carries ten men' (presumably the *Neptune* whose capture is described in Chapter 5), a 'huffler' also belonging to Dowsett, West Country-built, with eight or nine men (a curious description, for a huffler was generally a small boat engaged in pilotage or recovering anchors), a cutter with six men belonging to Wiseman's of Paglesham (another surprise, for Wiseman's were oyster merchants, later, as we shall see, distinguished for their respectability), a smaller boat with four or five men owned by Emberson (Dowsett's brother-in-law), a Folkestone-built cutter with six or seven men belonging to Adam King, the French-built cutter *Sprightly* owned by William Wright of Burnham, and 'one or two fishing boats which carry oysters to Dunkirk and bring smuggled goods back'. There were also two or three cutters, with crews of eight or twelve, landing goods at or near Bradwell in the Blackwater.

Against all these the chief boatman at Burnham, Isaac Dines, had only two regular men and two extra or 'glut' boatmen. The report begged for two more 'to row six oars and come up with and overpower such smuggling cutters'.

William Dowsett was not the only smuggler in this family, for John Dowsett [1] owned the *Big Jane*, 'carrying about six brass six-pounders' which had been in several contests with Government vessels. This may have been the 'large lugsail, commanded by – Dowsett' which was taken off the Essex coast by boats from the *Argus* and *Bee* cutters in 1780 after an eleven-hour chase, with 'smart firing on both sides, in which the lugger had three men wounded and her hull and sails damaged. The cutter's people received no hurt; their prize's cargo consists of 23 cwt of tea and 252 half-ankers of gin, brandy and rum; the smugglers made their escape by taking to their small boat'.

Headed by the Dowsetts and Emberson, the Paglesham smugglers were so well known that when a local landowner, John Harriott of Stambridge (who founded the Thames River Police in 1798) wanted a passage home from France he decided to make use of their service. At Dunkirk he found only the Kentish smugglers in port, but as they assured him the Essex men would be in that night he stopped to dine with them. The toast was given, 'Damnation to all Revenue laws and officers!' to which Harriott as a JP objected, pointing out that the abolition of Revenue laws would mean the end of smuggling, on which the chairman amended the toast to 'Revenue laws and officers for ever!'

Reports from the Crouch were plentiful throughout the 1770s. The Burnham Revenue officers, returning with some seized goods in 1784, were attacked by the crews of no fewer than five cutters lying in the river. In 1779 'a large smuggling vessel passed through Burnham to Hullbridge where she unloaded her cargo; she mounted six carriage guns and eighteen men, had on board 1700 halves and a large quantity of dry goods . . . The Maldon Custom House officers had a skirmish with some of the smugglers, but they proved too strong for them. We hear at least one of the smugglers is since dead of a wound.'

An even more formidable smuggler, of which warning was given in the same year, was a cutter 'of near 200 tons, mounting fourteen four-pounders and forty-seven men, belonging to one Wenham but commanded by a man nicknamed Swipes'. She 'made it a practice to bring a very large cargo of contraband goods which she lands in Colne and Burnham rivers as fast as she can perform the voyages between Flushing and this coast.'

The Maldon Collector's letters were much less detailed and graphic in the 1770s than they were to become fifty years later, and most of the previous instances are derived from newspaper reports.

Seizures are not described, the Collector's only reference to them being a request to send a writ. He does, however, describe Bradwell in 1783 as the home of 'a desperate gang', with 'three boats known to be kept for smuggling'. But he adds that there had been no seizures there for some time. And when in the following year all available officers were deployed at Bradwell, Tollesbury and the Burnham area to search for 'boats liable to forfeiture under the Act of the last Sessions' the search yielded nothing but one very old twenty-eight-foot boat, though the following year Isaac Dines of Burnham seized two old Kent-built cutters, the seventeen-ton *Gondola* and the ten-ton *Flying Fish*, 'both supposed to carry on the illicit trade from the nature of their business and common report'. The *Gondola* is oddly described as 'formerly a lighter'.

While the marshland estuaries were to see their busiest times in the nineteenth century, the open beaches of Clacton, Frinton and Walton were ideal for an old-style run, served as they were to seaward by a roadstead giving relatively sheltered conditions, and on the land side by roads leading to a deserted countryside, with the London market not too far away. Small wonder that this was a favourite shore, with Holland Gap, near Clacton, perhaps the hottest spot of all. In 1721 alone three finds were recorded. In April, twenty-seven gallons were found 'by spitting the sand' at Walton; in July eighteen half-ankers by tracing wagon tracks, and in September nineteen half-ankers when the ground at Frinton gave way under the feet of Mr Doyley.' 'Spitting' here described probing the sand, probably with tucks, a metal blade or rod in a wooden sheath, on the principle of a swordstick.

By 1742 the trade was well organised. In that year, 'some smugglers landed a large quantity of tea on the shore near Clacton where their riders were assembled in order to carry it off; but Mr Todd of Brightlingsea, and other Customs Officers, being appriz'd of their design, appeared on the Shore and attempted to make a Seizure of the Cargo, in which the smugglers opposed them and secured Mr Todd on board their Vessel and placed a Guard over the other officers till they had loaded the Goods on Horses; after which they released the Officers and rode off, being seventeen Horses and as many Men.'

The most notorious operator hereabouts in the mid–eighteenth century was Samuel Salmon, with his accomplice John Hallum, both of Thorpe-le-Soken. They were associated with or employed by

27

Harwich shipping in 1713. Apart from the two hoys, top left, all the craft are square rigged, including the packet, top right, which was rigged like the two-masted vessels in the foreground. Fore-and-aft cutter rig was adopted by the middle of the eighteenth century. Landguard Fort is on the right.

By the mid-eighteenth century fore and aft rig was generally adopted by small coasting vessels, as is shown by this scene on the Orwell, painted by John Clevely, senior, in 1753. The schooner-rigged craft on left may be one of the Ipswich-Harwich passenger wherries, the masters of which considered they must regard smuggling as part of their trade.

Sextroh & Cross, already mentioned, and did not confine themselves to the Clacton Shore, for in 1748 the Harwich Collector noted that Salmon, who had 'been smuggling all this last summer in Burnham' had gone to Dunkirk, taking a former member of the crew of the Revenue cutter *Walpole* as his pilot. But the Essex beaches were their favourite landing place.

Here is a typical example in 1750. The crew of the Handfleet boat patrolled along the beach to 'Walton Low' (between Walton and Frinton) where they saw a small boat ashore. It put off at once to a sloop lying in the Wallet, which immediately put to sea. Two men then called out 'Hallo!,' taking the officers for Salmon's and Hallum's men. They then made off, but soon ten armed men appeared, with five or six mastiff dogs which they set on the officers, who were beaten with whips and clubbed with their own pistols. One pistol was snapped, but 'it happened to misfire and flash'd in the pan.' The boatmen were threatened that if they ever left their watch house again they would not return to it alive, and between two and three a.m. the gang (with Salmon at their head) passed through Ramsey village with their booty. Observing that 'this vessel had landed twice in the past fortnight' the Collector asked for an order for about twenty Dragoons to be quartered in the three inns at Walton, the four at Kirby and the four at Thorpe.

Salmon evidently worked craft other than his own, for in 1749 the first and second mates of the *Walpole* were dismissed for embezzling money found aboard a cutter commanded by one Nathan Jacobs. Seeing the Revenue men approaching in 'Pennyhole' (as the bay outside the entrance to Handfleet Water is still called) Jacobs observed that he 'had more in his pocket than he was willing to lose, pull'd out six moidoores, two Portuguese pieces of 36s each, eighteen guineas and three half-guineas, which pieces Salmon minuted in his pocket book and put in a linen bag under the flint ballast.' There the *Walpole's* officers found them, and fell for the temptation, little knowing that their rummage was being observed through a chink in the bulkhead.

For a while Salmon was protected by the Colchester Superintendent of Riding Officers (as is recounted in Chapter 15) but his freedom came to an end, for in 1757, when he was on the run, he was described as a deserter from HMS *Vestal*, aboard which one may guess he had not shipped voluntarily.

A Great Holland farmer recalled how in 1778 he and his mates often kept gin in the stable, and after giving the horses their first 'bait' in the morning, used to drink it from a tin mug. [2] 'There was a gang of smugglers came regularly from London on horseback with ten to fifteen horses. They generally traded in gin, sometimes in dry goods. They arrived at Holland about five or six o' clock of a winter's night, would go down to the lower barn at the Hall and let the horses feed around the corn stacks, Mr Fisher receiving compensation by a constant supply of gin, of which he was very fond. When out of stock the old gentleman would call after some of his men to leave the lane gate "locked" – it was well understood what it meant – and the next morning there was sure to be a tub of gin under the horse block.' Not all these runs succeeded, for in 1781 'nine half-ankers and two asses carrying the same' were seized after a scuffle at Little Clacton.

This scene had changed little in 1814. One September evening a man came ashore at 'Daniel Gap' in a skiff from a small lugger and called at the house of Lieut Shirley, a Naval Officer in command of the troops at the Holland Semaphore. He asked Shirley's wife if a Mr Kaley lived there, perhaps meaning one J Scaley, at that time under a penalty of £6,120, treble value of 680 gallons each of brandy and rum unshipped six months before. He then made off, as did the lugger.

Mrs Shirley sent her maidservant to alert the troops, but she could only raise a sergeant and four privates of the 55th Regiment, the other thirty-five being absent. This force, with four late arrivals, but with only three muskets between them, made a search and discovered seventy-two tubs in a stubble field, and then 130 more in a ditch. These were taken into Harwich by the Revenue cutter *Active*, but on arrival they numbered only 197. Lieut Shirley explained that 'some of the tubs were stolen before the wagons got to my house. The state of inebriety among the guards was disgraceful.' The Riding Officer said he was told soldiers conveyed some spirits to Weeley to be sold. Perhaps thinking an alternative defence could do no harm, Shirley added that maybe the original total of 202 was not correct, for in the hurry he could not exactly count. The Customs addressed themselves to the nice point, whether a Naval officer was empowered to seize ashore. On the analogy of another Naval officer similarly employed at Bradwell fifteen years before (as described in Chapter 17), he was not. Nevertheless, a claim for rewards was still being pursued a year later on behalf of the military by Major Richard Jones of the 55th. (The armed forces, always an uneasy ally, regularly participated in the scramble for rewards. When in 1722 the Harwich Collector suggested the 'cantonment of HM Forces of Horse & Dragoons in parties on the coasts', he did not fail to add, 'with suitable reward'). Also in 1814, William Daniels, a farmer of Great Clacton (perhaps the owner of 'Daniel Gap') was asked by William Marsh, one of Scaley's accomplices in the previous run mentioned, and some companions, to lend them his boat to lift an anchor. He agreed, and then Marsh asked him for the use of his boathouse, as they had to walk to Harwich. Daniels then went to a friend's house, where his servants followed to tell him his boathouse was 'beset by soldiers, placed by the Lieutenant of the Holland Semaphore'.

All they could find to seize was a boat just over the legal length of fourteen feet, as to which Daniels protested his ignorance, saying he had ordered it to be built under this length. But when he sent a letter asking for its return, Lieut Shirley insisted that 'two soldiers of the 55th discovered from the tower Mr Daniels' boat lifting of tubs, and others conveyed them to his boathouse.' Daniels' letter, he added, was actually delivered by William Marsh, 'accompanied by the noted Captain Baxter' who was evidently another local desperado.

Another run by a galley in 1835 led to the recovery of seventeen half-ankers in a private house at Ardleigh. The Semaphore had by this time been removed, and the Colchester Collector was noting that ' the smugglers adopt the method of running by daylight after the night patrols have returned. This is easy as it is four and a half miles from the station at Walton and quite out of sight, and five miles from Clackton Wash.' He asked for three more men to join the six guarding 'Walton Gap' the nine-mile stretch of coast between Stone Point, Walton, and the Sluice beyond Holland Gap.

The regularity of unconcealed daylight landings as late as the 1830s, with local labourers joining in, is confirmed by the diary already quoted, which records that in 1830 'Richard Brett, a labourer belonging to Gt Holland, was at work with others on the sea wall. The day before Christmas they assisted some smugglers in getting a freight on shore. Having indulged too freely drinking gin, at night they were most of them drunk and could scarcely walk. Brett, in crossing the plank over the river from Little Holland battery to Gt Holland marshes, fell into the river [Holland Brook]. His companions with difficulty got him out on the sea side, laid him by the side of a haystack near the wall, covered him up and left him. The night was clear and a sharp frost; he was dead when they went to him the next morning. He left a widow and six children chargeable to the Parish. A few years after, a fine young man about twenty, named Martin Lott of Little Holland, who had been assisting the smugglers, died from the effect of having taken too much raw spirit.'

One explanation of these and many other cases of death from drinking may be that while most liquor was 70° over proof, it was sometimes smuggled as much as 180° degrees over proof. This saved tubs, but the mixing ashore after landing, and finding the extra tubs, was generally considered to involve more trouble than it was worth.

Another traditional Essex landing place was Handfleet Water, or Walton Backwaters, as it is now known, immortalised by Arthur Ransome as 'Secret Water', and today as beloved by yachtsmen as it was then detested by Revenue men – in each case for the same reason, its isolated seclusion. With its maze of tidal creeks the place would seem more attractive for the tub-sinking of the nineteenth century than for the earlier forays. But it offered the opportunity to slip in at night from the open sea, without having to negotiate an estuary, and then to hide for the next day's ebb in some rill where it was difficult to detect and where there was no water for a patrolling boat to search. There was also little risk of observation, for as the Collector observed in 1743 'it is little frequented by any but smugglers.'

At any rate the Customs always took Handfleet Water seriously. As early as the 1720s a boat with a Sitter and four men was allocated to it, and this force was maintained till 1778, when two men were withdrawn and replaced by a Riding Officer, Evan Brotherton.

Such a presence may have been sustained by tradition rather than necessity, for only six seizures were made both in 1786 and 1787, all small quantities, between two and thirteen gallons of geneva and wine, with half a gallon of something called levass, and in 1788 there was only one seizure of spirits and one of wool. One horse with its saddle and another with its cart were also gathered in. Describing these as 'trifling', the Board reached for its axe. The Collector observed that he would prefer a water-guard to the Riding Officer, but then, probably deciding he had better defend what he had, raised the alarm that corn was being loaded at Walton without an officer being present. It was therefore decided in 1789 to move Brotherton from Oakley to Thorpe (which was more central) and to give him additional powers as a temporary Coast Waiter. The poor chap was badly beaten up by smugglers in September 1800 and retired in 1805.

Walton Tide Mill, Great Oakley and Landermere were at this time the only landing places in Handfleet Water, so evidently Beaumont was little used till the quay was built there with stones from the old London Bridge in the 1830s. Arrivals and departures kept Brotherton quite busy, with an average of one vessel a month to be cleared inwards, and an average of four a month outwards, mostly loaded with copperas, but a few with corn.

The Walton copperas house, largest of many such works along the Essex coast, was still prosperous in the mid-eighteenth century, supplying green dye to the local clothiers and tanneries, but closing down in the early nineteenth century with the decline of these industries, though the raw material, nodules of copperas, continued to be collected on the beaches by fishermen's families for another half-century. Ships came to Walton laden with scrap iron (then termed bushel iron) with which the raw copperas was oxidised into green copperas in lead tanks. This iron was brought in containers weighing nearly a ton, too heavy for the scales of the Customs men who had to weigh it. Exports were to Rotterdam, but whether of the raw material or the manufactured product is not clear.

The Handfleet boat was not a popular posting, for in the days of ague the area was thought very unhealthy in winter. Several boatmen resigned the Service and others refused appointments for this reason. The official allowance for 'fire and candle' was changed in 1770 from £8 a year per vessel to 1s a month per man – an alteration which may have suited heavily-crewed craft but acted adversely for the five-man crew of the Handfleet boat in so chilly a place. The Collector tried to get this allowance increased, only to be met with the inevitable bureaucratic demand for details of the number of candles used and the quantity of coal consumed, but he did succeed in getting an extra £5 a year for each man, 'provided the seizures made shall annually amount to the whole of such increased salaries'.

As early as 1731 the Handfleet watch vessel was replaced by a Revenue cutter, the *Diligence*, but the employment of an eleven-man crew was not justified, and the following year the station reverted to a four-man watch vessel. To the surprise of the Collector, the Commander of the *Diligence*, Capt Hudson, accepted the position of Sitter in this boat, and his mate enrolled as one of his boatmen. Another boat was provided at 'Walton Low', so that in southerly weather, when the boatmen could not sail round the Pye Sand and the Naze Point, they could walk overland and launch off the beach. There was also a watch house built in 1745 on land owned by Lord Rochford, who was no friend of the Revenue. [3] This shore was being eroded in the 1750s, having receded 130 yards in five years, till in 1755 the watch house, which had been rebuilt after being washed away in 1749, again had nine feet of water in it at high water spring tides. But five years before this one of the boatmen, Samuel Webb, had taken three planks off the shore and as a result of this theft of his property his lordship refused new land. When the house was finally washed away the Customs asked for another watch vessel, preferring 'a full-built vessel which will ride easier than a cutter-built vessel at anchor and be more commodious.'

For a few years around 1770 this vessel was replaced or supplemented by the cruising cutter *Vigilant*, which was also expected to cruise to the Blackwater and Crouch, but when this was discontinued the Handfleet boatmen were again ordered back to their watch vessel.

Perhaps because of the boredom by day aboard a craft at anchor five miles from the nearest shop, and the hardships of the night patrols, quite an entertaining little miniature mutiny occurred in 1775. The Sitter, William Wilkinson, complained that his men spent the days 'drudging' (as oyster dredging is called to this day) in their own seven-ton boats.

'Tiring themselves at drudging by day renders them incapable of keeping a proper watch at night' he observed.

To which one of the boatmen, Nicholas Munt, replied, with a command of language that may well have prompted the Collector to speculate as to the identity of the actual writer: 'Now give me leave, good Sir, to represent to you the Nature of our going out at Night. First we row two or three miles more or less, then we have sometimes three, four, five or six miles more or less, which in winter time must be performed with a pair of Boots and a thick Jacket . . . and to walk the roads which sometimes in many places are full of water, and hardly passable by foot Passengers. When we have walked to the place desired, and all of a Sweat, we must secret ourselves in some place for fear of discovery, where we must stand or set, still, very cold, before tide is over. Now judge, Honoured Sir, if this duty can be performed every night.'

He and his mates took up the case against Wilkinson with equal eloquence: 'We might write several small articles little to his credit, but we forebear, being not willing to be thought malicious, but we cannot help repeating the frequent aggravations and abuse that we have received from him: such as calling us dogs and rogues, scoundrels, Liars, Vilains, Raskels, Savages, damning us for Blackguards, and using very approbious language, much unbecoming a Gentleman . . .'

The Honourable Board warned Wilkinson 'not to discredit himself by using ill language, but by his own example to learn them to behave properly to him', and ruled that one man should be reprimanded and three suspended for a month and until all four disposed of their dredging boats. The men first asked fancy prices, such as £20, and protested they could not find a buyer, then they tried selling the boats to each other and to their brothers. Ultimately two resigned, but Munt got reinstated, despite the fact he had only sold a share in his own boat.

Wilkinson was promoted two years later to the more pleasant job of Waiter-and-Searcher at Mistley. Thereafter the Acting Sitter who defied ague and the lack of fire and candle rejoiced in the name of Argalus Disborough. He departed this life in 1798, leaving the Harwich Collector's letters the poorer for the absence of so picturesque a name.

3

The War at Sea

Colne-side Contractors: Robert Martin and Daniel Harvey: A Commander's Triumph: The Repulses of Wivenhoe: Battles with the Bawdsey Boatmen.

THROUGHOUT the 'gallant' age of smuggling, if that is not too fine a description of a brutal and bloody period, interest focuses primarily on the Revenue cruisers, of which Colchester and Harwich had a long succession of splendid examples. Their story emerges in graphic detail, as they developed and evolved in a continual, and generally unsuccessful, effort to keep pace with the increasing size and fire-power of their smuggling adversaries. They ranged from little thirty-ton patrol boats, with a crew of half a dozen, up to powerfully armed cruisers of over 200 tons, with crews of over fifty. The earlier examples were clinker-built, but a Customs decision in 1783 that 'no clinker-built vessels over sixty tons should be built without the approval of the Admiralty' suggests that at this time carvel building was coming into favour, at any rate for the larger craft.

The Harwich cutters' 'beat' in 1737 was from Walton Naze to Orford Ness, extended in that year to Thorpeness, while the Colchester cutters worked from the Nore to the Swin. (An application to give them Bawdsey was refused.) Maldon, that is to say the Blackwater and the Crouch, was thus covered by the Colchester cruisers, and also seems to have received a good deal of attention from two cutters which belonged to the Excise, then a separate service, as described in Chapter 17 – the *Badger* and the *Fox*. Excise craft were fewer in number than the Customs' cruisers, and for that reason patrolled more widely; they may have paid special attention to the Blackwater because of the absence of a locally based Customs cutter.

Around 1730 the Customs, concerned at the expense of its growing fleet, turned to a system of putting many of the cutters in the hands of contractors. Some of the early craft were owned by the contractor and leased to the Customs at 4s 6d per ton per month. But most, if not all of the later contracts, were for the management of craft owned by the Crown.

The earliest arrangement was to allow the Commander thirty shillings per ton per year 'to keep the vessel and her boat in good repair, and find her with workmanship and materials, other necessaries and fire and candle.' This arrangement was accepted at Harwich in 1719 and 1728 by Capt Phillips of the *Walpole* and in 1731 by Capt Skeats of the *Waklyn*, both referred to later.

Subsequently a more elaborate arrangement was developed, with two alternative systems. In some cases no payment was made, but all expenses, including wages, victualling and repairs, were paid out of the gross seizures, after which the balance was divided between the Crown and the contractor. If there was a loss the deficiency was likewise shared, so that the Customs in effect were simply 'laying off' their risks.

Under the other system the contractor was paid 4s 6d per ton per month (the same rate as earlier contractors had received for the use of their own craft),for which he had to maintain the vessel, with wages, victualling and other expenses paid out of the gross seizures, after which the nett profit or loss was again divided between the contractor and the Crown. This latter system seems to have been favoured in Essex.

Finally, in 1784, a few years before the contract system was ended, the Customs introduced an arrangement under which the vessel remained the property of the Crown, with no charge for hire. If she was destroyed by accident, or taken by the enemy, half the loss fell on the Commander, with the profit or loss represented by gross seizures, less expenses also equally shared between Crown and contractor.

The only losses which the Customs as owners accepted in full were those arising from having to cut a cable, or cut away the mast and rigging, to save a cutter from total loss. A surgeon's bill for treating men injured by smugglers was paid by the contractor and claimed back from the Customs, but, up to the time of the final system, when Letters of Marque were issued in time of war damage inflicted by enemy action, or seizures of enemy ships, were the contractor's sole responsibility, with the Customs refusing to share in either gains or losses.

Colchester (or more accurately Wivenhoe) was a Revenue cutter station from very early times. Around 1680 the lawyer-historian Roger North, on a yaching trip from Harwich to London, anchored in the Swin in company with four East Indiamen. His pilot suggested taking a bale of goods from one of them, but North wisely refused, for 'next morning a Custom House smack came aboard us and searched every cranny, supposing we had been dabbling. It was not unpleasant to observe the desperate hatred the seamen had to these water waiters. One vowed he could scarce forbear to run his knife in their guts, for he was at his breakfast.'

Whether or no this smack was from the Colne (as seems likely), there was certainly a 'Wivenhoe smack' in 1698, and from the early days of the contract system till its end in 1788 the river supplied two notable contractors, Capt Robert Martin of Rowhedge (or East Donyland as it was then known) and Capt Daniel Harvey of Wivenhoe. Both were members of families prominent in the shipping affairs of Colneside in its heyday. A Capt Matthew Martin of Alresford, near Wivenhoe, achieved fame and fortune in 1718 by saving the East India Company's biggest ship, the 480-ton *Marlborough*, from three French warships by a daring stratagem.[1] His relationship to the Revenue cutter contractor I have not traced, but it is tempting to wonder whether the riches heaped upon him, including £1,000 from the East India Company, went into these ventures, and whether the social and political influence which he obtained helped to lay the foundations for the fortunes of both these families.

The Harveys were the most famous of the many Colneside ship and yacht builders, taking over the Wivenhoe yard in 1832 from the son of the smuggler Philip Sainty, described in Chapter 24. The yard reached the height of its prosperity in the 1870s when the proprietor apprenticed his son, John Martin Harvey, only to realise that the boy's heart was in the theatre. He went on to earn recognition and a knighthood as one of the greatest actor-managers of the nineteenth century, bearing a name which records the linking of the two families through the marriage of his grandfather, Thomas Harvey, to a Miss Martin.

Wivenhoe in 1832 – an idealised view by W. Bartlett.

The Excise *cutter* **Badger** *probably represents the sort of chubby, clinker-built hull favoured throughout most of the eighteenth century. She was built around 1788, at which time clinker building was probably going out of fashion (unless this was an earlier vessel of the same name). She was stationed at Bradwell, but this picture probably shows her at Dover, where she was also stationed.*

This aquatint of a chase, published by R. Dodd in 1803, shows a heavy, powerful cutter, with generous beam. It is not clear whether she is carvel built, nor is it possible to determine when this form of construction became generally accepted, though there is some evidence that the change was occurring in the 1780s, perhaps under the influence of the Admiralty.

Robert Martin lived in a house which still stands on the quay at Rowhedge.[2] He bought the Manor of Gt Holland near Clacton in 1748 and died in 1763. His daughter married the Collector at Colchester, John Kirby, a Freeman of Orford, who thus inherited both the manor and the house, where he died in 1777. Martin was one of the most important of all the contractor-commanders; so much so that around 1740 he was appointed Surveyor of Sloops for the East Coast, one of only two such appointments in the country, with a commission to cruise between Yarmouth and Portsmouth, inspecting and reporting on all the sloops.

He contracted five cruisers for the Colchester station in addition to one or two at Harwich and one on the Medway. The seventy-three ton *Princess Mary*, mounting two swivel and six carriage guns, with a crew of twelve, was contracted from 1729 to 1741, though during 1735 she was stationed at London. Her crew was increased by eight men in 1741, the year after Martin himself assumed command. In 1747 she was rebuilt and increased to eighty-one tons.

The Colchester cutters were very much the pride of the town, or perhaps it would be truer to say their commanders were proud to parade their prowess before their fellow-citizens, for the Customs presence was a prominent part of the social establishment of an eighteenth century town.

Robert Martin went so far as to organise a veritable Roman triumph following a seizure with his *Princess Mary* in July 1741.

Cruising in his new command off Beachy Head (in his capacity no doubt as Inspector) he encountered a Spanish privateer, which he took after an engagement lasting two hours, in which two Spaniards were wounded but none of the *Princess Mary's* men was hurt. She proved to be a former Hastings smuggler of thirty tons, the *Jolly Boys*, which had been captured a month previously and armed with two swivels. She had a crew of twenty-nine, who hailed from San Sebastian, 'that Sepulchre of our Shipping' as it was called during the War of Jenkins' Ear, when it was full of Spanish privateers and English prizes. This capture Martin brought all the way home to the Colne, where according to the *Ipswich Journal*:

'On Monday the Spanish prisoners were brought to the town, guarded by Captain Martin and his men, with drawn cutlasses, the Spanish colours, which they hoisted upon the Captain's attacking them, being carried before them. They were all confined to gaol, and are used with great humanity. The Captain is allowed to walk about the town, in company with two soldiers. Abundance of people flock daily to see them in gaol.'

Vigilant, *built in 1824, represents the ultimate in the development of the the Revenue cutter, with her long counter stern, beautiful sheer and generally yacht-like lines. The upper picture, a lithograph by J.C. Schetky, after a painting by T.G. Dutton, shows her towing the sailing barge* Charlotte *off Greenwich. The lower picture, a lithograph by T.G. Dutton, after a painting by H. Rolfe, published in 1845, shows her towing the sailing barge* Alfred. *The incidents are mentioned in Chapter 23.*

Three of the prisoners broke out of gaol (probably Colchester Castle) in September, but next month they were all sent to London under military escort.

In addition to the *Princess Mary*, Martin was contractor for the sixty-seven-ton *Essex* for the same period, 1729 – 1741, after which she went to Hull, for the smack *Wivenhoe*, commissioned in 1731, and the cutter *Good Intent*, brought from Dover in 1741 for use at Brightlingsea, perhaps as a watch vessel. He also commissioned the thirty-three-ton *Mayflower* with a crew of six, to watch the Medway at Chatham and Rochester. This hotbed of smuggling he had noted as a good prospect, and was not disappointed, with seizures in that year worth £974 against costs of only £267.

In 1760 Daniel Harvey was Commander of Martin's *Princess Mary*, and on Martin's death in 1763 he carried on the role of contractor, making a new contract which replaced the old 30s per ton per year maintenance allowance with the new profit-and-loss-sharing system based on 4s 6d a month. His craft at this time also included the *Rochford*, which he was commanding in 1774, but which does not feature in these tales, and the *Swift* whose fate is narrated in Chapter 7.

He then initiated a series of six cutters all named *Repulse*, the first four of which he also actively commanded.

The first *Repulse*, built in 1774, had a crew of eleven men and a boy; the second, built in 1776, was of 132 tons, with eight carriage guns, six swivels and a crew of thirty. The growth in size continued, for number three, built in 1778, was of 180 tons with a crew of forty-two; and number four, built in 1779, was of no less than 210 tons with a crew of fifty men and a boy, armed with sixteen carriage and twelve swivel guns. The fifth *Repulse*, built at Cowes in 1793, was of 143 tons, with fourteen carriage guns and a crew of twenty-seven; and the sixth, of 123 tons, with a crew of thirty-seven, including two mates and four boys, left Colchester for Grimsby in 1813 but was still serving under the Commander-in-Chief, Sheerness, in 1821.

The huge 210-tonner was among the largest of all the forty-four cutters in the Revenue service. This probably reflected the opportunity offered by privateering and also maybe Martin's elevation to Surveyor of Sloops eighteen years before her building, for the Surveyor of Sloops for the south coast, Warren Lisle, had the eighty-ton *Cholmondley* commissioned for him in 1740, and she was also in her time the largest cutter in the service. [3]

Harvey secured Letters of Marque for his *Repulse* IV, with the Board refusing to pay for her colours, warning him they would not bear any expense for engagements not resulting in the seizure of a smuggler, and ordering him not to quit his station under pretence of looking for captures. He was soon in action against a Dutch privateer, which unluckily for him was already a prize of HMS *La Prudente*. One man was killed and one wounded, and Harvey had to face an inquiry, which let him off with a caution after the mate of the Harwich cutter *Argus* had testified that the ship was under Dutch colours with 'all the appearance of an enemy'. Around this time he was also in continual trouble for overspending, and for desertions amongst his crew (or perhaps for claiming for more hands than he had shipped).

This *Repulse* was fitted with a new topsail and top gallant in 1782, with 'two iron clips for the masthead, and brass sheaves for topsail tye to carry full five-inch rope'. Perhaps this lofty rig was too much for her, for she carried away her mast, and had to cut all her rigging away, the following year. The Customs re-fitted her without demur, giving permission for her crew to fit out and use two condemned smuggling vessels while she was out of commission, though just previously they had reprimanded Harvey for helping himself without any authority to a vessel which had been seized but had not been condemned. At this time her crew was reduced from fifty-one to Commander, mate, thirty-one men and a boy because her seizures no longer paid for such a huge complement.

A mid-nineteenth century Revenue cutter of the Coastguard era, painted by J.C. and W. Joy in 1855. She retains the traditional squaresail yard, but hoists her boats in davits, apparently of the iron style still in use today.

Six years later, in 1789, the great *Repulse* was wrecked. How this happened is not clear, but it must have been within half a day's sail of Harwich, for her commander, Capt George Munnings (who had been appointed to succeed Harvey as Commander in January of this year, and who makes his appearance in Chapter 9) and his mate Jonas Woodward hired the private Harwich packet *Pocock* to salvage what they could. They could bring in only the mast, bowsprit and a yard and the Customs cut the promised payment of £7 7s to £4 4s on the ground that the *Pocock* was only employed for one day. Her predecessor (*Repulse* III) was also lost through stranding in 1780, but was recovered as described in Chapter 7.

Though there is a record of a 'smack' at Harwich in 1685, there was little enthusiasm for a Revenue cutter thirty years later.

Spirits and silks, tea and spices, were being run ashore everywhere on the coast, and seizures were made from the North Sea packets after almost every voyage. But in 1717 the Collector, Jacob Bury, observed that 'the Wivenhoe smack' and the Riding Officers must guard against 'smugglers landing goods in creeks and obscure places', and asked for a 'pinnace' to 'prevent the too common and pernicious practice of the pacquet boats sinking brandy etc without the harbour'. Such a pinnace would cost only about £34 and need only four men, whereas a 'smack or yacht' would cost £350 to build, and the salaries and victualling of her crew of ten would amount to £300 a year. Perhaps as important in his mind as the economy was the fact that the pinnace would be commanded and manned by the Tide Surveyors, who were doubtless loath to share their rewards with a cruiser.

The Customs, however, for once did not go for the cheapest option. They commissioned 'the *Weymouth* smack' whose origin is unknown, but which immediately found easy pickings from the unsophisticated smugglers of the period. Often her men had only to follow cart tracks leading from the beach to a hide inland. In 1721 'observing some smugglers to be very busy in a marsh near Kirby' they went ashore and picked up fifty-four half-ankers. In her first three years she made sixteen seizures, the proceeds of which were sold for £1176, with a large stock still unsold in the warehouse.

Most of the *Weymouth's* seizures were easy and bloodless. One day in January, 1725, she seized tea, brandy and handkerchiefs on shore near Walton, and then at Bawdsey a Folkestone-owned cutter from Middleburg with six bags containing 291 lbs of tea. The next day, near the same barn at Walton, she found another seven half-ankers of brandy, and a day or two later seized the sloop *Berry* of London from Holland with 22½ gallons of brandy and 16½ lbs of tea.

43

Sometimes, however, there was resistance. In 1726 the sloop *Margaret*, belonging to Richard Row of Walton (presumably Suffolk) was found in Woodbridge river. Row and about eighteen others, including Thomas Woods, an escaped convict under sentence of transportation, came off in four boats, seizing the *Weymouth's* boat and throwing the firearms in it overboard. In the scuffle the *Weymouth's* mate, Joseph Southgate, was wounded, despite which the *Margaret* was brought into Harwich and later burned.

Southgate had been similarly wounded three years before in a fight with the *Brass Castle* of Harwich, whose crew of six, commanded by Edward Russell, would only give up their cargo on being promised the vessel would not be seized. Russell thus escaped. But in 1725 he imprudently re-appeared to serve a writ for the return of another vessel that had been seized, the *Happy Return*. He was arrested at Aldeburgh, and secured in Harwich gaol till the Mayor and Justices held a Quarter Session at which he produced a witness to say Southgate had told him it was not Russell who struck him, on which the Grand Jury brought in a verdict of 'Ignoramus' and Russell again went free. Poor Southgate died soon after these adventures, and the Collector made a plea for a widow's pension on the ground that his hardships were the cause.

The first commander of the *Weymouth* was John Phillips, a member of a family as deeply involved as any in the web of Harwich political influence described later in connection with the packets. [5] In 1726 he and Capt Richard Clement, commander of the Dover cutter *Sewell* and supervisor of all the Revenue vessels between Harwich and Deal, put forward a proposal for a new sixty-ton cutter, forty-one feet long, sixteen feet eight inches beam, seven feet six inches deep, length on deck fifty-four feet, suggesting that she be 'fuller than the draft, both fore and aft, being frequently under water in a grown sea which commonly run short' – a picturesque way of explaining the sort of hull needed for the steep chops of the North Sea. Less explicably he asked for a round stern, 'for the better convenience of entering her men'.

This cutter was built by Clements [6] at Ipswich and named *Walpole*. Though it was noted that she 'really needed a false keel and gripe to add to her sailing' she was to serve for nearly half-a-century through many phases of the smuggling war. She was allowed a crew of fourteen including captain, mate and boy, and was soon as busy as her predecessor (which was sent to London), her captures including the Deal yawl *Dolphin*, belonging to Edward Langram, a notorious smuggler, which 'sailed so extraordinarily well in light winds' that she was spared destruction and used in the Revenue service at Dover.

The *Walpole* was contracted to Robert Martin, and during 1729 was stationed at Colchester. In that year, however, she was ordered to Wells, though remaining under the orders of Harwich. There she had a narrow escape, when under her mate, John Southgate (doubtless a relative of the former mate of the *Weymouth*) she attempted to seize two French shallops suspected of supplying brandy to a fleet of colliers anchored off the Norfolk shore. The shallops proved too strong for her and chased her into Holkham Bay where they overwhelmed her, seizing Southgate. The master of one shallop, taking him for Capt Harrold, commander of the Yarmouth cutter, threatened to kill him in cold blood, and only released him on discovering his true identity, with orders to convey the threat to Capt Harrold, who, however, died of natural causes the following year. Southgate went on to command the cutter at Hastings.

During her years at Wells Capt Phillips kept bringing the *Walpole* back to Harwich, each time with a new excuse – that he had broken a spar or been driven in by northerly gales, or on one occasion to collect the long-overdue wages of his crew. When the Collector chased her out again, he sometimes stayed ashore, on the pretext of super-vising the making of a sail or the state of his health, which evidently was no idle excuse, for he died in March 1733. The Customs appointed a Captain Wall to succeed him, but meanwhile one Samuel Phillips took possession, refusing to come to Harwich to hand the cutter over, but lying with her in Brightlingsea creek, 'to gain time for his friends to get your Honours' order reverted' observed the Collector. And it would seem that the old pals' network was stronger in Harwich than the rule of the Commissioners, for in May 1734 Samuel Phillips's appointment was confirmed.

He proved as troublesome as John. His crew mutinied in 1737, beating him and his mate, Samuel Langram. No sequel to this is recorded, but in 1744 both Phillips and his then mate, Phillips Baggott, were in trouble for leaving the cutter, falsely claiming they had been given leave, and were suspended. Both went into the packet service, where they attained command and became thorns in the Customs' flesh, as is recounted in Chapter 10.

With the *Walpole's* departure to Wells, a Capt Skeats took over in Harwich, first, in 1729, with a little sloop called *Robert & Anne*, which was fitted with cabins and raised a strake for her new work, and then the following year in the *Waklyn*, which seems to have been seized in 1729 as 'Wakelyn's boat' along with a gang of six smugglers who were sent to the county gaol with an escort of Dragoons, though the Collector noted they would have to be returned to Suffolk for trial as the seizure took place there. To name a King's cutter after her criminal former owner seems strange, but it is confirmed by a reference to a boat 'for the sloop that was Wakelyn's now in the service here'.

Skeats had his share of adventures, and one curious mishap when he laid the *Waklyn* ashore for a scrub near the quay. Caught in a gale there, she wrenched off her keel, and while she was on the yard Skeats took a condemned seizure, the cutter *Mayflower* – perhaps the same craft that Capt Martin of Colchester was to use in the Medway some years later. He then went to live at Orford, sharing a house with his brother-in-law who was a brandy merchant! The Collector thus had one cutter which should have been in Wells continually turning up in Harwich, and the other which should have been in Harwich finding excuses to put into Orford, till finally the Board ordered Skeats back to live in Harwich.

He was succeeded by Captain Ridley, whose chief claim to fame is that he permitted the escape of the most colourful of all the East Coast smugglers, John Pixley, 'otherwise Cursemother', a former Customs officer who was sentenced to transportation at Thetford Assizes in 1740 for armed smuggling, escaped from Norwich gaol, was re-arrested and in 1741 passed through Colchester on his way from Newgate to Norwich guarded by Dragoons. He escaped again, settled in Flushing and succeeded in rescuing an English brigantine captured by a French privateer. In the course of his adventures this remarkable character found himself a prisoner aboard the *Waklyn* where he was foolishly

John Pixley, 'alias Cursemother', a Customs officer turned smuggler, who after capture escaped from the Harwich Revenue cutter Waklyn *and settled in Flushing.*

left alone on deck. He jumped overboard, succeeded in getting ashore, walked some miles, bought a horse for six guineas, rode to Ipswich and 'is now in Holland.' The mortified Capt Ridley advertised in the *Ipswich News*, offering a reward of £40 for Pixley's arrest, in addition to the official reward offered by the Customs. The only puzzle about this story is that the escape took place in February 1732, which suggests that the dates quoted above from accounts hitherto published have become confused.

In 1733 the *Waklyn* was sent to another station. Her inventory showed a sixteen-fathom cable to be missing. Skeats said that as the Customs had refused to pay him for the rent of a boathouse he had seen fit to sell it!

Another comparatively short-lived Harwich cutter at this time was the little twenty-nine-ton *Cornelius* which was bought at Sandwich in 1738 by Capt Robert Martin of Colchester and contracted to the Crown at 4s per ton, per month. With a crew of only six she was profitable for a while, making seizures valued at £671 against costs of £265 in 1739, but in 1744 she made no seizures and her contract was ended. Her commander, Isaac Dekker, then went in the *Princess Mary*, nominally as mate, but as Robert Martin was seldom aboard, in practice usually as commander.

In 1742 Dekker was concerned in an incident at Bawdsey which was to be almost exactly repeated many times during the next half century. Bawdsey village lies on the north-east side of the entrance to the Deben, generally known as Bawdsey Haven or Woodbridge Haven, which is itself a few miles to the north-east of Harwich. Close by, on the intervening shore now occupied by the modern resort of Felixstowe, was then the village of Walton, leading inevitably to confusion with the Essex Walton on the Naze Point across Dovercourt Bay. It is also not always clear whether the smuggling mentions of Bawdsey refer to the village or the Haven.

However that may be, on this occasion a cutter Dekker was chasing sent off six men in a boat to land a load of tea. Dekker and five of his men followed in their boat, but when they came near the shore they were fired on by thirty of forty smugglers and horsemen. One of the Customs men, John Mills, was killed and his widow was awarded £50 'to encourage officers to do their duty'. The murderer, Thomas Fidgett, 'alias White Eyes', was ultimately brought to justice at Chelmsford Assizes in 1752. Other casualties among Martin's fleet resulted in payments in 1738 of £19 10s to the widows of men drowned from his vessels and in 1742 of £7 10s to the widow Durrell, with 30s for each of three children, after her husband had been lost from a boat chasing a smuggler – possibly the same incident which cost John Mills his life.

Another murderer met his fate as the result of a curiously similar incident at the same place in 1748, when the *Walpole* chased a smuggler ashore, finding aboard one Stephen Pettit, who was wanted for the murder of Joseph Keys, one of the Ipswich Town Serjeants, a fortnight before. His clasp knife, eight inches long, with a seven inch blade, was identified as the murder weapon and he was soon convicted and hanged. As a result of this seizure, 'sixteen stout seamen' were sent by Admiralty tender to HMS *Namur*. (One who was wounded escaped while visiting the surgeon.)

The Cutters Grow Up

End of the Walpole: *Troubles of the* Argus *and* Bee: *More Bawdsey Battles*

TO return to the *Walpole*, Phillips's successor in 1744 was Isaac Dagnett, formerly master of the Harwich hoys *Goodwill* and *Isaac and Rose*, which the Customs employed to take goods to London, the high freight charges being defended by the cost of 'losses from theft and expense in getting the goods ashore in London'.

In 1750 he seized the cutter *Turpin*, 'which is the best sailer in England, the same in which the French did at first design to carry the Young Pretender to Scotland, and afterwards was employed as a Privateer and did great damage'. One Samuel Freeman presented the Harwich Collector with a writ of delivery for her return, but the Collector insisted on a Letter of Attorney from her owner, John Bentley of Flushing. So anxious was Bentley to get this vessel back that he sent the letter direct 'in one of his smuggling vessels, for fear a fresh information should be laid against the cutter'.

The *Walpole* now worked closely with the *Princess Mary*, which seems usually to have been commanded in practice by her mate, Dekker. One night in 1749 they joined forces in a search, with the *Princess Mary* cruising from Orford to Sizewell and the *Walpole* from Bawdsey to Orford. They agreed to show a candle and lanthorn at the stern if starting a chase, and 'three candles and lanthorns half shroud up' if they came up with a smuggler. After jointly seizing the cutter *Queen of Hungary* with a cargo of tea they fell out over the rewards, but Captain Martin arrived on the scene and arranged a settlement.

In 1760 the *Princess Mary*, now under Captain Harvey, came into Harwich to report she had chased a French lugger for twelve hours, but lost her through carrying away her bowsprit. In the morning the lugger was seen at anchor in full sight of the town. A lieutenant and twenty men from HMS *Rye* were put aboard the *Walpole*, which chased her down the Suffolk coast. It was blowing so hard that the lugger was afraid to leave the lee of the land. They lost her in the dark but next morning found her at anchor off Dunwich. She proved to be *L'Esperance* of Dunkirk, which despite being an open boat of only about eighteen tons had a crew of sixteen men and a boy, armed with four swivels, four blunderbusses, twelve muskets, six pistols and twelve cutlasses. They were five days out of Dunkirk but had taken nothing. All finished their venture as prisoners aboard the *Rye*. Two years before this, the *Walpole* was caught by a south-westerly gale lying at anchor in Hollesley Bay. Her boat was swamped and when

The Walpole *drives foul of the* Royal Caroline.

the windlass pawls gave way Dagnett had to cut his cable and run below Orford Ness, splitting a foresail and two jibs. There was an embarrassing sequel, as the lost anchor was found some years later in the possession of a Harwich smackman named Farley Spratlin, who was an ex-mate of the *Walpole*, and Dagnett's brother-in-law. He admitted he had swept it up in Hollesley Bay, and it is not difficult to guess who had told him where to look.

Dagnett had a still more embarrassing experience in 1752 when no less a dignitary than King George II was expected at Harwich to embark in the *Royal Caroline*. Lord Anson and Sir Charles Molloy were ashore with the reception party, along with the Mayor, Aldermen and Capital Burgesses of Harwich, when under their eyes, not two hundred yards from the shore, the *Walpole* drove foul of the *Royal Caroline*, doing some damage. The officers of the *Royal Caroline* had refused to allow the *Walpole's* men to go ashore to fetch their captain and mate, who were also in the official party, but had compelled them to attempt to move the cutter 'at an improper state of the tide'.

One of Dagnett's many adventures is of special interest as demonstrating the way the slightest numerical superiority gave one side or the other the advantage in an encounter with smugglers.

One day in 1746 he seized a tea-laden sloop named *Friends Adventure*, commanded by John Batten (a good Harwich name) with a crew of eight. He took four of these aboard the *Walpole* and put his mate and two hands aboard the sloop, which he then imprudently allowed to drop three miles astern. The four smugglers took advantage of this to fetch swords, and bundled the three Revenue men into their boat, in which they reached Felixstowe. The four aboard the *Walpole* were lodged in Harwich gaol, from which they broke out at midnight, probably with the connivance of the gaoler, who did not report the escape till six o' clock the next morning. A few days later the Levington boat (this creek, just above the present yacht marina, was considered worth its own watch boat as early as the 1720s) dropped down to Harwich to report that the *John & Rachel* of Ipswich was under sail for Flushing with suspects on board. The Revenue men went after her in the Levington boat, having no time to launch their own, and overtook her near Landguard Fort. She refused to lay to, and when they boarded refused to open the hatches. The fore hatch was then broken open, to reveal three men, one of whom was Batten of the *Friends Adventure*. But the *John & Rachel* was now well outside the harbour, driving out on the ebb, and the officers had no alternative but to leave in their boat while they could. Had the *Walpole* been in harbour Batten's luck might have turned at last, but fortunately for him she was away on a cruise.

Dagnett seems to have been something of an honest simpleton. Certainly he was not a very dashing commander, spending at least half of his time in harbour, his three-or four-day cruises alternating with at least three days loading stores or carrying out minor repairs. He was not, however, the only commander whom a Collector kept trying to chase out to sea.

But in 1746 he was in more serious trouble for embezzling part of several seizures, having given each of his mariners a 'stope' bottle of brandy. The worst result of this, in the Collector's view, was not the loss of duty nor the effect on the sobriety of the crew, but the fact that brandy obtained free removed the incentive to get rewards by seizure. 'If the mate sells a gallon of brandy he gains as much as if he seized twelve gallons' he calculated, 'and a mariner as much as if he seized 144 gallons, so the gift of a gallon is better than the seizing of twenty half-ankers.' But, he added, 'Dagnett has not a head capable to perceive the ill consequences of such a precedent.'

A similar indiscretion finished his career ingloriously twenty years later, after twenty-four years in command. A remarkably ferocious Inspector's report in 1768 found fault with much of the Harwich establishment, and in particular declared that the *Walpole's* seizures were not adequate to her expenses for seven years, amounting to £3100, whereas the King's share of her seizures was no more than £462 11s. 'The inactivity of Capt Dagnett is occasioned by his great age . . . it is proper to discontinue the Commander and dismiss the mate' (John Hiblett, who had been in the position for eighteen years.) The fact that the Admiralty cutters with Customs commissions had also 'fallen very short' was considered no excuse.

Worse was to follow. For it then appeared that Dagnett had been privy to a fraud over the supply of sails. The Collector, who had known him for forty-three years, and the Comptroller, who had known him from his infancy, pleaded on his behalf that 'about five years ago his intellect began to fail him, and have gradually got worse ever since, so that he was very liable to be imposed upon by such a skilful and designing man as Smith' — evidently the sailmaker by whom, he

Cyprian Bridge (1738–1814) Commander of the Harwich Revenue cutters Walpole *and* Argus. *He seems to have started in the Harwich packets, and may have still been serving in that service when this portrait was painted at the age of twenty-one. After thirteen years as a Revenue cutter commander he returned to the packets, and died at the ripe age of seventy-six, honoured by Harwich as 'father of the Corporation.' His uniform cannot be identified as belonging to either of the services.*

believed, 'the fraud was wholly committed'. This restored his superannuation.

During this trouble the *Walpole* lay idle, despite the Collector's plea for a deputation for one of the mariners as Second Mate, in order to take her to sea. (The award of a deputation to seize was the first step in seniority for a mariner. Preferably there were three deputed men aboard a cutter, so that two boats could be used, leaving one deputed man still aboard.) Cyprian Bridge,[1] one of the great men of Harwich in its heyday, was then appointed Commander, with John Hobday as his mate, but the following year the *Walpole* was discontinued, to be followed by a succession of cutters named *Bee* and *Argus*.

The origins of both series are curious. There were during the final years of the *Walpole* two other small cutters, *Vigilant* and *Letitia*, under the command of Thomas Shearman, Inspector of Water Guard, and used originally for boarding the packet boats at sea. The former (which in 1771 had also been 'occasionally employed to guard ships in quarantine here') was transferred to Handfleet Water the following year, but after two years the experiment was discontinued and the Sitter and his boatmen were ordered to return aboard their watch vessel. The *Vigilant* was ordered to be sold, but a survey showed her to be rotten from stem to stern. In the same year (1774) the *Letitia* was renamed *Bee*, 'to be employed on the same terms as you are pleased to allow a cutter to Capt Harvey', though the Customs with unusual open-handedness then added 'Since the vessel is condemned, nothing to be charged for rent'.[2]

The first *Argus* in Harwich was an interloper. A little craft of only twenty-four tons, she arrived in April 1763, unannounced and unwelcome, under the command of a Mr Caley, who claimed the title of Inspector General, but produced no papers to prove it, refusing to visit the Custom House or give reasons for his presence. The *Argus* lay in the harbour for fourteen weeks, only going to sea once, and made a great nuisance of herself. Her first action was to rummage a corn vessel, finding some liquor which Caley chose to send to Ipswich. Then Caley stirred up trouble by telling the crews of the packets that they were entitled to two gallons of spirits per man – an allowance permitted to the crews of foreign-going ships which would, as the Collector was not slow to point out, have made nonsense if applied to packets with average crews of fifteen making thirty voyages a year.

Caley, wrote the Collector, is 'famous here for being nothing more than a great drinker, and sometimes to such excess aboard ships that Mr Shearman and his men have been obliged to help him into his boat to prevent him tumbling overboard, but drunk or sober he never forgets to get liquor to carry aboard his own cutter.' One of his tricks was to take liquor aboard the *Argus* to prevent its seizure, returning it after the rummage.

What happened to Caley is not clear. But the *Argus* which replaced the *Walpole* does not seem to have been his cutter, but a new sixty-eight-ton vessel built at Folkestone, with orders to extend her cruising area from the Swin to Lowestoft. Cyprian Bridge took her on contract and commanded her and her successor, *Argus* III, till he resigned in 1783 to take the Post Office packet *Prince of Orange*. The *Argus* III arrived at Harwich in 1777, a fine new craft of 133 tons, 'built at the expense of the Crown'. Having regard to her size the Board allowed six more men, giving her a crew of twenty-four.

This continual growth in the size of cutters was reflected also in their boats. The first *Bee* had only a six-oar galley, but in 1774 Cyprian Bridge asked for a twenty-eight-foot eight-oar galley for the *Argus* on the grounds that he could carry it on deck and that 'most of the smugglers use them and by the swiftness of their going easily elude the pursuit of the boats at present employed in the Revenue service.' Yet by the time the Revenue cutters had their eight-oar galleys the smugglers were using forty-foot craft rowing twelve oars. Probably these big boats were hoisted aboard by heaving the stem to the mast-head before the stern was manhandled over the rail and the boat lowered down on deck.

The *Bees* were also put out to contract, in this case to the Harwich Collector, Griffith Davies (succeeded in 1772 by his son, Henry Pelham Davies), in partnership with his two Tide Surveyors, Thomas Shearman (who lost his obsolete title as Superintendent of Waterguard a few years later) and Joseph Orlibar.

To have given its servants a financial interest in a system they were required to control may seem a curious idea, but it was a policy favoured, for in 1784 sixteen of the Board's twenty-four contract cruisers were contracted by the Collectors and Comptrollers, jointly or severally, at the ports where they were stationed. Indeed, the contract for the *Bee* of 1776 was based on a decision of the Board, taken six years earlier, that there should be 'no contract but to persons interested in the seizures made by the vessel contracted for, unless for short temporary services'.

A partnership between the chief officer and two subordinates also seems doubtful policy, and perhaps it was, for the arrangement broke up not only in a financial difference of opinion, referred to later, but also in a furious row between the Collector and his Tide Surveyors, who accused him of lack of support over the seizures of the Post Office packets (a problem, explained in Chapter 10, which must have put him in a highly difficult situation). The Collector brought counter-charges of neglect of duty, and the two Tide Surveyors resigned. Shearman secured the same position at Maldon, where he retired in 1798, aged sixty-seven, with a rupture and bad eyesight after thirty-two years as a Tide Surveyor, twenty-one of them at Maldon.

This was an unhappy time at Harwich Custom House, for while the Comptroller was ill the Collector's clerk was also accused by Shearman of taking bribes from his fellow officers, who all testified that they merely followed tradition by giving him a tip out of rewards they received. After being threatened in front of the whole staff that he must repay every penny or face dismissal, the poor fellow went out of his mind, leaving the Collector to cope single-handed with his problems and his enemies.

Despite this he continued to run the *Bee*, making representations on her behalf 'from motives of duty as well as interest', till his death in 1782, when the contract was taken over by his successor, William Crowder, who agreed that all expenses, including repairs and salaries, should be paid for out of the gross value of her seizures, and accepted that he would not make any claim for the expense of repairs when the contract ended, which in fact it did in 1788. After this the *Bee* did not continue as a cruiser but went to the Downs as a quarantine vessel, with a reduced crew.

Just how profitable these contracts were is difficult to determine. Shearman and Orlibar asked to be released from their obligations for a new *Bee* in 1776. on the ground that they 'made the proposal before being acquainted with the risque and expense as they now found it to be upon the account of the *Bee* for one year being made out'. But as has been mentioned the Collector was prepared to carry on with the contract.

When William Crowder was asked to pay £784 costs to the Board in 1784 he was 'much surprised, having reference to the letter of 13 October 1784 promising indemnification to the contractors of cutters in the service of the Revenue.' The terms of this indemnity are not revealed, but it may have been concerned with war conditions, for when Letters of Marque were issued to the *Argus* and the *Bee* in 1780 it was confirmed there would be no benefit to the Crown rising out of seizures from the enemy and no claims for damage would be admitted.

The first *Bee*, as has been mentioned, was the *Letitia*, re-named in 1774. The following year she seems to have been replaced by the *Peggy*, another craft under condemnation, similarly re-named *Bee*, with a crew of fourteen including her master and mate. In 1777 the same procedure was apparently applied to yet another seizure, the *Amelia*, though there was also a proposal in 1776 to build a new hundred-ton *Bee* with a crew of twenty, and it is impossible to discover which of these alternatives was adopted.

Whatever their origins, these busy *Bees* were involved in more than their share of hardship and adventure, possibly because Edward Hart, who was their mate till his promotion to Commander in 1776, was an officer of unusual dash, perhaps to the point of rashness.

An incident in 1775 had an extraordinary sequel. Hart, then still mate, took four men off to a large smuggler in the Wallet. They were 'greatly abused and would probably have been murdered had not a boat appeared belonging to the *Swift* (commonly called the *Beehive*) under Capt Harvey's mate', upon which the captain of the smuggler ordered his men to search for arms in the *Bee's* boat. They found two muskets, two pistols and a blunderbuss, and with these put to sea, taking the boat's oars for luck. This is the only reference to the *Swift's* nickname, and its connection if any with the *Bee* is not explained.

A week later the *Pretty Sally* of Harwich, under James Mason, presumably the former mate of the *Argus*, put in from Dunkirk, returning the *Bee's* arms and boat's oars, but this was not the end of the matter, for the Collector declared that 'it has been universally repeated among the smugglers that the *Bee* is not a Custom House vessel, and has no authority to seize . . . We are convinced from many other circumstances that they had been incited to resist that cutter, and illtreat the crew.' The smugglers, he asserted, had 'bound themselves by an oath to destroy the *Bee*.' He even added that 'the Commanders and mates of some of the Revenue vessels, jealous of the *Bee*, have taken this method to render her unsuccessful.' Charged with such an attitude Cyprian Bridge of the *Argus* strongly denied it.

The Collector demanded that the Captain of the smuggler be arrested as a pirate to obtain publicity and put an end to the scandal, for 'as soon as the smugglers' threat to destroy the *Bee* comes to be known we shall not be able to get men to go in her.' Despite this fear the *Bee* and *Argus* continued to give and take hard knocks, making between them twenty-five seizures in 1777 and the first half of 1778, mostly mixed cargoes of gin and tea. Several of these involved bloodshed.

The *Argus* had one of the many clashes with the boatmen at Bawdsey in December 1777 when she challenged a landing there. Sixteen of her crew had seized a load of tubs when they were attacked by the Bawdsey men who re-captured twenty-two half-ankers and a boat in which they took them up to Woodbridge. 'We generally see Bawdsey men among the smugglers' observed the Collector, adding that 'every week there is a landing close to where the Bawdsey Preventive boat is stationed.' This was confirmed by the sacking of the Sitter and the four Boatmen at Bawdsey in 1797, but reading between the lines it is clear that on the many occasions when the Revenue men secured only a small part of a landing both parties must have been playing a game by the only rules which avoided bloodshed. The Customs men seized enough goods to avoid censure and disgrace, as well as saving their skins, while the smugglers made sure of retaining enough to provide a profit on the run.

The following year (1778) the *Argus* went to a cutter off Dunwich which had chain halyards for her main and headsails – a defence against being disabled by gunfire. The Revenue cutter hoisted her ensign and opened fire, but 'finding her a large cutter with ten carriage guns besides a number of swivels, and full of men, could not tell if she was a smuggler or a privateer, and having neither shelter for her men nor chains for her sails, prudently put about.' The smuggling cutter set her large jib and pursued, but finding herself outsailed bore up and fired her two stern guns. Two days later the same cutter found the *Argus* off Southwold and chased her to Orford Ness, where an Aldeburgh boat reported she had just picked up two smugglers off the beach.

In the same year the *Argus* joined the Yarmouth cutter *Hunter* which she found engaged with 'a large cutter with four carriage guns, two-pounders, and six swivels.' Following these engagements she had her bulwarks pierced with 'a tier of portholes for the guns.'

5

The Cutters Outgunned

'Horney Cock' and William Dowsett: Doing a deal with a Smuggler: Stinging the Bee.

THOUGH the small cutters of the mid-eighteenth century had been replaced by larger craft, and these had received more and better guns, the Revenue men were now again consistently outmanned and outgunned.

The *Bee* in 1778 recognised in the East Swin a big cutter commanded by 'one Cocks or Cox known as Horney Cock', and chased it to Orford Ness. There the smuggler made a signal by 'hoisting a jack at his gaff end' to another large cutter which her Commander Edward Hart, perceived 'to mount many carriage guns and to be full of men.' The hunter was then herself pursued almost into Harwich harbour.

Guessing that the goods would be landed that night, Hart sent fourteen men in boats to cruise off the likely landing place. In the morning they fell in with a forty-foot galley rowing twelve oars, but as she was empty they realised the landing had taken place. At Ramsholt, on the Deben, cart tracks across a field led them to an underground cache, containing nearly thirty-three half-ankers. But before they could load them into their boats they were surrounded by nearly 100 armed men, who rescued most of the spirits and 'beat and wounded the officers in a very barbarous manner.' 'Smuggling is carried on on the Suffolk coast in a more open and daring manner than ever before, by very large armed vessels for which neither cutter is anything like a match', reported the Collector in 1778. Cyprian Bridge of the *Argus* observed, 'Frequently they have about a hundred horsemen, besides carriages of all sorts to receive the goods. When our officers meet with them and make seizures from them, it is only what the smugglers please to give them.'

The *Bee* had her revenge a few years later, for in 1783 she seized 'the fine Clench cutter, except as to the bowsprit which is fixed as a sloop . . . owned by the notorious Henry Cock, known as Horney Cock, with four men aboard. Five more men came off and threatened to re-capture her, but were repelled.' Cock offered Capt Batten of the *Bee* an unlimited sum for her release, but the eight-year-old cutter, sixty-three feet by twenty-two feet, named *Achilles*, was sent to The Tobacco Ground at Rotherhithe with a view no doubt either to fetching a good price or to entering the Preventive service. But though she was valued at £591 a sale by auction failed to raise a bid, and when she was subsequently offered for £300 there were no takers – perhaps a reflection of the awe in which 'Horney Cock' was held on the coast.

In the same year as her first unsuccessful encounter with the redoubtable 'Horney Cock' (1778) the *Bee* had a more successful encounter with the *Neptune*, owned by the notorious William Dowsett of Paglesham, with a crew of eleven armed with six swivels. The *Bee*, lying in Burnham River, saw her in the Whitaker, and giving chase, drove her ashore on the Barrow Sands – a mishap which suggests some panic among the smugglers, unless they were trying to entice the *Bee* into

A swivel of 1776, based on Chapman: Architectura Navalis. *This type of gun was popular in privateers and other small craft, and was the forerunner of the later carronade.*

the same situation, for she must have drawn more water than the forty-ton *Neptune*. The eleven smugglers, who as well as their six swivels had plenty of small arms, would not surrender, and when the *Neptune* came afloat on the flood tide Hart fired a blank shot, after which the engagement started in earnest. After an hour the *Neptune* struck her flag with two of her crew dead, William Richardson (a native of Shottisham, Suffolk, who had fled to Flushing to escape a murder charge) and James Anderson. The *Neptune* was found to have '391 half-ankers and two wholes of brandy, rum and geneva, 8 cwt tea, 3 cwt tobacco, 2 cwt coffee.' The *Bee* suffered no casualties, though her sails, rigging and mast were damaged by shot. The Harwich coroner's jury brought in a verdict of 'Chance Medley.'

Within a few weeks the *Argus* brought in another forty-ton cutter, the *Waggon* commanded by the same William Dowsett. How had he been allowed to go free after the taking of the *Neptune*, when six or seven of his crew were sent to the Navy? Thirty years later he would have been hustled into prison without ceremony or delay. It seems possible that at this time the Revenue men were still more concerned with seizing contraband than with capturing smugglers, partly perhaps because they were so motivated by rewards, and partly because despite all the ferocity and the bloodshed, the smugglers were still such a familiar feature of the scene that they were treated as opponents rather than enemies or criminals. This sort of attitude is also suggested by the *Argus's* seizure of the cutter *Friendship*, with spirits and tea, 'hovering without the Galloper.' Because this was outside the territorial limits the Board declined to prosecute, but allowed Captain Bridge to do so. He, however, could not get enough evidence, so made a deal with the owner of the *Friendship* to restore the cutter if he would relinquish any claim to the cargo.

Three years before this, in 1775, Bridge had been involved in two curiously similar incidents in the space of a month, which caused the Board to murmur about 'the appearance of collusion', and which suggest that Bridge was a more cautious and pragmatic performer than his colleague Edward Hart, and for that reason lived longer.

Off Lowestoft one morning the *Argus* saw a lugger lying-to, and chased her as she made off. It fell calm, and Bridge boarded, finding geneva, arrack and tea. The captain made the normal excuse that he was bound for Bergen, but refused to show bills of lading or to go aboard the *Argus*. Having not enough men to man both vessels and secure the crew, Bridge took the cargo, 'which they consented to' and let the lugger go.

Three weeks later, off Southwold, the *Argus* chased a seventy-ton cutter, and again it fell calm. Haggis, the mate, boarded, to hear the same story that they were for Bergen, with the same refusal to show bills of lading. When the *Argus's* boat fetched Bridge, the captain said he would give up her cargo, and even ordered his men to assist in loading it into the *Argus's* boats.

Yet ten years before this, in 1765, when the Board complained about this type of dealing the Collector was already insisting, 'the only way is to seize the vessel, for all the smugglers confess that they would rather lose three cargoes than one vessel. We always insist officers do seize the vessels and boats. The contrary practice is the way some officers get money . . .' Clearly, however, it was one thing for the Collector to lay down a policy, and quite another for outmanned Revenue cutters to carry it out. In any case, while it is easy to bring the familiar charge of collusion, and in these instances difficult to refute it, it also has to be remembered that the Revenue men, their wives and their families, had to live in the same communities as the smugglers, and a curiously ambivalent attitude was probably the inevitable result.

As these adventures continued, the Harwich Collector observed that the *Bee* could scarcely go out without falling in with a smuggler who fired on her. He asked that she be supplied with 'proper netting and stancheons, filled in with the usual things that are proof against musket shot', and be given four two-pound guns. A month later he asked for 'the new carronades', suggesting they could be paid for out of her seizures.

In 1779 she encountered a lugger of about 100 tons, apparently unarmed, but when Hart made to board her she put out five guns and chased the *Bee* through 'Goldeyman's Gap' into the Wallet. Hart went into the Colne and rode overland to report that the lugger was landing her cargo at Clacton. The *Argus* was lying offshore, and Hart went off to her with five men of the press gang. Thus reinforced the *Argus* should have been able to make a capture, but the lugger, having finished her business, made off into the night.

In February 1780, the mate of the *Bee*, James Frost, and his crew were beaten up by a large party of smugglers who rescued from them the *William & Mary* which had been seized in Herne Bay. Nine years after this Frost was appointed to a cutter at Liverpool but was still too ill to go and it was suggested he could be better employed ashore as a Superintendent of Warehouses. (On this occasion the date of the melée was given as August 1783, but there can hardly have been two such fracas).

Again in 1780, the *Bee* seized in Hollesley Bay the 250-ton brig *Isabella* of Buckhaven, with forty-four half-ankers from Middleburg, and, along with the *Argus*, took a large lugger off Bradwell with 'ten large wall pieces mounted on swivels'. This engagement had to be fought from boats as there was not enough wind to bring up the cutters. The smugglers escaped, leaving 250 half-ankers and about a ton of tea.

The *Bee* then spent the last four months of the year at the Nore, at the end of which service she was retained on salvaging from the wreck of the store ship *Cato* on the Pan Sand, off Whitstable, losing her galley during the operation. A few months later Edward Hart, worn out by his exertions and his wounds, died, 'one of the most active, spirited and valuable officers' observed the Collector in a tribute rare among the many formal notifications of death.

Joining the Navy

*Special Services: Wartime Regulations: Private Enterprise: Arrogant
Lieutenants.*

CYPRIAN BRIDGE'S successor in command of the *Argus* III was
Capt William Haggis, her former mate, who kept her till 1791 when
he was succeeded by Captain John Saunders. Whether this *Argus* came
to an accidental end is not clear, but certainly there was an interval
before *Argus* IV was commissioned. During this time Capt Saunders
fitted out the cutter *Liberty*, for which he 'craved' certificates of protection against impressment for four men in November 1793. The Board
granted protections to mariners discharged from 'the late *Argus* cutter.'
   The new commander of the *Bee* after Edward Hart's death was Capt
John Batten. Both the new commanders soon began to experience the
tribulations of their predecessors. Haggis was lying in the Rolling
Grounds off Harwich in May 1780, only a few months after his
appointment, when he saw a lugger reaching in for Bawdsey. Giving
chase he saw men and horses ashore taking oilskin bags from her.
Then she put off and sailed to the north. Sending the *Argus* in pursuit
of her, Haggis took six men ashore. Leaving three of them to load
half-ankers into the cutter's boat he went with the other three among
thirty or forty horsemen, all loaded with oilskin bags, who attacked
them. Haggis defended himself with his hanger (a short sword), but
was wounded in the hand, knocked to the ground and whipped, while
the men tried to make their horses trample on him. He was finally left
unconscious in the water, and only saved by some locals who had
been watching. The lugger reached Orford, where the crew got ashore
and disappeared.

The cutters now became increasingly concerned in an even tougher
struggle – the war against Napoleon. This affected them in two ways.
   On the one hand a bewildering succession of regulations was
imposed on small craft of all kinds, which the Revenue men had to
oversee and enforce. The regulations prohibiting many kinds of hull
and many trivial details of rig meant that vessel after vessel was arrested
as 'not adaptable for the fair mercantile trade'. These repressive rules
are dealt with in Chapter Twelve; it may merely be observed here that
for the cutters they involved some easy rewards for some humdrum
labour as a change from their harsher ordeals. Warlike stores aboard
neutral ships were also for the seizing, a definition stretched in 1780

to include 750 casks of beef and pork aboard a ship bound for Bordeaux, along with 'any copper fit for sheathing'.

More important, the Revenue cruisers were drafted into the Navy and the Navy was drafted into the Revenue service. The Admiralty had long had a claim on the Customs' cutters in time of national emergency, with the Customs probably not sorry to be relieved of their cost. In 1744 twelve of the total fleet of nineteen had been transferred to naval duties, with the *Walpole* attached to Commodore Smith's squadron at the Nore. Now, with war again dominating national issues and straining national resources, the cutters were again repeatedly sent on special services.

They gathered in Harwich in January 1795 under orders to proceed to Flushing, when news came that that town had fallen and they asked leave to return to their stations. (All communications with Holland were finally cut in February after the Harwich Customs had coped with 'immense quantities of baggage from thence.') They also served in the Texel expedition in 1799 and in a blockade of the French ports, undertaken in 1801 by Nelson, fresh from his triumphs in the Baltic. Such cutters as remained had their stations much extended, with the *Argus* IV under John Saunders cruising in 1795 from the Swin Middle to Lowestoft, and the *Repulse* under Munnings having a roving commission from Gt Yarmouth to Portsmouth.

In March of that year however the *Argus* was sent to Emden, Saunders protesting that he was 'not furnished with such private signals as are used by the British cruisers upon that coast to which he is under orders to proceed'. She returned after a few months without completing her service, along with other Revenue cutters from Emden, which gathered at Harwich, again asking if they were now at liberty to return to their stations. She then resumed her routine duties on the coast, including assisting HMS *Edgar*, dismasted near Orford Ness.

One of the special duties of the Revenue cutters was to take up navigation marks as a defence against invasion. Mrs Mary Rebow, of Wivenhoe Park (herself a member of the Martin family) recorded in her diary [1] in August 1779, 'Capt Harvey is to return on Friday with his new cutter with Mr Gascoign.' Then on the Saturday she added, 'I was mistaken about the cutter, for it is the old one there has been all the fuss about, and she is expected down today with the Admiralty colours flying on board. The business, it seems, is for Mr Gascoign and some others to go in her the beginning of the week to fix small cutters at all the principal buoys on the coast, which are to take them up and destroy them as soon as any of the French fleet appears in sight and after that she is to go as a privateer.' 'Mr Gascoign' probably refers to Bamber Gascoyne, MP for Maldon, 1761–1763, and later MP for several other places. 'All the fuss' may refer to the attack on the *La Prudente's* prize already recounted.

The same tactics were employed for another purpose in 1797, when Capt Bromfield, an elder brother of Trinity House, arrived at Harwich to assemble a squadron of fishing smacks, led by the *Argus*, to remove or sink the Whiting, Rough and Gunfleet buoys at the Northern approaches to the Thames Estuary, and so thwart the plans of the mutineers at the Nore to defect to republican France or the new Dutch Republic. The little squadron also warned London-bound provision ships to avoid capture by the mutineers.

This scare led to a plan for the Revenue cutters to be placed under the orders of Trinity House in the event of a future emergency. In 1798 a rehearsal was staged, using five hired Harwich smacks, with the *Pocock*, which had been used for the salvage of the *Repulse* ten years before, serving as tender to the Trinity House buoy yachts and Revenue cutters on station. After this Trinity House does not seem to have pursued its bid to control the Revenue cutters, though it did take over the name *Argus*, which throughout the nineteenth century was used for a succession of lightship tenders.

The *Argus* herself returned from the exercise in trouble for 'craving' new sails while her old suit was not worn out, and went to Deptford for repairs, after which she returned to special service for the whole of the year 1799, serving under Admiral Mitchell in the Texel expedition. For this year the cutter *Union* was employed as temporary cruiser in her absence. Thomas Collis, the *Argus's* deputed mariner, sailed in the lugger *Brave* to collect her from Colchester. He was at first officiously prevented from leaving Harwich by the gun brig *Furious*, as one of the frequent embargoes on sailing was in force, and on arrival at Colchester the Collector refused to retain the *Brave* which had to return with the *Union*.

Three years later Saunders resigned, blaming ill-health. (He died in 1811, aged sixty-five.) Perhaps he had also had enough of Navy ways, for, asked for a reference on behalf of his first mate, twenty-one-year-old John Turner, as his successor, he sent this splendid broadside, addressed from Grimsby Roads 'under orders of the Officer Commanding Ships'. 'You call on me to state whether John Turner has Navigation and understands the management of ships. I can only say that he has Navigation, but whether he understands all of the etiquette of a ship of war I cannot adjudge, being entirely ignorant of it myself . . . I know he understands the management of a cutter better than any Navy officer that has yet been on board the *Argus*'.

John Turner got his promotion after a probationary stint in command of the *Hunter* at Yarmouth, but faced problems, reporting that he had only succeeded in recruiting five men, making a total crew of seventeen including himself, and that he did not 'see any prospect of getting the cutter her full complement'. He made repeated applications for the renewal of Captain Saunders's Letters of Marque, which were perhaps an attraction to recruits.

In 1805, when the *Argus* was having a re-fit at Deptford, 'the *Rose in June* cutter, under condemnation at this port [Harwich], fitted out as a temporary cruiser by the Commander of the *Argus*, Captain Turner, sailed with twelve men', including Turner and his Deputed Mariner. This was apparently his own private venture to employ himself and his crew. It would be interesting to know how many small craft were armed at this time. The little *Adventure* of Harwich, clinker-built at Dover in 1785, with a total crew of four and a value of £200, was licensed in 1793 for two swivels, four muskets and four cutlasses. Such a provision was presumably offensive, with a view to pouncing on some wretched little Dutch schuyt, for it would have been quite inadequate against any conventional privateer. The year after Turner fitted out the *Rose in June* the Commanders of the packets applied to fit out a lugger called the *Tar* of Deal, also under condemnation, 'as a private ship to cruize against the enemy'. The licence application was urgent, as 'in the event of hostilities with Prussia the greatest expedition will be necessary.' The *Rose in June* [2] was rewarded by the capture of the Folkestone lugger *Dolphin*, with 298 half-ankers, four bales of tobacco and 144 packs of playing cards, before she was dismantled in July 1805, when Turner brought the *Argus* back from Deptford, only to lose her and his own life two years later.

Foreign toy-town privateers were quite common. In 1747 Dagnett of the *Walpole* saw a little ten-tonner anchored off Felixstowe, and sent a boat off to her. She proved to be the *Guillaume Gouteux* of Calais, with nine men and a boy, armed with a musket and a cutlass apiece and three or four pistols. She had worked up on the flood tide from Dunwich in company with a brigantine bound from Hull to London, and anchored near her, intending to board her as soon as it was dark. Nor was privateering confined to action against enemies. It was also applied to the Revenue service, for in 1771 Cyprian Bridge unsuccessfully asked for 'a large lugg sail boat' seized by him 'to be used by him for the Service', and in 1773 Capt O'Hara, of HM Sloop *Alderney*, having purchased a small cutter to cruise against the smugglers, borrowed a condemned boat for her. When his own boat was ready the borrowed one was duly burned. John Loten, the Collector at Leigh, also procured a small decked vessel equipped with three swivels, and made many seizures.

An aversion to the Navy was not confined to John Saunders – and it was returned with an arrogant contempt for the Customs on the part of some of the naval lieutenants in command of the eight Admiralty cutters ordered in 1784 to cruise against the smugglers between Yarmouth and Portsmouth.

Lieutenant Leggett, commander of one of these, the *Surprise*, in 1792 seized the *Adventure*, a cutter trading between Harwich and Holland, but owned in Bristol, and presumably the Letter of Marque already mentioned. When asked for details he sent 'a few lines on a dirty piece of paper'. The Collector deemed it a 'painful task to make any comment upon the conduct of officers in the Navy when in service of the Revenue, but though we produced Acts of Parliament . . . and offered our opinion with many admonitions it appeared all in vain, and he declared in our presence he would not give a Fig (or Farthing) for a man who had no an opinion of his own . . . His language and manner were highly contemptuous and insolent, accompanied with the most dirty, mean insinuations and suspicions . . .'

Capt Hardy in 1786, soon after his appointment to HMS *Otter*, seized a vessel which he asserted was a smuggler without even going aboard her. Asked for evidence he said he had none, and later he casually mentioned that he had released the vessel. The Collector 'gave him friendly hints and opinions.'

Naval involvement increased in the post-war years, for the cutter fleet came under Admiralty control in 1816 and was not returned to the Customs till 1821. This provided employment for lieutenants who would otherwise have been 'on the beach', but it was not popular, since for many years such service did not count for seniority. Nor was it welcomed by the Customs, who would have preferred to accept the 'more roughly educated sailing masters, who are the standing pilots of HM Ships.' Hence it is interesting to find two Commanders at this time insisting that they needed to carry a pilot. Capt Hearn of the *Drake* at Harwich was allowed in 1814 'to take a pilot for the present but to report his reason for not being sufficiently acquainted with his present station', which was Yarmouth to Sheerness. Five years earlier Capt Smith of the *Leopard*, also of Harwich, gave his reason for employing a local branch pilot, Stonehouse Stewart, at 6s a day. 'Because of the weather he has not been able to cruise so as to obtain a complete knowledge of the coast on the northern part of this station.'

Cyprian Bridge, John Saunders and other members of old Harwich families, who had attained to command by working up the hard ladder from Deputed Mariner to Mate, must have been turning in their graves.

7

Cutters captured

Loss of the Repulse, Swift, *and* Argus: *Murder of the* Fox's *Crew: Revenue Cutters' Race*

DURING the long years of the wars against France several of the cutters were captured, either by smugglers or by the French. Both the Colchester cutters fell into enemy hands within a few years of each other.

The third *Repulse*, in direct defiance of her orders not to quit her station, set off for the French coast to pick up prizes under her Letters of Marque, but ran ashore near Calais in May 1780. The mate in charge, Martin Hopkins, his mate, Mr Harlow, and the crew of nineteen were imprisoned in Calais for thirteen months before being released on payment of a fine and ransom. On his return Hopkins applied to the Board to reimburse these sums, but was refused, because the capture was due to 'willful misconduct and negligence'. The *Repulse* herself became a French privateer but was recaptured and repossessed by Capt Harvey. Rather surprisingly Hopkins was reinstated as mate.

The little forty-seven-ton *Swift* fell in with a smuggling yawl in 1781 off the Essex coast. Hauling the yawl alongside, she took on board the master, a man named Knight, along with about twenty-five half-ankers of brandy and geneva. But Knight realised that the *Swift* had a crew of only ten men, fewer than his own. On his signal about forty men emerged from concealment, boarded the *Swift*, bundled her crew into a boat and put to sea. The *Argus* pursued them but without success. Six years later one of the smugglers' crew was spotted in Ipswich gaol, confined for a minor assult. He was brought to trial for 'piratically seizing and sailing away' the *Swift* and sentenced to death. The *Swift* herself was recovered while smuggling off Hastings the year after her capture, when Capt Harvey had his claim 'to be repaid his interest in the late *Swift* cutter' refused on the ground she was 'the sole property of the Crown'. The Board also declared it was 'determined never to suffer the commander of an established vessel to have one under contract at the same time', probably with the intention of maintaining competition among the cutters and discouraging them from hunting in pairs or packs.

At the time of her capture the *Swift* was under the command of Jonas Woodward, but John Harlow, formerly of the *Repulse*, was with him. The Customs decided that Harlow was to blame and dismissed him, giving Woodward a chance to secure his place as second mate of the *Repulse* after her recovery, or possibly the *Repulse* IV commissioned round this time. Soon after this, in 1782, the *Repulse* joined with HM cutter *Liberty* in seizing the *William & Mary* off Southwold. The lieutenant in command of the Naval cutter offered to take the prize into Harwich, or to provide the *Repulse* with men to do so, but Martin Hopkins, again in command of the *Repulse*, took her under the shelter of the Gunfleet Sand, off the Essex coast, unloaded her contraband and delivered her back to the smugglers. This time he did not get away with it, but was also dismissed, with the Board ordering the total rewards of £200 to go to the *Liberty* with no share to the *Repulse*. Woodward again got promotion, to first mate, in which capacity he was serving when the *Repulse* was lost, as has already been mentioned.

The reaction of Henry Davies, the Collector, to the loss of the *Swift* was to offer to provide a replacement of about sixty to eighty tons, with a crew of fourteen to sixteen men. 'A number of small vessels, none above forty tons, many under fifteen, are employed working from Dunkirk to Essex, between the Naze and the Thames. Large cutters cannot follow them among the sands' he pointed out hopefully. Soon afterwards he suggested employing one of the *Bee's* recent captures, a lugger named *Musquito*, under John Batten's command, with seven additional men, 'on several or joint cruises' with the *Bee*. Batten himself was more concerned to increase his own complement, observing that 'when two boats are manned from the cutter the vessel is scarce safe.'

The *Argus* had already had her ten two-pounders replaced by fourteen carron guns, but now, alarmed by the capture of the *Swift*, she also begged for more arms lest she too was overpowered. Her fears were well founded, for her successor was in fact captured some twenty years later in 1807 under Capt John Turner. The story of this disaster can be reconstructed in vivid detail from the reports of many who took part.

She sailed from Harwich on 12 September 1807 for Hollesley Bay, where she lay a while at anchor before getting under way for the Galloper. There she hove-to for the night, intending to cruise between this sandbank and the North Foreland. In the morning she hailed the gun brig *Starling*, reaching down for Orford Ness, and in the evening about eight o'clock saw a brig 'within the Galloper' steering southeast. In a strong north-north-east wind the *Argus* set off in pursuit under double-reefed mainsail, full foresail and fourth jib. No ship was in sight till she saw a lugger, apparently giving chase. At 9.30 pm she fired a bow chaser to bring the brig to, and hailed her. The reply confirmed Turner's suspicion that she had been captured, and he sent his Deputed Mariner, Isaac Siggers, off to her with five men in the four-oar boat, at the same time ordering the lashings of the boarding

The Argus *athwart the French lugger* L'Etoile, *with the captured brig* Endeavour *lying off.*

pikes to be cut away. Siggers was at this time acting as mate in place of William Deane, who was relieving the mate of the Yarmouth Revenue cutter *Hunter*. He found the brig to be the *Endeavour* of Arundel, in charge of a French prize-master, with four Frenchmen and an English boy aboard. He set out to take the five Frenchmen aboard the *Argus*, but as he did so she opened fire on the lugger, which proved to be *L'Etoile* of Boulogne, a sixty-tonner with a crew of seventy-three (though only sixty were then aboard), mounting fourteen guns, three- and four-pounders.

Night had now fallen, and Siggers, his men and his prisoners could do nothing but watch the engagement from the *Endeavour*, lying hove-to in the moonlight. As they did so the Frenchmen told them the brig was the lugger's first capture on that voyage, though later Captain Turner was to report that he had re-captured another brig from her on his previous cruise, and that she had 'done great damage on our coast for a long time.'

After her first broadside from her weather guns at a range of about 200 yards, they saw the *Argus* tack, firing her two bow guns. She did not, however, pay away enough to bring her other broadside to bear, perhaps unwilling to expose her whole side to the volleys of musket

71

shots from the lugger. The lugger was now described as luffing into the *Argus's* weather quarter, but ultimately the *Argus's* bowsprit rode across the lugger's deck between her fore and main masts, giving the Frenchmen a chance to board. Watching the scene, Siggers realised the *Argus* was taken, and as he could no longer see the lugger correctly assumed she had sunk. He got the *Endeavour* under way and returned to Harwich. The *Argus* was taken into Dunkirk next day.

Subsequent reports came from Captain Turner in hospital in Dunkirk, and later from two former members of the lugger's crew, captured aboard the Danish frigate *Frederick Waardt*, one of whom had visited Turner in hospital. Five men had been killed in the *Argus* and six wounded, including the captain. Of the dead two were from Harwich, one from Ipswich, one from Manningtree and one was an Irishman. Four were killed in the lugger and eight wounded, including the captain and one officer. Four of the lugger's crew and five prisoners from the brig went down in the lugger when she sank.

Turner had only struck after being wounded three times and having his left arm shattered above the elbow. It was not a discreditable outcome against such odds, though Turner's claim that the fight lasted an hour and a half must be less accurate than Siggers' estimate of a quarter of an hour, unless one was describing the whole incident, and the other the actual hand-to-hand melée. He was well cared for in hospital and allowed to be attended by the *Argus's* steward. First reports were full of hopes that his arm could be saved without amputation. Then came news that he had died of his wounds.

Eighteen prisoners were marched to Arras goal where they petitioned for their prize money to be sent through an agent 'as our captain is dead and we have no other refuge to turn to'. A number of them did not survive the eight long years of imprisonment, dying in various French prisons, mostly at Givet, where their funerals were attended by their shipmates and the pay due to them at a shilling a day was then meticulously made up. Some, however, returned in 1815, including Edward Catchpole, who at the time of his capture had written a brave letter to his wife, copied into the Collector's notebook: 'My dear, I would have you make yourself as happy as possible, for I hope to see you again.' His faith was rewarded and his wish granted, for in 1815, then employed in the Preventive boat at Southwold, he was asked for a reference to support the plea of another ex-prisoner, Enoch Hitchcock of Manningtree, who had got home from France but like many another old sailor after many another war could find no work.

Isaac Siggers incurred no censure for his passive role, but it may not have done his career much good. He was put in command of the *Argus's* eight-oar galley, and in February 1808 was complaining that life in an open boat in mid-winter was affecting his health, and begging for 'some small decked vessel'. This plea seems to have been ignored, and he does not appear to have found further advancement, whereas William Deane, the *Argus's* regular mate whom he was relieving, went on to be mate of the new *Argus* and then commander of the *Iris* and later of the *Hawk*.

With the end of the French wars, heavily armed smuggling cutters were largely replaced by luggers and galleys, often carrying mixed crews, half French and half English, for aliens could not be charged with offences committed outside British waters. With a few notable exceptions such craft relied on concealment rather than armed defiance. Many galleys were painted white and worked under oars, making them inconspicuous. The Revenue men had to play the same game, and relied increasingly on night patrols in their boats.

The Harwich cruisers were now the *Active*, which had been on the station in 1792, returning to Faversham when the new *Argus* arrived, and which was again at Harwich in 1814, the seventy-six-ton *Hawk*, built in 1807, and stationed at Harwich in 1822, and the eighty-one-ton *Viper*, built at Cowes in 1805 and, unusually, schooner-rigged. She was paid off at Harwich in 1817, her crew being transferred to the 'Revenue boat service'. Just before this one of her boats, 'employed on the newly adopted system for the prevention of smuggling', was lost at sea with all hands. She also refloated a smuggler ashore on Landguard Point, Harwich, in 1811 after the crew had jettisoned 600 tubs of geneva and made their escape. The liquor was found by soldiers, four of whom died from drinking it. This schooner succeeded a smaller *Viper* of forty-four tons which belonged to the Excise and was based at Harwich from 1792 to 1804. Her last commander, Edward Morgan, was appointed to the schooner, suggesting that this may also have been an Excise craft.

Another Excise cutter, the *Fox* of Colchester, fell in with a large open lugger at sea in August 1815 and sent off a boat with a boarding party thirteen strong. Seeing the strength of the lugger's crew, the officer in charge said he would not molest her, lowered his sail and dropped astern. The smugglers, however, bore down and rammed the boat. They then fired into her and in the melée the officer, his brother and two other men were killed, with three wounded. Two of the smuggling gang, Thomas Gilham and William Brockman, were hanged at Execution Dock the following February. According to the contemporary Press they shook hands with friends and declared they were 'going on a more prosperous voyage than any they had undertaken.'

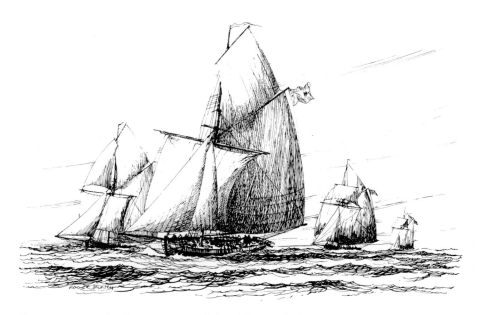

Revenue cutters in the race to test their sailing qualities.

Many of the cutters were after 1816 under Naval command. One of them, the *Eagle*, had such an outstanding record of captures that in 1819 the officer in command of her, Lieut Pogson, was promoted to the rank of Commander in recognition of his zeal. In 1818 she had seized two luggers with spirits, and an eleven-oar boat with seventy-six tubs of brandy and 432 packs of cards, which were burned by order of the Stamp Office. Commander Pogson celebrated his promotion by seizing the lugger *Huzzar* of Boulogne, with a crew of eleven Frenchmen and twelve Englishmen, who put up a resistance in the course of which one smuggler was shot, and in the following year the lugger *L'Argus* with five Englishmen and seven Frenchmen. This *Eagle* was replaced in 1822 by a big 125-tonner of the same name built by Goode at Bridport in 1816, which went on to Weymouth in 1844 and finally became a watch vessel at Stockton in 1845.

Naval appointments became universal in 1831, at first as a compulsory three-year posting which did not count for seniority, and so was highly unpopular, but after 1841 on a five-year contract carrying full Naval pay and privileges. How much the change was part of the general enthusiasm for re-organisation, and the ending of traditions which included some questionable practices, and how much it was simply to relieve naval unemployment, is not clear, but it must have been another nail in the coffin of Harwich, where the great cod fishery had collapsed, the Admiralty turned its back on its Navy Yard in 1827 and the Post Office packet contract was lost in 1832 – a collection of calamities which plunged the town into a century of depression.

An apparently unique exception was made for one Harwich civilian Customs officer, Isaac Saxby, who was appointed mate of the *Desmond* in 1841 and promoted to command the *Scout* two years later. He, however, led a very different life to his predecessors in the *Argus* and the *Repulse*, for while he made some seizures of contraband he was largely concerned with another activity of increasing importance, the salvaging of cargoes and the saving of life from the innumerable wrecks on the Thames Estuary sandbanks, an occupation in which he policed the local smacks and also played a leading part himself. This story I have already told in *The Salvagers*.

Before Saxby's time, in 1824, the *Scout* had the distinction of winning a unique race for Revenue cutters to test their sailing qualities. The course was from the Cork round the Kentish Knock to Margate. The *Fly* came second, the *New Charter* third and the *Lively* fourth, with the *Eagle*, *Sealark* and *Desmond* several miles astern. While this sporting occasion was organised with an eye on future improvements, it now by hindsight seems like a valedictory farewell to an age that was ending, for the Customs fleet, numbering forty-four in 1821, was reduced to thirty-two years later, and the cutters were increasingly relegated to a secondary role by the reforms of the 1820s and 1830s. The new-style smugglers were to be looked after by the cruising tenders of the Preventive Water Guard and the later Coastguard cutters, which were much less ambitious craft.

8

Sharing the Spoils

Rewards and Expenses: Rich Pickings from Salvage: First Come First Served: 'The Opportunity of Getting Money'

THE foregoing chapters have dealt with the evolution and adventures of the Revenue cutters through succeeding phrases in their affairs. Let us conclude with a less romantic aspect which was all-important to those concerned – the system of rewards.

In 1721 the Commander was paid £50 a year, his mate £25, his servant £8, and the mariners £15 each. But these modest sums were nothing to the value of seizures. The *Argus* grossed £17,526 in the years 1774 to 1778, her best year being June 1777 to June 1778, which yielded £7,099. These seizures were shared out on the basis of half for the King and half for the ship's company. The division of the latter varied from age to age. In 1749 the Harwich Collector pointed out that the system was unduly complicated and suggested it be tidied up on the basis of dividing a notional £20 as £10 for the Commander, £3 for the First Mate, £2 for the Second Mate and 10s for each of ten mariners. In 1781 the arrangement was a quarter of the total sum to the Commander, one-eighth to the Chief Mate (who had to pay one-fifth of this to the Second Mate, who also received a mariner's share) and the remaining eighth to the mariners. In 1841, however, the Harwich Collector observed that rewards for seizures 'are now a quarter, a third, a half or two thirds' and 'should be a moiety' (half), referring presumably to the proportion paid to the ship's company.

The King's share was balanced against the cost of the cutters, with the sort of thrifty bookkeeping typical of the period. For the first quarter of 1786, the *Argus* and the *Bee* cost £330, salaries being £102 and £60 respectively, and victualling £85 and £56, with tradesmen's bills and repairs amounting to £22 for the pair of them. The King's share of their seizures was £214, leaving a 'deficit' of £116. On the same basis the whole Harwich establishment was costed like a shop. Gross receipts from Michaelmas 1777–1778 were £7,250, of which £3,066 went on salaries and expenses, with the balance of £4,183 to the Receiver General. But since the figures were 'intended for the information of the House of Commons' the Collector went on to point out that the King's share of seizures, £4,548, exceeded by £1,481 the salaries and expenses of those collecting the money. Some recent Government policies have been branded as 'monetarist', but it is difficult to imagine, say, today's Traffic Wardens being costed on the basis of subtracting parking penalties from their wages, or the Police returning a 'deficit' after deducting fines and payments by organisations hiring their services.

Many of the individual seizures and their resulting rewards were quite small. Robert Martin's cutters in 1733 earned £7 10s from the fifteen-ton *Dolphin* and £12 from the twenty-four-ton well smack *Deary*. In 1798 the boat *Rodney*, valued at £7, brought William Haggis £1 9s 5d after payment of charges, and the cutter *Peggy*, valued at £79, brought John Batten £35. But the value of the cargo was often many times that of the vessel carrying it. The little nine-ton smack *King George* of Woodbridge, seized there in 1799 with five bales of woollen cloth and two bales of Norwich stuffs, ordered by a merchant at Middleburg in Holland, was sold for a mere £4 5s, but the sale of the cargo brought the Commander of the *Argus* £49, the Mate £24, the Deputed Mariner £10 and twenty-nine mariners £27.

When two Revenue cutters were engaged on the same seizure the custom was that the first to board claimed the whole reward. This, according to Capt Haggis of the *Argus*, had been established by Capt Harvey of the *Repulse* when her boats and those of the *Bee* took a smuggler and he refused any share to the *Bee* – though, added Haggis, 'lately Capt Harvey has attempted to break a custom established by himself' – a reference to a row over the seizure of the schooner *Nassau* of London for illegally having an all-foreign crew. The custom was defended on the ground that 'if altered, cutters will keep an eye on each other, and the moment a chase is perceived another cutter will instantly do the same in order to set up a claim, whereby much trouble and vexation may ensue.'

Many of the more substantial rewards came from salvage, which was throughout both the periods convered by this book an important activity and a valuable source of income. The claims of salvagers were met before duties were levied, provoking a protest in 1754 at the 'extraordinary allowances made by Justices of the Peace on goods salved from stranded ships, to the great detriment of the Revenue.'

During the nineteenth century the assistance of ships in distress, and the saving of life and of cargo and stores from those which could not be assisted, became the work of specialist salvaging smacks. These were already active throughout the eighteenth century, but at this time the Revenue cutters probably had the pick of the many valuable prizes to be found stranded on the sand banks of the Thames Estuary or still afloat in the channels between them. Isaac Dagnett in the *Walpole* found the Whitby collier *John's Goodwill* ashore on the Whiting in 1764, her rudder broken off. The master wanted to cut her masts away, but

The chance of a salvage job.

Dagnett laid out three anchors, hove her off and got her into Harwich. With her cargo she was worth £1,000, but the master refused reasonable salvage, so Dagnett 'have stopt the ship.'

One of the most remunerative jobs was the *Cupid* of Bridlington, stranded on the Gunfleet in 1797. After £177 had been earned for getting her off, a sale of the ship and her cargo of hemp yielded £618 for thirty men of the *Argus*, £659 for thirty-two men of the *Repulse*, £234 for ten men of the smack *Friends*, £229 for ten men of another smack, and £55 for the gun brig *Furious* 'for services' – a total of £1800. This was justified as being less than a quarter of the value of the ship, put at £1,750, and her cargo, put at £6,466.

The *Bee* found the *Fortuna*, bound from Oporto to London, with wine and cork, adrift in the Wallet in 1784, derelict and unmanned – the salvager's dream. Though the hull was sold for only £170 the wine was valued at £1,503. John Batten and his crew presumably received half this amount, but soon afterwards he was ordered to refund to the owners an overpayment of £193, and to pay to the Collector £278 as the Crown's share.

In 1782 his colleague William Haggis in the *Argus* got £237 when the *St George* (Charente to Ostend) was wrecked off Bawdsey and her cargo sold for £438, and in 1797 Munnings and the *Repulse* shared in an award of £126 for assistance to the *Belle Flora* (London to Dantzic) ashore on the Blacktail.

When after the French wars salvaging became principally the prerogative of the specialist smacks, the Revenue men were left with the task of supervising its landing and seeing it properly declared at the Custom House. This was less rewarding and agreeable. Colchester and Burnham were asking in 1822 for rewards for the Tide Surveyor and boatmen 'out night and day to Fishing smacks bringing in wrecked cargoes.' The Colchester Comptroller suggested 5s for the Tide Surveyor for every day and night and 2s 6d for each boatman.

It was the custom to put a Tidesman aboard each smack to see the salvage safely handed in, and the application may have arisen from the wreck of the Dundee brig *Neptune* on the Maplins, bound from Memel to London with hides. Four men of the Crouch Preventive station were put aboard the smacks *Beulah*, *Corsair* and *Union*, and Robert Sainty's lugger *Thetis*, all of Colchester, which were taking part of her cargo to Wivenhoe. From there they had to walk back to Foulness – a distance of thirty-four miles. Nor was this their only tribulation, for a plea in 1828 for a subsistence allowance of a shilling a day to be paid to Preventive men aboard salvaged ships observed that they 'are treated in many instances not only with great neglect but with gross abuse.'

Many other rewards and perks were available to Revenue men of all kinds and ranks, recalling Pepys' observation that 'it is not the salary of any place that did make a man rich, but the opportunity of getting money while he is in place.'

Revenue cutter Commanders earned a reward of £15 'head money' for every smuggler convicted, or £20 for every man impressed, with an annual prize of £500 for the greatest number. This was won in 1810 by Matthew Gunthorpe in the *Viper* of Yarmouth with a bag of no less than thirty heads.

When a vessel was not sold but burned or cut up (presumably without being valued), the reward was sometimes paid at the rate of ten shillings per registered ton; by this formula the *Argus* received £36 for the cutter *Chumbly* (perhaps the Collector's rather delightful spelling of *Cholmondley*) which she had seized in 1778.

Tobacco and snuff, which were also burned, earned their captors 3d per lb. The Collector also got 4d in the £, and the Comptroller 3d, on the value of spirits. This also mounted up, for between October

79

1784 and July 1786, spirits to the value of £8,122 were sent from Harwich, bringing these officers £135 and £101 respectively.

Finally there were a few perks for various extra duties. Tending of ships in quarantine brought payments at the rate of £1 per ship for the Collector, 15s per ship for the Comptroller, 2s 6d a day for the Tide Surveyor, and 1s a day for the boatmen. The Rolling Grounds at Harwich and Latchingdon Hole in the Blackwater (between Osea and Northey Islands) were nominated as quarantine stations. During the cholera outbreak of 1832 extra boatmen were retained at Crouch River Coastguard Station (two), at Bradwell (one), Tillingham (one), Wakering Steps (one), Shoebury (three), and 'Haven Hole'. An extra man was also retained for the Burnham quarantine boat *Fanny*, and while she was under repair Stubbins' smack *Sisters* was hired. Maldon paid three doctors' bills for examining crews of colliers and 'craved' quarantine flags for the *Maria* and *Fanny*, both of which are referred to in later chapters.

This work involved not only a watch on crews, some of whom occasionally got ashore and made a get-away, but also the handling of some cargoes. In 1770 a cargo of hemp from Riga was ordered 'to be aired for at least a fortnight.' The Harwich Collector protested that he had only one small craft available, and that a single bunch when opened would fill it. He asked for the ship to go to 'Standgate Creek' (presumably Stangate, in the Medway) under the orders of the *Argus*.

Any contact with a ship from a restricted country involved quarantine. Robert Liveing of the smack *Robert & Martha* found himself in trouble in 1768 after bringing ashore the pilot of the brigantine *Lyon* of Exeter, but on this occasion the letter of the law was not enforced. A trickier problem arose in 1816 when the Bawdsey pilots went off in their salvage smack *John & Hannah* and brought into Harwich a ship they took to be a Dane, bound from Hamburg, which was free from quarantine. The captain demanded a King's Pilot, so Henry Newson tricked him by showing the card of his father-in-law, James Passiful of Orford Ness, who was a King's pilot. Then he found he himself had been deceived, for the vessel was the *San Rafael* from Malaga. With the card ('duly fumigated') as evidence the Customs proceeded against Passiful, only to find they had this tangled tale to sort out.

Two Colourful Adversaries

THE Commander of the Revenue cutters *Repulse* V and VI, Capt George Garnett Huske Munnings, was a fascinating character.

A miniature surviving in the family's possession shows him to have worn a pigtail and to have had red hair, a sign perhaps of his choleric temper, reminiscent of the similar disposition of Sir Alfred Munnings, that most provocative President of the Royal Academy, who stemmed from another branch of the family. He lived at Thorpe-le-Soken, a village near Clacton, at 'Thorpe Cottage', which despite its name was a substantial farmhouse with 'ten airy bedrooms'. He was clearly proud of his command, for he had a thirty-six ton smack built by Cole at Rowhedge in 1791, which he registered as *Repulse* in 1793, recording that he, the sole owner, was 'commander of the *Repulse* cutter'.

The Essex Customs officers had plenty of experience of his hot temper. In 1790 he visited Maldon, pressing for the Navy, and actually impressed one of the crew of 'the King's boat', Arthur Bull, despite being shown his Commission. When the Tide Surveyor remonstrated, he said Bull had 'acted impertinent', and sent the man aboard the *Repulse*, which then sailed. The Collector sat down to write a furious letter to the Board about this 'extraordinary case', but next day Bull walked in and reported for duty, having been put ashore at Mersea.

Munnings had another brush with the Customs in 1804, this time at Harwich.

The Collector, Richard Wordsworth, was still enjoying a leisurely lunch at a quarter-to-four one afternoon when he was sent for to return to the Custom House. In the public room he found his clerk, the Comptroller (Mr Runnacles), Munnings and four men, one of whom was his agent. He went through to his private office to get a pen with Munnings shouting after him 'I have been waiting for you to have a property registered'. 'Have you so? How long have you been waiting?' replied the Collector as he returned. The following elegant conversation then ensued.

'You are never here to do your duty. I have been at the office twenty times without finding anyone.'

'I do not believe it.'

'I suppose you mean I tell a lie. You are a damned poverty struck fellow and if I was to meet you in the street I should think you so far beneath my notice that I would trample on you and even kick you.'

'That is more than you dare do for I understand that you bear the character of a coward. You must take care, or you will get a good horsewhipping.'

They then cooled down, the Collector observing that he had been at the office from ten till two o'clock, and Munnings returned to the Three Cups, grumbling to his agent, 'This is the way you involve me in disputes.' The necessary papers having been completed, he returned to the office, but as the register was being delivered to the master of the vessel he interjected, 'Have you done with me?' 'Yes' replied the Collector. To which Munnings replied, 'Then I have not done with you' and struck both the Collector and his clerk, who tried to intervene. Later in the year the Collector took Munnings to court and got £20 damages in the Assizes. The Collector observed that the Department 'has long been obnoxious to him', and recalled a previous abusive exchange when he had refused to endorse a young man as master of one of Munnings' vessels as he appeared to be under twenty-one and could not produce a Birth Certificate.

As well as his more dramatic adventures, Munnings was active in the prosaic occupation of catching neutral vessels for technical breaches of their licences, or seizing poor dredgermen's boats because they infringed one of the absurd scantlings regulations.[1] He was also a noted scourge of the active smacksmen smugglers, who nevertheless constantly turned to their arch-enemy as their spokesman and advocate. The owners of six smacks which got the *Phoenix* of Whitby off the

Geroge Garnett Huske Munnings, Commander of the Wivenhoe Revenue cutter Repulse, *owner of the privateer* Courier, *proprietor of Landermere Quay, and scourge of the Customs.*

Middle Sand and into Burnham in 1804 employed him at the subsequent arbitration, when he got them £345 for their assistance, with £45 costs. Five years later he performed the same service for the salvors of the British ship *Speculation*, stranded on the Essex coast on a voyage from Gothenburg to London, and in 1818 the Revenue cutter *Lapwing* and the Aldeburgh pilots employed him after they had assisted the Aberdeen ship *Canada* bound from Quebec to London with timber. This relationship between adversaries was not unique, for it was closely reproduced in the respect shown by the next generation of salvagers for a later Harwich Revenue cutter Commander, Isaac Saxby,[2] but it throws an interesting light on an aspect of the war between 'free traders' and Revenue men.

After commanding (and wrecking) one of the largest Revenue cutters in the service, Munnings decided in 1811 to go into prize-taking on his own account, and obtained Letters of Marque and six six-pound carronade carriage guns for his 150-ton London-registered schooner *Courier*, 'now bound on a voyage from London in and about the German ocean and in the coasting trade and back to London'.

Part of his new crew was signed on at Handfleet Water, near his home, in October 1811. They were a First Lieutenant and Chief Mate at £3 15s a month, another mate at £3 5s, a Mate and Pilot at £11 4s (the high figure is not explained), a Surgeon 'as per Agreement', a Cook at £3 12s, a Steward at £3, a Boatswain at £3 5s, a Carpenter at £3 12s, a Gunner at £3, no fewer than three sailmakers at £3, two Landsmen at £3 and one at £1 15s. On 4 January 1812 more hands were signed on at Harwich – a Chief Mate at £3 12s, four ratings unspecified at £3 and one at £1 10s, two Landsmen at £3 and two at £2, with three names against which neither rating nor wage is shown.

Under the agreement they signed, 'Officers, seamen and other persons' were to receive £1 1s for each capture and 'not claim or be entitled unto any of the proceeds of any prize'. They also received a little extra which throws some light on prevailing conditions, for, said the agreement, 'whereas it often happens that part of the cargo is embezzled after being safely delivered into lighters, and as such losses are made good by the owners of the ship, it is further agreed that whatever officer or seaman the Commander shall appoint shall take charge of the lighter and go therewith to the legal quay and deliver to the ship's husband . . . Such Officers to be entitled to 2s 6d for each lighter and sixpence for each four hours.'

Not all these men were in the end shipped. The final crew for which a Press Protection Certificate was issued in October 1812, numbered twenty-four men and boys. Only three of these were aged over thirty, none was over five feet eight inches and more than half were 'pocked' from smallpox.

One of the *Courier*'s exploits was an attempt to seize a Prussian ship named (by a curious coincidence) *Curier* in 1813. After searching for her at sea for three weeks, the *Courier* came into Harwich to learn that she had been wrecked on the Shipwash, bound from Holland to London with a cargo of butter, cheese and gin. Munnings took charge of the smacks engaged on salvaging this cargo, with a remarkable sequel, to be recounted shortly. Apart from this rather inglorious episode there are no records of the *Courier*'s adventures, beyond reports by Charles Bull, the Burnham Tide Surveyor, that in 1812 Munnings brought in three neutral vessels laden with flour, butter and cheese, with out-of-date licences. All three were restored to their owners by the Court of Claims, but in March of that year the *Vrouw Debora* (also cheese-laden) was condemned by the Court as his lawful prize.

With the end of the French wars Munnings gave up privateering. In 1815 he asked for the *Courier* to be surveyed and registered 'at Harwich, where she has been raised upon' (meaning probably building up a rakish privateer into a cargo-carrier). 'The above vessel has no former licence, having been recently a Letter of Marque' the Collector noted on the application. He had by this time a business address in Bishopsgate as well as interests in Essex near his home, including the little quay at Landermere village, which was a port of call for the weekly Manningtree-to-London packet service. From this he supplied coal to Harwich Barracks and shingle for road repairs. He also owned the lime kiln and malting there, along with the King's Head Inn, in addition to his extensive farm nearby.

Despite all these interests he did not 'swallow the anchor', for in August 1828 he was at Calcutta in a ship named *Sunbury*[3] receiving approval from a Parsee merchant in Bombay to spend 2,000 rupees, 'with Naujee's sanction', to repair and 'cork' (*sic*) his ship after 'a most boisterous passage from Madras' with a freight of horses.

In 1831 he was back at home, winning first prize at Walton Regatta with his yacht *Ann*. Then in 1837 he was found dead in a cab taking him home to Peel's Hotel (perhaps his London lodging). When his effects were sold at Thorpe they included, as well as farming stock and two carriages, 700 volumes of books (a good selection of literature, history and travel) and 2,000 feet of well seasoned teak planking. The meticulous accounts for his funeral include the item, 'Paid to two reporters not to insert £1'.

'Thorpe Cottage,' later renamed Thorpe Grange, was later the home of the Victorian antiquarian, Yellolly Watson, who after the fashion of Victorian antiquarians did not deem his predecessor worth a mention in his book, *The Tendring Hundred in the Olden Times*. The house is now demolished, though the Grange Farm remains.[4]

The salvage of the *Curier*'s cargo led to a major scandal when most of the spirits from the wreck were later stolen. Even in the age of informers the advertisement of a £50 reward for information was in vain. Of 869 gallons put into store, 722 gallons disappeared, though it was claimed that only sixty-seven gallons were stolen and the rest were lost 'through leakage or unavoidable accident, the casks being much damaged in saving them from the wreck'. Faced with many claims by owners and salvors of goods, the Customs haughtily replied that the warehouse was 'a good weather boarded building erected not more than six years'.

The plunder began at the time of the wreck, when the lugger *Fox*, belonging to Daniel Sutton, refused to obey Munnings' orders. Tubs marked with the *Fox*'s name were carried through the streets of Harwich, and one of them was later found in a wildfowler's boat, as a result of which the master and crew were apprehended. The marking of smuggled tubs seems an astonishingly brazen act of foolhardiness.

Daniel Sutton[5] was a noted smuggler with the *Fox*. A son of Dr Robert Sutton of Ingatestone, a pioneer of inoculation against smallpox, he was born in 1767. He set up as a solicitor in Colchester, but his heart was in his boats rather than his office. He lived at Wivenhoe, where he constructed a quay. He was Town Clerk of Colchester from 1813 to 1818, and he also liked to describe himself as a Vice-Admiral of Essex, a more questionable claim,[6] though he managed to find himself some niche during the last years of this ancient office, employing the Burnham Tide Surveyor for the purpose. He bought the forty-seven-ton cutter *Success* (built at Brightlingsea in 1794) from John Brand of West Mersea in 1814, but he was bankrupt the following year, when the *Fox* was sold to a Mr Bloomfield, a good Brightlingsea smuggling name. (Sutton tried to prevent her re-registration but without success.) Three years later, however, he was owner of the schooner *Maria* of Dover when she was wrecked with twenty cases of geneva aboard. The sale of this realised £879, and there must have been other sales, for the Colchester Comptroller was authorised to pay out no less than £1,462 to the salvagers.

Two years after this his boat store at Wivenhoe was sold up, the contents including three boats, sails and spars, six guns and carriages. Sutton had to be helped by his relations to emigrate to Tasmania where he ultimately died at Hobart, impecunious to the end. His wife, née Annie Richardson of Bury St Edmunds, died of cholera in 1790, but his three daughters all made good marriages, one to Sir Charles Cowper, Governor of New South Wales. His son, Robert, was less fortunate. He went on an expedition to the Sandwich Isles, where it is said he was eaten by cannibals – a sick-sounding joke if ever there was one.

10

Packet Boat Smugglers

Winning 'A Vice-Admiral's Place': At Loggerheads with the Post Office:
Troubles with Passengers: Spars and Sails: Passage Boats, Scoots and Lobster
Smacks

THE North Sea packets, precursors of the Sealink of to-day, were
constantly at loggerheads with the law. They engaged regularly in
smuggling, and their privileged position made it difficult to apply the
draconian penalties imposed on humbler craft. Thus, despite all its
efforts, this was a war the Customs could never finally win, and which
it found frustrating to fight.

The commanders of the packets were also their owners, contracting
them to the Post Office, quite a different system to that adopted by
the Customs for the Revenue cutters. The Post Office contract in 1736
was to provide a good vessel with at least eight hands including the
commander. This, however, was not sufficient crew, so three or four
extra hands were shipped. These mariners took it in turns to act as
cook, so the fare served must have been variable! The established
seamen were paid £1 2s 6d a month and their victuals, but in practice
they were only victualled while at sea or in Holland, and were left to
provide for themselves while at home in Harwich, which was one
third of the time. At a living rate of 7½d a day, the Collector reckoned
that this meant the wages were cut by £40 a year, which the men had
to make up from smuggling.

Private ownership was inappropriate to the risks of war, and in 1744
the Treasury observed that 'the Harwich and Ostend packets stay on
the other side for fear of being taken, the property of them not being
in the Crown'.

The rivalry between the packets and the Revenue cutters must have
been intense, and was at its height in 1777 when the Customs decided
to put its officers in uniform, significantly observing that 'the officers
of the Navy, the masters of the Packet Boats and other persons in the
public Sea Service wear uniforms.' The Commanders of the cutters
were accordingly allowed blue coats, with orange lapels and cuffs, and
white waistcoats and breeches. The mates had similar coats but without
lapels. Both had to provide their own, the Customs' contribution
being confined to the first set of crested silver buttons, worn on sleeves
and pockets.

The packets themselves were cutters around fifty to sixty feet long, of
about ninety tons. They were thus bigger than the early Revenue

cutters, which however outgrew them in size in the 1770s. They had been carrying the Royal Mails, as well as passengers of all ranks and degrees, between Harwich and Helvoetsluys since the seventeenth century, but just before that destination was finally closed by Napoleon in 1795 they transferred their base in 1794 to Yarmouth, regarded as more suitable for the new continental destination, Hamburg. This caused such distress at Harwich, which largely depended on the service for its existence, that they returned in 1801, by which time the French stranglehold on Europe was extending beyond the Elbe, and relations with Denmark were soon to be broken. By 1807 the only North Sea crossing for passengers was the long and stormy voyage to Gothenburg, while for the mails, so vital to sustain both commerce and the war, the Post Office was reduced to landing its bags at Heligoland, then a British possession, and leaving it to the local smugglers to get them to the mainland. During an earlier French war, in 1740, when Calais was closed, two Dover packets filled in the time acting as reserves on the North Sea service. One lay in Harwich, the other in Helvoetsluys, exchanging stations every two months. They stepped in whenever the regular packets were not available, through foul winds or other causes, and seem to have made sufficient passages to make this worth while.

The Customs and the packet service were both involved in an extraordinary tangle of political corruption. The Parliamentary franchise was in the Corporation, which consisted of eight Aldermen and twenty-four Capital Burgesses, recruited by co-option. The Government in its turn also controlled the Corporation by its patronage particularly over the appointment of packet commanders, who were mostly members of the Corporation, and it used as its 'manager' the Collector of Customs, who also in the 1760s acted as Agent for the packets, paying out 'pensions' on behalf of the Treasury amounting to £100 a year, to secure the political allegiance of the privileged voters.

How this racket worked is shown in a report of 1764 by the Collector, Griffith Davies, who was himself many times Mayor of Harwich. When he paid these 'pensions' to two Government supporters he 'observed an unusual coolness in their behaviour'. The reason proved to be their 'mortification' at seeing 'Phillips Baggott, a boy and no voter [and the former mate of the Revenue cutter *Walpole*], made a Captain of a Packet over their heads . . . It was a provoking circumstance that this man . . . should now have interest enough to perpetuate an employment of £1500 per annum in wartime and above £1,000 per annum in peacetime . . . I assured them I was not privy in any part. They clamoured pretty loudly . . . when the Packet Boats, which are as good as a Vice Admiral's place, are given to those who oppose the Government.'

A few years before this, in 1752, Davies had been concerned in a tussle with the packet service over Land Tax, introduced in 1699. 'The Commissioners for the Borough' he explained 'have always till very lately been employed in the pacquet Boats or dependent on them which enabled them to ease themselves out of Land Tax on their houses and kept the captains . . . from being taxed at all. At the same time they have loaded the officers of the Customs with much more than they ought to pay. Last year, by a little management, I got a majority of the Commission to my side and appointed such assessors as moderately assessed the Captains of the Pacquet Boats and properly eased the officers of the Customs.'

The solicitor of The Post Office, however, refused payment, on the ground that the captains were contractors and not officers, so that their pay was wages and not salaries. Davies asked the Board to get an opinion from the Attorney General, 'the expense of which I had rather pay out of my own pocket than suffer such a sum taken so unjustly from the Revenue every year by people who think it meritorious to injure the revenue of the Customs!' (Evidently the departments, not their officers personally, paid this tax, which was costing the Customs only £36 to be reduced to £10 if the captains were assessed on their nominal salaries of £50, which were in fact a small part of their total earnings.)

Since the packet crews depended on smuggling for a living wage, relations between the two services would in any case inevitably have been fraught, but with this sort of political background they became particularly bitter and confused.

The rows went back to the 1730s, when the Agent for the Packets was complaining that the Customs did not report the 'concealments', or hiding places, in the packets, and the Collector was countering with the charge that 'the principal people at the Post Office in London treat Customs letters as a Meer Joke'. Around this time the Customs made a tactical error when two members of the crew of the *Carteret and Harrison* who acted as informers were nevertheless dismissed. Twenty years later this was still remembered, making it impossible to obtain any information.

According to the Harwich Collector in 1735 (at the time Samuel Phillips secured the command of the *Walpole*) officers were afraid of losing their posts if they offended the rival faction. 'None of these frauds occurred before the last election of Members of Parliament for then the Custom House interest prevailed and we were not afraid to do our duty', he explained. 'But since that, the Pacquet people and their friends have had the governing power of the Corporation, and the ears of Members of Parliament, who are always willing to hear any insinuation to our prejudice.'

Apart from straightforward smuggling, the allowance of spirits which the mariners were permitted, already mentioned in connection with the trouble-making Captain Caley, was a continual bone of contention. In 1736 the packet-men were insisting on their right to two gallons a head, having been told by 'the yachts and Hollands traders at Helvoets-luys' that this was the custom in London. The Collector noted that 'it used to be five or six gallons a man.' Trying for a more reasonable ration, he sought the support of the Mayor and Magistrates, but found them backing 'the packet men'. 'But as we observed they were deluded into this mad humour we forebore using violence with them, but by cool reasoning they at last submitted.' In 1744 captains were permitted a 1½ gallon bottle of brandy, a pound of tea, six to ten bottles of Spanish wine and 36 lbs of raisins, and the mates a bottle of brandy, six bottles of wine and six to twelve lbs of raisins – 'about double what is allowed' the Collector noted. The allowance for fishing boats (which of course were not making a foreign voyage a fortnight) stood at two gallons till 1772, when it was reduced to two quarts.

Since, as has been observed, the Revenue men behaved ambivalently towards the smugglers who were their neighbours, it was inevitable that there should be still more double-dealing towards their mates in the packets. The rummagers behaved so variously that in 1736 an Inspector was appointed to check and oversee the searchers. The appointment went to Henry Stevens, who was immediately engaged in a furious row with the Tide Surveyor, John Coleman. The Collector sided in no uncertain terms with the Inspector, declaring of Coleman (who was sacked) that 'the whole town is witness he never could agree long with any creature, either male or female, for setting aside his being frequently drunk, and quarrelsome, he has such a spirit of contradiction and perverseness that it is impossible for anyone to agree with him.' Yet within a few years the gamekeeper had also turned poacher, and Stevens himself was 'endeavouring to raise a party in the Corporation to intimidate the Collector from examining into these frauds.' One of his tricks was to go aboard a packet carrying a covered basket to receive 'food for his dog' – and in fact to have it filled with beef and bottles.

'Private concealments' were built into most of the packets, on deck and below. Their stone ballast was also favoured. The Customs officers would be below, laboriously shifting the slabs of stone to discover the bottles in the bilge. As they passed these up on deck members of the crew handed them over the rail into boats waiting alongside!

The barefaced audacity of the packets was shown by an incident in 1756 when Isaac Dagnett was despatched in the *Walpole* to look for a notorious smuggler, Robert Eastee's cutter *Soken* of Harwich. He sighted a sail which looked like her, but which on closing was found to be the packet *Prince of Orange,* under Capt Madison Hunt. The packet refused to give Dagnett a rope, but he succeeded in throwing his boat's rope over the 'bill' of the packet's anchor and got aboard that way. Hunt told him the *Soken* was in Rotterdam waiting for a convoy, which answer was confirmed by all his men. But when later the Tide Surveyor picked the *Soken* up, it was found she had been towed across the North Sea from Holland by the *Prince of Orange,* well freighted with Hunt's own goods, and only dropped an hour before the sighting by the *Walpole!*

Madison Hunt was also the Agent for the Packets, standing towards the Post Office much as the Collector did towards the Board of Customs. He carried on his vendetta to the extent that when he found himself executor for the landlord of the Custom House he allowed the rent to get in arrears, issued a writ and refused to accept the money, hoping to be able to arrest the Collector!

On at least two occasions the whole packet service, vital to the conduct of the war, was nearly brought to a standstill, and was only saved by one Government department intervening against another.

In 1774 the Customs seized the packets *Prince of Wales* and *Earl of Bessborough.* These were two of the most notorious smugglers, and it is amusing to note that when that arch-enemy of smuggling, Rev John Wesley, was a passenger in the *Bessborough* he praised her as the cleanest vessel he had seen, with the most obliging captain.

Aboard the *Prince of Wales* had been found 258 lbs of tea and 9½ lbs of coffee, and aboard the *Bessborough* 4½ lbs of coffee and 100 gallons of geneva, and these were not isolated seizures for 'not a single voyage had these two boats made during the past two years [i.e. 1772–1774] without committing similar infringements of the law. The Commissioners of Customs commenced proceedings in the Court of Exchequer but were prevailed upon to abandon them upon the Captains paying . . . two-thirds of their profits, amounting to £306 and £272.'[1] The mates of both packets were also dismissed, and the Commanders of two other packets put up £2,000 as security to answer for their conduct. This was at least an improvement on 1739, when John Deane and Nathaniel Saunders 'both under prosecution' declined to sign bonds, 'for that they do design to continue The Packet service where they must do little things that would forfeit their bonds'. The Customs observed that 'the contractors or owners . . . have (perhaps inadvertently) furnished but too just an occasion to the illegal practices of these mariners by paying them less than what is given on board merchant ships in general, and what is obviously incompetent for the support of them and their families . . . and unless their wages shall be raised by a more liberal allowance from the Post Office, we have little hopes that this evil will be redressed, but on the contrary rather encouraged by any favour that may be obtained on the present occasion.'

The fear was soon fulfilled. In 1777 the Collector received orders to seize both the *Bessborough* and the *Dolphin,* but as this would have left no packet to take the Dutch mail he let the *Bessborough* sail, enquiring at the same time if he was also to seize the *Prince of Orange,* 'in the same predicament as regards smuggling'. Then within a few days a King's Messenger arrived from the Postmaster General requiring a packet to take an express to the Ambassador at the Hague. The *Dolphin,* already under seizure, was the only packet in. Then the *Prince of Wales* and *Bessborough* were sighted, both due to be seized. As she was next on turn the Collector let the *Bessborough* go and seized the *Prince of Wales.* The next year there was another seizure aboard the *Dolphin,* but as bail had already been given to produce her whenever required she was allowed to sail. The *Prince of Wales* was again seized in 1784, and when the private packet *Pocock* was sent to warn the *Prince of Orange* she was also arrested as an accessory.

During these proceedings the Post Office decided to resume the offensive, declaring that 'certain facts when investigated proved beyond a doubt that there had for years past been collusion of the grossest character. On every voyage contraband goods, chiefly tea, coffee and gin, had, with the connivance of the local officers of the Customs, been imported in large quantities, and of this only a comparatively small part had been seized.'

Little had changed thirty years later. In 1809 the Customs suggested that packet crews should be kept aboard till the rummage was done, and that their boats should be locked to prevent them escaping 'as they did in the recent seizure of the *Lord Duncan*'. This does not seem to have been done, for when in 1812 a hired extra packet, the *Anholt,* was seized, her crew tried to get away in her boat to escape impressment. The Captain, John Rutter, fired on them, killing one man. For this he stood trial, but after several witnesses had testified to his good character he was fined one shilling.

A year after this, in 1815, when silks were found aboard the *King George* on her arrival from Heligoland, her crew were mustered and two offenders were sent to the Navy, prompting a protest by the Commanders that 'it is hard that property so valuable as our packets should be continually at risk of forfeiture for the conduct of others on board who have nothing at stake, to which we are not privy, and cannot prevent.' But this plea that packets should be exempt from seizure on account of the malpractice of their crews was refused 'as it is open to the Treasury to give relief in cases of hardship where the Commander can show he has used all diligence to prevent, and is entirely ignorant of, the fraudulent transaction.'

The Senior Commander in the service, Thomas Hammond, found himself in similar trouble in 1816, following the discovery of cloth in the cabin of the steward of one of his vessels, the *Earl of Leicester*, valued at £1,500. The packet, which five years previously had got away with the piratical seizure of two Danish merchantmen at Marstrand,[2] was detained, and only released on payment of £5 satisfaction as a result of the intervention of the Secretary General of the Post Office, Francis Freeling, who observed that 'the General Post Office is inclined to hope that the Honourable Commissioners will be pleased to order the packet to be restored' – a nice example of the diplomatic language adopted by one imperious Government Department towards another, avoiding the twin pitfalls of peremptory demand and obsequious entreaty.

Three more packets were seized in 1817, *Charlotte*, *Alliance* and *Beaufoy*. Captain Norris of the *Beaufoy* (who was to be lost overboard from her two years later) came aboard at Cuxhaven, and, noticing suspicious goings-on, made a search which disclosed that parts of her ceiling had been made removable for the concealment of goods. But despite the anxiety and expense caused to them, the Commanders do not seem to have taken offences sufficiently seriously to prevent re-employment, for when Roger Rolfe, mate of the *Prince of Wales*, was sacked for smuggling in 1772, it was mentioned that he had been dismissed from a similar position in the *Dolphin* for the same reason a few years before.

In addition to their crews, the passengers also gave trouble. Many pages of the Harwich Collector's letter books are filled with pleas by humble passengers begging for the release of their baggage, and by haughty letters from grandees demanding it.

The packets were forbidden to carry merchandise, but the passengers succeeded in including a rich variety of illegal items in their personal baggage. In addition to the familiar spirits, tea and tobacco, the Harwich warehouse in the 1770s contained at one time or another: India taffety and chintz, Hollands sheets, Barcelona silk, 'diaper for clouting', 'Mother of Pearl stands for a lady's toilet', 'twelve heads of Roman Emperors and a parcel of Agate and Cat's Eye Stones', ruffles, 'a piece of Red silk embroidered with green silk, belonging to the Baroness Dieden, Lady to the Ambassador for his Danish Majesty . . . stopt out of the trunk of Mr Henry Zinck, Danish Consul at Liverpool', a 'petticoat from the Hereditary Princess of Brunswick as a present to her Majesty' (sent on its Royal way after two letters to the Board from Lord Harcourt), bunches of garnets, 'a nightgown lined with skins and two old sheets of Germany linen', Tambour waistcoats, Brussels lace, pinchbeck watchchains, '18 pairs of ladies' lappets, catgut stitched', '36 silk shapes for shoes, embroidered with silk', 'some catlings and a pound of tea' and 'three Baggs of Buggles'. Methods of concealment were as various and picturesque as the items concealed. A woman passenger in the *Bessborough* in 1763 'had about her cloaths seven yards and a half of Brussels lace, eight yards and a half of chinks, thirty-six toothpick cases, one snuff box and one ink horn, all japann'd.' The Customs had 'no person here a proper judge if the toothpick cases are of foreign or English manufacture.'

For men the breeches were favoured. A parcel containing 'one double handkerchief and two child's Cambrick frocks' was seized in 1764 from a passenger 'supposed to be a Gentleman's Man, on board the *Prince of Orange* Pacquet, which said goods were found secreted in his britches.' Eight years later some silver snuff boxes were similarly discovered. This sort of detail really turned the Honourable Board on. 'What part of the breeches and how concealed?' they enquired. 'We desired him to unbutton' replied the Collector 'and found the said boxes concealed in the back part within his breeches, next his Backside', adding for good measure, 'This is a practice greatly favoured by gentlemen as well as their servants.' Firearms were also common in gentlemen's baggage, including in 1773 a remarkable German wild boar gun, 'with a bayonet that fixes itself at the muzzle by a spring as soon as the piece is discharged.'. Even the silver coins in passengers' pockets or purses might give trouble. They were weighed, and if short of the correct weight, 62s to the pound troy, were seized on suspicion that they had been illegally clipped. Indeed, coinage featured extensively among the problems of the Customs. Chests of coins were brought by Jews to be cleared and loaded aboard packets which had to sail the moment the mails were aboard, keeping the officers up till midnight counting their contents. The Collector reported in 1759 that there are 'now lying here Six Casks of Spanish dollars and Pieces of Eight that are near a ton weight. A larger quantity is expected tomorrow without licence [for merchandise]. The carrying hence sometimes of £100,000 in a packet boat to Holland has had several ill consequences. It has rendered the public correspondence very precarious, and a great part of the millions which have been exported have been consigned to part-owners of every French privateer that belongs to Dunkirk.' These owners no doubt often received such coinage as ransoms for shipping they seized.

At the other extreme passengers arriving at Harwich sometimes had every penny taken from them. The Collector reported in 1774 that 'from motives of humanity he had more than once been obliged to give them money out of his own pocket to proceed on their journey', and a year or two later the Commander of the *Dolphin* likewise accommodated a passenger 'destitute through having all his money seized.' Yet almost at the same time the Collector was asking, 'can £5 be brought in? If so, all the defective British coinage in Holland will soon find its way into this Kingdom.'

Among the VIPs, diplomats were particularly troublesome, despite being allowed the privilege of clearance at any time, whereas ordinary passengers' baggage was, up to 1813, landed under the charge of the Tide Waiter only between nine and twelve in the morning and two and four in the afternoon.

A Mr Fagel, 'Ambassador to our Court for the Hague', arrived in the *Earl of Leicester* in 1813 and was asked for a schedule 'agreeable to the Act of 1764.' He, however, flatly refused any examination – 'not the only unpleasant instance since the re-opening of communication with the Continent', observed the Collector. Lest it be thought the immunity was claimed only for a diplomatic bag, the Ambassador's luggage was listed as five trunks, one portmanteau, two baskets, two bags, one hat box and six small parcels! When Lady Elliot took passage to Helvoetsluys in 1794 she was sufficiently important or influential for the Customs to order the *Argus, Repulse* or *Active* to convoy the packet in which she was to travel. Even this, however, was not good enough for Her Ladyship, 'who prefers to wait a week for a frigate.' In 1744 the wife of one of the Pages of the Backstairs first tried bribery, and when this failed threatened that her husband would complain to His Majesty. The Collector replied that she 'could do no greater favour, as His Majesty would know he had some officers that could do their duty.'

King's Messengers also abused their position of trust. A package covered with Royal seals and addressed 'Au Roy' presented problems, for it was difficult to tell from rustling it whether it contained papers or silk handkerchiefs. In 1750, the King's Messengers were 'insufferable', and 'unless a speedy stop be put to these people's insolence, officers will not be able to do their duty.' In 1756, 'whenever Mr Butson, a King's Messenger passed this way he has never missed of quarrelling with some officer or other.' One ingenious smuggler used the ruse of posing as a King's Messenger, coming ashore with the Captain and the mail, and having his portmanteau carried to the Post Office for him.

Sometimes, however, those in authority showed a human face. One of the Tide Surveyors, J B Haggis, was reported by Lord Temple, Col Freemantle and the officers of the Royal Bucks Militia for bad behaviour in 1804. The Collector was usually ready to defend his subordinates right or wrong, but on this occasion he had to report that on hearing the commotion in the street he had gone out to find Haggis 'dressed and accoutred as a sergeant of the Loyal Harwich Volunteers, not only intoxicated but extremely drunk'. Haggis must have expected this to end his career, but within a few weeks he received the forgiveness of the gallant officers for 'his great insolence and contempt'.

The packets also engaged in a bit of illegal importing on their own account, or were charged with doing so. The *Active* arrived in 1815 with a spare bowsprit aboard. It was seized as being much too large for the packet, which anyway did not need one. The Customs alleged it was for a vessel at Ipswich, adding that deals, timber and oars said to be for the ship's use had been smuggled ashore. 'The Packets (some excepted) devise every means to get their vessels' materials from foreign, but when detained or seized pretend it is an act of necessity' complained the Collector.

The cod smacks[3] had the same habits, particularly on their voyages from Norway with lobsters. Another bowsprit, aboard the smack *Freeling,* which arrived with lobsters in 1816, was seized on the 'strong suspicion' that this was how her owner, Mr Hart, fitted out his fleet. In 1795 the *Betsey* had arrived, in the same trade, with a dozen pairs of boats' oars and a dozen boats' scoops. She was seized, and her skipper, Robert Barker, was arrested on a penalty of £100 to £200, with only £5 in his possession, which he optimistically offered in settlement. By the 1820s, when a co-operative was formed for the lobster smacks to share both profits and losses, the rules limited imports to 'twelve of double or one dozen of single deals, three fathoms of firewood, three boathooks or buoy staves and three spare yards', and the losses covered excluded forfeits from smuggling, along with damage to sails.

Sail cloth was another bone of contention in the 1770s, when Capt Flynn of the packet *Dolphin* asked permission to import his own canvas, explaining that he had no English sail cloth, 'the Dutch being so very preferred'. This import duty provides one of many examples of what happened when a levy was slapped on anything that moved from one place to another, without much thought as to the complications involved. William Shearman, the Harwich sailmaker, observed that some Custom Houses were stamping imported sail cloth so faintly that within a year or two it would be obliterated by weather, leaving an incriminating maker's stamp on foreign cloth which bore no proof it had paid duty. And anyway what was the point of stamping each bolt of canvas once when two or three sails might be made from it? The Commissioners patiently ordered that the stamps be dipped in red lead and linseed oil, with authority to stamp several times if required.

The Post Office packets did not provide the only North Sea passenger services. Any vessel, fishing or coasting, was liable to have a passenger aboard, and to put him ashore on some unwatched Suffolk beach. The *Speedwell* of Colchester (to be in serious trouble thirty years later) was caught in 1814 putting a foreign passenger ashore in Hollesley Bay out of a ship from Bremen. (Her master's name was given as Brown, but if this was indeed the same *Speedwell* I suspect this was a mistake for Bacon, father of the two violent sons mentioned in Chapter 12). The forty-ton *Friendship*, over which Cyprian Bridge of the *Argus* had earlier done a deal when she was seized, was 'wholly employed between Harwich and Heligoland carrying provisions for the garrison there' in 1813 when she was again under suspicion.

There were also unofficial 'passage boats', particularly during the absence of the Post Office packets, such as the *Pocock* already mentioned. Such craft were allowed to sail without clearing with the Customs, since the urgency of their trade often necessitated their sailing at night. Unlike the packets, however, they had to report on arrival. Masters and mates of both packets and passage boats were required to sign the smuggling bond. The *Queen*, regularly employed plying to Hamburg in 1796, was fitted with proper passenger accommodation, but conditions must have been spartan aboard 'several craft trading with oysters out, passengers back, to Husum [on the North Friesland coast] and Heligoland'. Yet they were in demand, for in 1807 the Collector was asking for licences for lobster smacks 'frequently engaged and at a moment's notice to go to the Continent with Passengers and Expresses upon mercantile affairs'.

Foreign craft were also busy, and sometimes put the Collector in a quandary comparable to that which he faced when ordered to arrest packets essential for the conduct of the war. An order in 1795 to detain 'all Dutch scoots' (many of which were turning up claiming to belong to Emden or Papenburg, and thus to be Prussian neutrals) arrived just as a Dutch fishing boat brought the Secretary of the Commission of the States General under a flag of truce. 'Does this order include Sheveling boats with flags of truce with passengers, messengers with despatches and families of English prisoners of war?' asked the Collector.

There was also in 1771 a regular traffic between Southwold and Holland by Dutch 'scoots' which were accustomed to export thirty or more bags of flour beyond their own needs. The Barking smacks in 1767 'do under cover of catching fish on the coast of Holland make it a practice to bring over Jews and other persons with prohibited articles to land on the coast of Kent.' As for the 'Hollands traders' to London, 'it is the custom of these sloops [in 1753] to have boats meet them in the Swin, at the Nore or else at Hole Haven, into which they put all, or most, of their prohibited goods so that when the officers board them at Gravesend there is nothing to be found and they pass as fair traders.'

All in all, it is small wonder that the most elaborate defences failed to provide against every eventuality.

11

A smugglers' town

Military Militancy: The Reluctant Constable: Ben Points to the Rescue: A Smuggling Wife: Part-time Pilots: A Postmaster Joins In: A Teenager's Adventures.

HARWICH, as one would expect, was very much a smugglers' town. As has been shown, the Customs had to count the Navy, the Post Office, the King's Messengers and the Lords of the Manor among their adversaries. As to the populace, when the ever-smouldering feud with the packets was fanned up by some incident (as in 1744) the Collector 'could not walk the town without being insulted, and threatened to be shot or thrown overboard.'

The constables and the Army were no more helpful. As far back as 1714 – a reminder that smuggling was by no means confined to 'the smugglers' century' – two Tidesmen-Boatmen were going their rounds in West Street, where they seized five half-ankers being conveyed out of the town by two men on horseback and one or two on foot, armed with clubs and other weapons. These men 'furiously assaulted the officers, beating and wounding them inhumanly', and succeeded in making off with three of the casks. One man forced an officer into a house where 'he beat him unmercifully that murder was cried out.' Finally he was rescued by a local tailor after one of the constables had refused to help and 'seemed well pleased to see the officers barbarously used.'

As for the military, two dealings with Landguard Fort, both in 1739, tell their own story. This strategically placed stronghold of law and order, commanding the northern approach to Harwich harbour, with the notorious Bawdsey Haven only a few miles on its other side, should have been a powerful deterrent to the offences which in fact it cheerfully encouraged.

On one occasion the Collector was told to prepare a new chart of the harbour. Taking his theodolite and measuring wheel he crossed the harbour to the fort and asked the permission of the Deputy Governor, Mr Hayes. 'Don't you know not to measure fortifications?' came the reply. The Collector explained that he had orders to take bearings on the churches. 'We pay no regard to any orders' replied Hayes, who then seized the instruments and turned the Collector out. He then wrote a furious letter to the Treasury demanding to know what orders had been given and adding that he 'would have secured the Collector, who acted insolently towards him, but that he thought the Revenue might suffer.' One wonders why their Lordships at the

99

Treasury, and if it comes to that the Commissioners of Customs, did not sometimes warn their officers not to behave like children.

A few months before this, the *Middleburg Merchant* broke an embargo on sailing by getting under way, with two Customs tidesmen aboard, 'presumably for London'. The Collector went to Landguard for help from the Garrison, but found only a sergeant, from who he 'desired assistance to stop the vessel and two others', presumably by warning gunfire. 'He told us in plain terms he durst not, for that his captain had told him not to assist us.'

Many of the town's fine cod smacks made smuggling runs; the story of the *Providence* and the *Good Intent* will be found in Chapter 25 (along with another yarn about the governor of Landguard Fort). Another member of the smack-owning fraternity was Benjamin Points, whose *Prince of Wales* was generally in the forefront of a salvage job, including the wrecks of the German passenger liner *Maria Francesca,* a galliot named *Three Brothers* lost on the Shipwash, and the Newcastle snow *Contest,* lost on the Gunfleet, all in 1814.

Whether he was also a smuggler I do not know, but he showed where his sympathies lay by attempting to rescue two of his fellow-townsmen from the custody of the Customs in September 1815. Before confusing ourselves with facts it is worth savouring his own account of the set-to, for it is sublimely romantic. He was, he declared, at his door, oiling his boots (a ritual necessary in the days of leather seaboots) when he saw a crowd of people and was told some impostors were searching houses in the next street without any authority.

'Knowing that a short time previously there had been several persons in the town of that description', he went to the scene and 'found several hundred people assembled crying "impostors!" and "informers!" ' Several voices cried 'Points! Points!' so he got near and shoved one with his elbow, but not to injure him. His only purpose, he declared, was 'to protect persons from the mob, particularly from the women, who appeared to act more violently than the men.'

Whether such flights of fancy were expected to be taken seriously or were merely to provide the satisfaction of a colourful and dramatic exit is a conundrum which arises over and over again in these stories. At any rate the freedom secured by Points' nudging elbow and the militant ladies of Harwich did not last long for the prisoners, Samuel Nalborough and William Parsons, or for Points either. Before long all three were behind bars at Chelmsford.

Parsons' misdemeanours are not revealed, but Nalborough was a local tradesman who bought pieces of foreign silk from mariners in the Post Office packets. He had, he confessed, over the past three years bought twenty pieces from each of five such suppliers, selling twenty-eight pieces to a Colchester auctioneer named Linton and smaller parcels to the landlords of the Cups and Angel inns and to a Manningtree grocer as well as to buyers in London.

As a receiver, he seems to have been treated as a serious offender, for he was among prisoners to be sent to the Fleet prison in 1817, a full two years after the Harwich street fracas. The Customs, however, observed that it would be useless to move him as, unlike the smugglers proper, he was 'under sentence of the Court of King's Bench and would only be remanded'. Points and Parsons seem to have served shorter terms, for the former with his *Prince of Wales* was on a list of suspected smugglers in 1817.

Most of the silk smuggling was done in this way, as was confirmed by another case in the same year which landed James Scott of Harwich in gaol following the discovery of bandanas on his premises. The Customs were convinced that poor James was honest and industrious and that his wife was the villain of the piece, saying that the silks had been obtained from a member of the crew of the packet *Lark* who had since gone to Woolwich (where in the days before a police force there seemed no thought of finding him), and were part of an order given to Mrs Scott by 'Mr Edward Duke, lately a shopkeeper, now in Chelmsford gaol for debt'.

The Harwich Collector's manifest sympathy for Scott did not influence the Board to release him. He spent his year in gaol, while at home his wife had all her household goods seized and had to depend on the minimal support of the parish.

Harwich Harbour in 1808, showing the old High and Low lighthouses, whose lights in line showed the fairway, with Landguard Fort in the background.

101

All this is further evidence that most of the small-scale Essex smuggling in the early nineteenth century was financed and organised by local traders and innkeepers. Many of them finished up at Chelmsford, but no doubt many more went undetected and hence do not enjoy the doubtful privilege of appearing in these pages.

One such operator who particularly irritated the Customs was Roger Hines, who kept the White Hart inn in West Street, and worked in collusion with his brother John Hines, who was Deputy-Postmaster. The Customs had to work with the Post Office and to deal with passengers, including King's Messengers, at the White Hart, and as they could be sure of abuse and obstruction at both places relations were far from cordial.

Hines would lie alongside an incoming packet in a boat, and obligingly take ashore any parcels dropped into it. Another of his interests was illegally exporting fine worsted yarn, or crewels, which arrived at Harwich in the Ipswich wherries. (The Collector asked the owner of one wherry, John Norman, if he had left off smuggling, to be given the engaging answer that 'he must not leave off while he was a wherryman'.) Finally in 1759 the packet *Prince of Wales* was seized for having crewels aboard, and her Commander, Capt Phillips, set about securing evidence to get her released. As a result Roger Hines, along with Isaac Peache and Robert Chapman, were successfully prosecuted the following year.

A curious little example of international co-operation between citizens of countries at war to engage in a little trade which in the eyes of the Customs clearly covered some illegal importation occurred in 1814. A Frenchman met five English fishermen in Ostend and agreed with them to deliver twenty hams, 3cwt of butter and 5000 eggs in England, 'they defraying all costs and demands of Customs'. Off the Essex coast the Frenchman met small craft from Colchester into which he loaded this innocent sounding cargo (and what else?) and after being paid he put about for France. Unluckily for him he was driven into Harwich where his crew of two deserted and he shipped two local men for the return to Dunkirk. On the way they were boarded by the Revenue cutter *Drake* which, despite there being only one bottle of gin and 2½ gallons of beer aboard seized the boat and delivered the men to HMS *Namur* at Sheerness. The Frenchman claimed that 'a native of France cannot be kept in the English Service' and demanded a trial.

One of the Harwich men signed on was Jonathan Easter, and the reason he was out of work was that a few months previously he had bought a boat called the *Lord Nelson* to deal in mackerel, and sailed to join the boats fishing off the Galloper. Here he was arrested by the

Revenue cutter *Hawk*, which alleged he had thrown overboard twenty-seven tubs. Lacking proof of this, they found that though Easter had erased the previous owner's name, he had failed to paint in his own, for which technicality the *Lord Nelson* was seized and sent into Yarmouth. All in all, having lost first his boat and then his freedom for no proven offence, Easter's feelings about the preventive service cannot have been very amicable – and on this occasion there is no record of previous offences to justify the evident suspicion he aroused.

The little outports, such as Burnham and Handfleet Water, tended to produce attractive characters and entertaining stories. Manningtree and Mistley, lying a few miles from Harwich at the head of the navigable Stour estuary, were no exception.

The Stour Navigation had opened up a barge trade to Sudbury in 1713, a few years before the birth of the Rt. Hon. Richard Rigby of Mistley Hall, whose orgies scandalised even eighteenth century society. A notorious politician and place-man, he became Paymaster of the Forces, and on his death in 1788, left, it was said, 'near half a million pounds of public money'. He spent some of his ill-gotten gains on converting Mistley Thorn into Mistley Spa, with shipyard, quays and warehouses to the design of Robert Adam. Today the Hall has gone, and only the Swan Pool, the towers of the Adam church and some Georgian houses remain, to recall his efforts to develop his new port, which extended to interference in the work of the Customs. His steward, a Mr White, who owned a large farm, was recognised in 1748 as a 'Gentleman Coal Meter'. 'He neither tops nor turns the bushels, as other meters do, but stands to see a porter do it', the Collector explained.

Michael Hinde, the Waiter-and-Searcher in charge of the place, made several ingenious arrangements. In 1732 he received 6d per last on all corn shipped, provided the Harwich Surveyor did not attend. If that officer had to be paid, the charge was deducted from Hinde's allowance. His coal meters also received 2d per chaldron from the merchants – ostensibly for helping to fill the bushel measures and working overtime, but also, noted the Collector, 'we fear making large measures'. He had his own philosophy, which was to be strict with foreign shipping but lenient (sometimes to the point of laxity) with coasters. 'We must not fall out with our Neighbours for Trifles where we are fix'd and oblig'd to live all our lifetime' he observed, as he allowed twenty bushels of salt to be unloaded. The outraged Salt Officer[1] shopped him, and reported his heretical remark to the Commissioners, who however let him off. A few years later (in 1768), he was dismissed for 'notorious neglect and breach of duty', in the same purge which

Mistley quay in 1832, showing the Adam church.

Eighteenth century Manningtree.

ended the careers of the Commander and mate of the *Walpole,* but again he was reprieved. Then in 1772 he yielded to the persuasions of Richard Rigby, who wanted five hampers of wine loaded at his own common quay in the local hoy *Thorn,* and got away with that as well. Finally he died in harness in 1776, to be succeeded by William Wilkinson, the unpopular sitter of the Handfleet boat.

The Mistley officers had a tradition of piloting vessels on the river, as did the Burnham Tide Surveyor, referred to in Chapter 21. This was the speciality of the Warner family. William Warner, a Tidesman-Boatman who had previously been a full-time pilot, was sacked for carrying on his old occupation in 1761, but crisply replied that he had written to Mr Rigby, who advised him to follow his piloting. According to the Collector, 'he would continue to Pilot ships and we might kiss his arse for that he had a friend at the helm would protect him.' Told to return his Deputation, he 'saucily told us his friend Mr Rigby advised him not to deliver it.' But the Collector considered this patronage was a delusion, and the Deputation was in fact soon surrendered.

Thirty years later, in 1793, another William Warner, perhaps his son, was employed as a coal meter at Mistley and also insisted on combining this with piloting, along with William Jacobs, apparently with the Collector's approval, but to the annoyance of the regular pilots, Robert Eteen, G Warner and S Warner. The Collecter disposed of them by declaring there were 'not three more worthless fellows in the parish'. The same dispute arose five years later when the Collector referred to the objectors as 'idle drunken fellows', and added that Warner and Jacobs seldom earned more than £9 or £10 each. But while Warner defended this use of his spare time he was outraged when the Justices appointed him an overseer of the poor, declaring it would 'retard his duties as a coal meter'. The Customs threw the thirteenth clause of HM Letters Patent at the Justices, 'but they still remain obstinate and are determined to try the legality of Mr Warner's exemption at Chelmsford the ensuing Assizes.'[2]

Let us end these little cameos of Harwich and the Stour in their lustiest age with the story of Joseph Holdee, who at the time we meet him, in prison at Harwich in 1798, claimed to be only twelve years old, though the Customs, impressed by his knowledge and shrewdness, thought he was fifteen or sixteen.

The son of an English father and a Dutch woman who kept a pub at Flushing, Joseph started his amazing career by shipping aboard the *Maria,* supposedly of Boston, Massachusetts, when she came to

Flushing, unloaded two bales of woollen cloth, and loaded 600 half-ankers, two bales containing about 100cwt of tobacco, and two oilskin parcels which others in the crew said contained lace.

This *Maria* had been launched by Bayley of Ipswich only a year or two before, a clinker-built thirty-three-tonner. When in 1797 she tried to clear at Harwich, bound from Ipswich to Hamburg with three men and a boy, the Customs found her claim to American nationality was supported only by a bill of sale from Bayley to Charles Cowing 'of Boston in America'. They asked authority to detain her on suspicion, but had to be content with pressing one of her men for the Navy.

Now, on a June day in 1798, with Joseph Holdee aboard and still under Cowing, she set out from Flushing for 'Sizely' (Sizewell, Suffolk), but when that evening she was seven or eight miles off the beach they spotted a lugger. Cowing had everything bar the lace bundled overboard before the lugger came alongside, under the second mate of the Revenue cutter *Hunter*, with eight or ten Revenue men. They detained the *Maria* on suspicion, which was confirmed when next day they fell in with half the jettisoned tubs. They picked up 300, of which twenty were given to the crew of the *Maria*, the master refusing to accept any, and the cutter was then released. This extraordinary procedure was recorded without comment or explanation by the Harwich Collector. If it was a ploy to tempt the smugglers into deeper involvement it did not work, for they went straight in to 'Sizely' where they landed their twenty tubs and their lace.

They then on 7 June went into Harwich and unloaded the baggage of an American passenger (so-called), and after lying there a week sailed to Woodbridge, where as a result of a dispute between Cowing and his merchant the *Maria* was laid up and dismantled. Joseph Holdee made his way home to Flushing and had a look round. He saw there the small open lugger *Bee* of Dover, owned by 'Little Dick', loading 300 tubs for 'Sizely Gap', and a small schuyt, crewed by three Dutchmen and an Englishman, also loading 300 tubs for the same destination. Under repair he saw the thiry-six-ton square-stern cutter *Charles* of Emden, owned by Rowland Debney[3] of Orford, a yellow hull with black strake in the middle and a black top strake. She had a red vane at the head of a lofty topmast and a short bowsprit supported by a stem knee.

Joseph, however, chose the *Success* of Woodbridge (was his father a Woodbridge man, I wonder?) but on her voyage to her home port she was taken by a French privateer and the crew were held in Ostend. After four days they set out to march to Lille, but Joseph escaped on the journey and again made his way home.

This time his father shipped him in the *Fanny* of Emden, with 200 half-ankers to be unloaded at 'Walton Gap'. They sailed on 7 September, and on 11 September Evan Brotherton, the Thorpe Riding Officer, saw a boat with two men in it towing tubs up Handfleet Water. Having a horse instead of a boat he could not pursue them, but once detected they were soon apprehended. They proved to be Joseph and an older man named Anthony Martens, a native of Bruges, and a baker by trade. Having a wife and three children to support, 'necessity compelled him to engage himself as a mariner aboard the small vessel *Fanny*'. The *Fanny* herself, with the remaining crew, seems to have escaped, having perhaps left the riskiest part of the job to the new recruits.

Joseph and Anthony soon found themselves under lock and key in Harwich, perhaps in that basement under the Guildhall where to this day you may see the splendid pictures of chasse-marée luggers scratched deep in the wall by French prisoners. The Customs sought a ruling: should they be delivered as prisoners of war, put aboard a man-of-war or released? 'Having complied with the regulations of the Alien Act' they were released, only to be immediately re-arrested by the Mayor of Harwich as suspected persons. (As Chief Magistrate this was probably his only alternative to issuing them with the passports that would have sent them on their way.)

The Customs applied to an attorney for affidavits, presumably to protect them from the Mayor next time, but the attorney observed that 'objection might be taken to their validity while they were in custody.' The prisoners did not wait for these legal points to be settled. Early in November they 'made escape out of prison by sawing the iron gates thereof asunder.' A hue-and-cry was raised but without result. 'We are inclined to believe both left the country in a smuggling vessel bound to some foreign port', observed the Collector.

One would like to know what became of young Joseph. Three disastrous smuggling attempts and two escapes from custody in two foreign countries must be counted a fair six months' adventures in any teenager's life.

12

Laws and Licences

The Web of Regulations: What was a Cutter?: Owners in Bond: Luggage Boat or Tub Boat?: Rough Justice.

FOR three-quarters of a century authority laboured under the delusion that smugglers could be caught in a web of laws and regulations of ever-increasing size and complexity.

Licensing of shipping was first introduced by the Admiralty in 1721, and was made applicable to all vessels of over fifteen tons in 1786, following the American War of Independence, as many American vessels were still trying to obtain the privileges of British ownership. Control passed from the Admiralty to the Customs in 1807 – a recognition that the war was now against the smuggler.

Act after Act was passed through Parliament between 1770 and 1850 regulating the size, shape and build of vessels, the limits of their navigation, the number and nationality of the crews, the nature of the cargoes they might carry and of course the duties levied on them. Legislation became so complicated that every few years a Consolidation Act had to be passed, summarising a situation which was becoming incomprehensible to mariners and Revenue officers alike. Then the process of amendment and addition began again till a new Consolidation Act was required. In this way fore-and-aft rigged vessels and rowing boats were subject to tortuous technical limitations (attention to square-riggers, which could not outsail the Revenue cruisers, was confined to their cargoes, their crews and the limits of their permitted voyages).

One of the most tortuous regulations endeavoured to distinguish between the sloop, which was considered acceptable, and the cutter, which was one of the commonest and most dangerous types of smuggler, specially after the Smugglers' Act of 1816 forbade the rigging of any vessel over fifty tons as a lugger. Today a sloop is commonly defined as a single-masted fore-and-after setting only one headsail, while the cutter sets two, a foresail and a jib. But the traditional distinction was that the sloop had a fixed bowsprit and topmast, while the cutter could reef both these spars. This enabled the cutter to set a big spread of canvas, and to outsail any other vessel, with the possible exception of some luggers, for which purpose she usually had a finer, faster hull than was associated with the sloop. Yet, as an example of the confusion which bedevilled the whole distinction, the Revenue cutters themselves, as we should now describe them, and as they in fact were by contemporary standards, were nevertheless always referred to as 'sloops', 'smacks' or sometimes 'yachts'. Possibly its association with the illicit trade made even the word 'cutter' disreputable.

A very long bowsprit was the key to the cutter's speed, both because a big headsail could be set on it and because it complemented a big mainsail with a long boom. As a result it was ruled in 1787 that bowsprits must not only be fixed, but also that they must not exceed two-thirds of the length of the hull. The rambling wording of Georgian legislation also mentioned that the legal sloop must set her jib on a stay of two-inch rope for craft up to twenty tons, increasing by a half-inch for each additional ten tons. This made a lot of trouble for the Essex oyster smacks, which probably managed to secure their bowsprits, but could not dispense with flying jibs set on travellers. In 1791 John Heard of Tollesbury had his six-ton smack seized. He 'had a fast bowsprit, same as other vessels deemed sloop rigged, but without a jib stay – the only cause of seizure.' As the Collector noted, 'in these very small vessels [the law] cannot be complied with, without great danger in going out to furl the sails.'

The year before this Charles Bones of Burnham had a little twenty-three-footer seized by the redoubtable Captain Munnings both for having too long a bowsprit and 'for having no stays whatever'. The Customs found her registered length was twenty-four feet six inches which just made her bowsprit legal, and noted she 'certainly had a forestay, fast or standing bowsprit, according to the words of the Act, in which no mention is made of a jibb stay, neither can such be used in these small dredging vessels.'

The situation was particularly preposterous because even if the distinction could be made in principle, it was easily overcome in practice. The Harwich Collector observed in 1784 that 'smuggling cutters are fitted with boltsprits standing, by the help of a bolt through the bitts, clink'd . . . yet in gales the bolt and clink are easily removed and the boltsprit let in to any length for the ease of the vessel in a perilous situation.' Yet this obsession with bowsprits continued year after year. In 1798 the Harwich Collector was still protesting that smugglers were buying up small vessels liable to forfeiture and fitting them with standing bowsprits, thus making them into sloops which did not require a licence. His proposal was to 'extend licensing to all vessels under forty tons of whatever build, rig or other description.'

Rake of keel and size of scantlings also received attention. A note in the 1824–5 Colchester registry of the thirty-three-foot sloop *Success*, built at Rochester in 1798, reads 'By the Act 57 of Geo 3 Cap 87 Sec 27, the difference in draught fore and aft not to exceed one-and-a-quarter inches for every foot of the breadth of the vessel. Present draught forward 3 foot 10 inches, aft 5 foot 1 inch – difference 1 foot 3 inches.' As the beam of the *Success* was twelve feet this was exactly the permitted limit. What would have happened had she been an inch outside the limit is not stated.

A twenty-one foot boat blown ashore on the Essex coat in 1805 was seized, 'her planking being less than three-quarter inch thick and timbers less than one-and-a-quarter inches square as required by Sec 12, 28 Geo 3, Cap 34'.[1]

In 1779 a ban on boats rowing more than four oars on the south-east coast was extended to include those rowing more than six oars elsewhere. By 1818 boats with more than four rowlocks were forfeit even in Essex.

Licences were needed for any boat over eighteen feet long in 1789, and fourteen feet up to 1826, when it was noted, 'A late Act of Parliament subjects all boats to obtain a licence, of whatever dimension.' This was strictly enforced when it suited the Revenue men's book. The *Whim* of Colchester was seized in 1814 for being fourteen feet one-and-a-half inches long.

Even when licences were granted they were not for unlimited use. In 1817 fast rowing boats (that is long boats or boats lightly built) might not go more than four leagues from the coast between the North Foreland and Beachy Head, or six leagues elsewhere, nor voyage more than twenty leagues along the coast.

Open boats of under fifteen tons were confined to four leagues off the coast between the Foreland and Beachy Head, eight leagues elsewhere and fifty leagues along the coast, and no open boats might go foreign. Decked vessels of under fifteen tons might go four leagues from the coast between Folkestone and Beachy Head, twelve leagues elsewhere and seventy leagues along the coast. Decked boats between fifteen and seventy tons 'intended to be employed foreign' were restricted to fifty leagues along the French coast, but 'allowed along the English coast and coasting trade generally.' These regulations were broadly reconfirmed in 1841.

In 1805, vessels were compelled to have at least half the crews British. Yet small craft were not allowed to employ large crews. When the smack *Star* sought a licence in 1812 the Maldon Collector noted, 'If in coasting cannot be granted the number of hands requested.'

Nor were the indespensable licences granted automatically – specially the extended licences giving the right to navigate 'round Great Britain and foreign between Scheveling and the Seven Islands' (The Channel Islands), or from Leith to Weymouth.

When J Cottee, in 1828, bought the smack *Providence* for trade with Holland and France the Maldon Tide Surveyor observed that 'the Nunn family (by part of which she is manned) are old offenders' and that 'Cottee's principal reference was a person known to have been convicted of smuggling.'

Samuel Ellingford of Great Wigborough, Essex, applied for a licence for his smack *Dolphin* in 1836. It was noted that he 'had been convicted and was now a suspicious character.' After William Cook had gone to gaol in 1836, following the seizure of his smack *Friends*, Alexander Hall, 'a most notorious convicted smuggler,' applied to be endorsed as the smack's master.

Whether these offenders were given another chance is not revealed, but a glimpse of the way the official mind worked is given by Thomas Turpin's application for his smack *Triune*, newly built in 1836 by Read and Page of Ipswich, and prize-winner that year at Walton regatta. Whether to grant this perplexed the Customs. Turpin was of good character, but he was in partnership with a notorious smuggler named Daniel Rich, whose part in the seizure of the smack *Dagger* is recounted in Chapter 14. In the end the Customs decided that no one was likely to risk a vessel worth £400 in smuggling, and as there was then much oystering on the Dudgeon it seemed best to give Turpin a chance to make an honest living. He got a provisional licence for six months.

Even when they succeeded in getting a licence owners were put in an impossible position, since as signatories to the bond they could be held responsible for the misdemeanours of masters and crews over whom they had no control.

When the *Decoy Duck* was seized by the Colchester Tide Surveyor in 1815 (her licence doctored 'by some chymical process') her owner petitioned that as a result of his signing the bond 'the Sheriff's bailiff . . . have siezed all the household goods and even the shirt from his Back of your Honours' Petitioner.' The Customs view of this sort of plea was that owners were seldom as ignorant as they pretended to be, though the Maldon Collector urged that all ships' masters ought also to be automatically a party to the bond – a suggestion that was apparently ignored.

One of Samuel Groom Hart's well smacks, the *Phoenix* of Harwich, landed her cargo of Norway lobsters at 'Holy Haven' (Hole Haven) and returned home, to be seized for having silk handkerchiefs aboard, while Hart himself was at sea on another lobster voyage. The Harwich smack-owners petitioned, less concerned about her master and owner than because 'lobsters waiting in corves at Eke Sound will die and future ones become tainted.'

Daniel Cole, the Wivenhoe boatbuilder, repaired the smack *William and Hannah*, and when her owner could not pay the £70 bill he took her for the debt and fitted her out. When she sailed she was seized by the Revenue cutter *Active* for a smuggling exploit two years previously when owned by one William Shakeshank Banks of Wivenhoe 'who destroy'd himself.'

Another builder, George Bayley of the Stoke Yard, Ipswich, had a small smack named *Felicity* in his charge to sell in 1797. He decided to use her to deliver a 'luggage boat' to a customer. In Orford River the master showed his papers and went home. When he returned he found the *Felicity* had been seized and taken into Harwich because she no longer had the boat with her. But the real reason was that 'Bayley was employed to build for smugglers' and in the eyes of the Harwich Collector the 'luggage boat' was in fact a tub boat.

Tub boats were indeed one of Bayley's specialities. According to a Harwich report of 1789 they were 'very deep, flat floor, very full fore and aft. Timbers small and boards thin. Thwarts high and bound with iron knees to increase stowage underneath. They have in general wash strakes above the gunwales.' The report added that 'since the Act they are built about a hair's breadth under the length of eighteen feet and width increased.' One of Bayley's tub boats, belonging to the *Charles* of Harwich, was in 1798 credited with carrying 200 to 300 tubs, not a bad freight, since a four-gallon half-anker cask weighed half a cwt.

A Colne Smack, the *Speedwell* of Brightlingsea, was bequeathed by her owner to his widow, Ann Bacon, for life and then to their five sons. Two of them, John and Thomas Bacon, were picked up at Littlehampton and consigned to Horsham gaol in 1835. But Ann Bacon had signed the security bond in a penalty of £170 and found herself in Chelmsford gaol. According to her story her trouble began with her husband's death twelve years before, when she had the *Speedwell* repaired by Bayley of Ipswich, and the estate could not pay the bill. The firm's lawyer had threatened to stop the vessel, and she had heard her son mutter on leaving home that 'King William shall have her first.' The Customs insisted the *Speedwell* had been long suspected, and that Mrs Bacon knew what her sons were up to, though they admitted she could not prevent it. 'Her only means was by giving information, which she did not like to do, both these sons being violent characters.'

The *Speedwell* when seized was found to have a false bottom, here illustrated.

Violent or not, Thomas Bacon returned to the smuggling, having perhaps no alternative with the *Speedwell* lost. He was picked up in an open boat off the Branklet (at the mouth of the Crouch) in 1838 with 149 half-ankers and three quarter casks. Then still only thirty and single, he was given the chance to compare the amenities of Chelmsford gaol with those of Horsham.

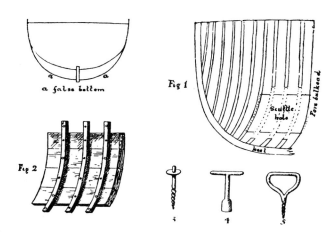

a false bottom

Fig 1

Scuttle hole

Fore bulkhead

Fig 2

The Speedwell's *concealment was unusually elaborate for an Essex smack. It is perhaps significant that she worked down Channel well away from the Ipswich shipyard where the work was probably done, and where one would assume it must have been the subject of waterside gossip. The space under the false bottom (a) was reached by removing a section shown in Figs. 1 and 2. This was fixed in place by screws countersunk in the false frames, their heads covered with corks to represent trenails. The ends of the section were hidden under a timber at one end and behind the fore bulkhead at the other. The fixing screws were operated by a special key and there was a hand screw to insert in the screw hole to lift out the removable section. These tools were surrendered by the smugglers after the seizure. (From* Smuggling Days and Smuggling Ways.)

Liability to penalties sometimes caused owners to turn informer.

The Wivenhoe smack-owner William Goodwin in 1837 informed the Customs that one of his vessels, the *Bethseda*, was attempting to run a cargo of quicksilver and glass without his knowledge. As a result she was seized at St Osyth Stone with fourteen cases hidden under her ballast. Her master and his four hands 'consented to remain with Lieut

Roberts, Chief Officer of the Coastguard' in preference to being sent to the Navy or to gaol.

The vital licences were often got rid of when a vessel was boarded, either to avoid incriminating owners or others not aboard at the time, or perhaps because they may have been endorsed with details of previous convictions (like a modern driving licence). The *Nancy* of Ramsgate was seized at Harwich in 1815 because her licence was 'secured in lead – a practice much resorted to in smuggling, and the boat herself being calculated for fast rowing and sailing it is conceived that the vessel may have been employed in the illicit trade.' Even the Customs, however, could not convict on such suspicions as these, so the next thing was to find an irregularity. It was duly discovered that her skipper had not made the necessary amendment when he also became her owner, and that was good enough to detain the *Nancy*. A petition for her release after a month was rejected.

Securing the licence in lead was to permit it to be thrown overboard in the event of seizure – a ploy unsuccessfully attempted by the *Friends Goodwill* in the Blackwater (as described in chapter eighteen). When the yawl *Liberty* was taken and condemned in 1812 'the crew escaped with the register and other papers and as the owners cannot be met with all hopes of recovery are unavailing.' This suggests that no register of licences issued was kept, a surprising omission. Copies of bonds were kept in the King's Chest at Maldon, but as they were only between twelve and twenty-seven in number in the years 1802 to 1806 they represent only a small number of the licences issued.

Sailing without a licence, or with one which was deficient or out-of-date, was a serious matter. There was no warning for a first offence.

Ben Cackett, the Crouch barge-owner, had an old boat called the *Village Maid*, used for no more dangerous purpose than carrying 'Pile-woods' from Hullbridge to Burnham for sea wall repairs. He delayed taking out a licence and had her seized in 1822.

The Maldon barge *Sally* was stopped in 1828 off the Nore by the Revenue cutter *Surly* with her licence two days out of date. In addition, the separate licence for her boat had been issued by George King, the Burnham Tide Surveyor, who had not the authority to do so. William Bragg's Brightlingsea smack *Zephyr* was similarly hustled into Harwich by the *Surly* in 1831 because the date of her licence was February 2 instead of February 5.

There was a panic among the Tollesbury smacks in 1791 when the *Slowly* was seized at Portsmouth for having a licence showing the length of her keel instead of the length 'aloft' (overall). This was found to be a mistake on the part of the Tide Surveyor, repeated on the licences for ten other Tollesbury smacks, all of which had to be corrected. Nine of these were for the limits Spurn to Poole, showing that eighteenth century Tollesbury, along with Burnham and West Mersea, had more in the way of big sea-going smacks than has hitherto been suspected.

It will thus be seen that if a vessel was suspected of smuggling it was not difficult to find a pretext to seize her, and that is in fact how the game was played. Black lists of wanted craft were periodically issued, and when one was picked up some irregularity was generally discovered. Even a coil of small rope 'convenient for sinking tubs' was enough. Failing that, suspicious behaviour, such as the absence of a smack's boat, would do. It was rough justice, but reading between the lines one can see the Revenue men were usually well informed, and a strict adherence to the sort of legal code that would nowadays be demanded would probably have left them in a hopelessly impotent position.

The Honourable Board periodically invited Collectors to submit suggestions for improving the system. (A little consultation at the time of framing the measures might have made more sense.) Many of the answers are quoted elsewhere but the Harwich reply for 1805 is a good example.

'Firstly, to prevent losses of tobacco and spirits on their transmission from the outports to London let the Crown own three or more vessels specially for the work. Their commanders would not hazard a good situation through neglect or embezzlement.

'Secondly, why not entirely prohibit the sale to foreigners of British vessels under thirty tons? Most of those sold foreign were now fitting out for smuggling and will soon be ready to go to Flushing or Embden to return with neutral papers.' By a less convincing bit of logic the Collector insisted this would not injure English shipbuilders, as 'English vessels are sharp built and foreign vessels are built for burthen'.

Sweeping bureaucratic rules and prohibitions made without knowledge of local circumstances did, however, produce innumerable unforeseen conundrums.

The system of making owners a party to licences caused confusion at Harwich in 1795 because the fishing fleet had been built up on the old system of Bottomry. Owners mortgaged shares in their vessels, usually one-eigth or a quarter, thus spreading risks and raising capital for new ventures. The lenders were issued with Bottomry Bonds, along with a bill of sale as security. They shared neither in profits nor losses, but received a fixed rate of interest, usually ten per cent. Were these people 'owners' for the purposes of the new enactment or weren't they, enquired the perplexed Collector.

These smacks raised another problem when a duty on tonnage was imposed, payable only on loaded vessels. (The Harwich packets were exempt unless they were carrying a carriage.) Were the smacks loaded merchantmen when they brought a cargo of lobsters from Norway, as the Act referred to 'any kind of goods'?

13

Prison Life on 4½d a Day

*Debtors and Convicts: Customs versus County: Pleas and Petitions: Sent to
the Navy: John Pewter and the Boadicea.*

ONCE caught, smugglers were usually dealt with under the ancient
Exchequer law, now obsolete.

The Smugglers Act of 1736 (the real declaration of war) imposed
the death penalty on smugglers using arms, and transportation,
flogging, or hard labour for resisting arrest. There were also severe
penalties for gathering in gangs. But most of the smuggling acts also
permitted the imposition of compromise penalties at the Customs'
own discretion – a principle which, as mentioned in the Introduction,
serves to the present day – and this course was usually followed.

Throughout the first half of the eighteenth century there seems to
have been little disposition to prosecute the routine casual smuggler.
It was considered sufficient at best to seize his goods (which rewarded
the Customs officer without unduly distressing the smuggler), or at
worst to condemn his vessel also (which caused him real distress). Petty
prosecutions of men of straw were not felt worth the cost and trouble.

When smugglers gathered in gangs and opposed, or 'obstructed',
the forces of law and order it was a different matter. Arrests on the
spot were rare, since the Customs men were usually outnumbered, but
subsequent apprehension on the affidavit of an informer was common,
particularly in the case of regular or 'notorious' offenders. The usual
outcome was imprisonment (for periods not revealed in the eighteenth
century letters), but occasionally transportation was ordered. The local
gaols, particularly Harwich, were quite insecure. When one considers
that a room well barred and locked, guarded by an honest warder,
should have been able to contain a prisoner, one is tempted to wonder
how often an element of this insecurity was the susceptibility of the
gaoler to bribes or threats. However that may be, the Collector's mind
was not easy till he had his man inside the County Gaol at Chelmsford,
and the journey there was a problem unless an escort of Dragoons
could be found. In 1727 one Dean Briant was arrested. He offered to
turn King's evidence, but the problem was to get him to Chelmsford,
for, said the Collector, 'I dare not trust him on horseback.' Briant
settled the matter by absconding from Harwich Gaol.

Even Chelmsford Gaol was not always secure. Three notorious
smugglers broke out there in 1733 – Jacob White, Thomas Forgan and
Edward Carbold. Carbold was a Wrabness merchant, informed on
after a big run of tea and declared to be 'worth £400'. There were no

soldiers in Ipswich to escort him to Chelmsford, so the *Waklyn* was employed to take him to Maldon, where he was met by the two Riding Officers who had arrested him and taken by them to the gaol. The Collector said he could not even send witnesses to London for his trial 'for fear of being corrupted or carried off by smugglers', but would have to escort him there himself. Forgan was arrested in 1729 after obstructing officers in Handford Water where he was running ten cwt of tea in the *Young Johanna* of Middleburg. Of White I have no details, but if he was also a man of substance again one wonders if the breakout was fixed by bribery. Oft-quoted stories of convictions being impossible to obtain because of the partiality of juries for smugglers find little corroboration, but on several occasions the Collector reported bitterly that 'he was robbed' by judges or magistrates. In addition to cases quoted elsewhere, in 1731 the Harwich Collector attended the Assizes at Chelmsford for the trial of John Lilley, who had obstructed officers. The case was taken on a Saturday night, and (according to the disgruntled Collector) Lilley perjured himself after which, despite the evidence to the Grand Jury, which had found a true bill, the Judge told them to acquit Lilley without even allowing the prosecution evidence to be heard.

As well as condemning smugglers, the Justices also had to condemn smuggled goods before they could be sold or destroyed. In 1731 the Harwich Collector reported that it was 'always the customs at this Port, at the condemnation of goods before the Justices to give the Mayor and Justices a small treat, but the present Mayor, not content with that, has taken on him to order what victuals and liquor he pleases . . . If the Commissioners of Excise have but a trifle to condemn they allow 40s expenses!' (The greedy Mayor in 1731 was James Clements, already mentioned in connection with the building of the *Walpole*.)

With the general imposition of bonds and licences in the second half of the eighteenth century the picture changes. Most smugglers were now in bond to the Customs, making it an easy and almost automatic operation to impose penalties.

These penalties were often three times the value of the smuggled goods, or for an infringement of a vessel's licence the Coast Smuggling Security of £100 was often imposed – a considerable sum, equivalent to £3,000 by today's values. Such penalties were paid only in a minority of cases. A plea of poverty was almost universal, as a result of which most smugglers found themselves in gaol as Crown debtors. (One exception was Ambrose Ballanger, later to be landlord of the George & Dragon at Foulness, who had £130 of his father's money with him when he was caught driving a cart containing four half-ankers to

Rankin's mill at Stambridge in 1839. The Customs found the money and kept it.)

This procedure involved no trial, but left the Customs in the position of prosecution, judge and Court of Appeal with convenient opportunity for extorting information as the price of ultimate release. So casual were they as to the legal processes that when in 1771 the Revenue cutter *Vigilance's* mooring was stolen by a fisherman, the Harwich Collector, Griffith Davies, who was also Mayor (and thus Chief Magistrate) used that authority to commit the man to prison to stand trial at the next Assizes. He had also immediately issued a Warrant when in 1759 he arrived at the office to find it had been robbed, though on this occasion he did arrange for his Clerk to prosecute, as it would 'not be right for the Collector as Mayor, and the only Magistrate in the Corporation who can commit to the County Gaol, to be prosecutor also'.

In view of the profits made from smuggling, the almost universal inability or unwillingness to pay the £100 penalty suggests that imprisonment was sometimes accepted as a lesser evil. The Harwich Collector in 1813 thought this considerable sum inadequate in the case of licensed illegally built vessels, urging that it should be double the value of the craft, with a minimum of £300.

The procedure followed well-established lines. A case was first formally referred to the Customs' solicitor, who issued the writ for the debt due. Assuming the offender could not or would not pay the sum demanded he was taken before a magistrate, whose decision to commit to prison seems to have been largely another formality.

The smugglers were committed to the debtors' side of the county gaol, which in most of the cases described was at Chelmsford. (In fact after 1829 a new gaol at Springfield, just outside Chelmsford was used, but to save confusion I have not differentiated.) Debtors were kept in a special part of the prison with 'free access to a commodious airing yard, day room etc' whereas other prisoners were allowed only an hour's exercise morning and afternoon 'in the small airing yards, of which there are twelve for the men and twelve for the women.'[1]

There must have been a regular smugglers' community in the gaol, averaging ten between 1812 and 1819, in which year it had increased to twenty-three. After this date the total decreased for some years to single figures, with another increase to twenty-five in 1825, nineteen in 1826 and fifteen in 1836. These Crown debtors had a special officer in charge of them and were regarded as distinct from the common debtors, who averaged thirty-eight in number between 1812 and 1819. The distinction added a complication to an already confused situation,

119

for all debtors were expected to pay for their keep, and while those in prison for 'debts from losses on trade and other unavoidable circumstances' pleaded inability to pay by reason of 'absolute poverty' the Customs were expected to furnish the subsistence of the smugglers.

The Justices in 1797 established a scale of charges claiming fourpence a night rent for 'chamber, bed and bedding, provided that no more than two be put in each bed and not more than two beds in one room.' The Act under which this charge was made also permitted debtors to bring in their own beds and in this case the charge was reduced to one shilling a week for 'chamber rent'.

The gaoler was quite unable to recover either charge from the common debtors, who in 1819 unsuccessfully petitioned for an allowance of 1s a week from the county. The Crown debtors, then twenty-six in number, and including several of the smugglers who feature in these chapters, petitioned separately in the same year, declaring that they could not find anything in the rules to justify the deduction of a shilling a week from their subsistence, and claiming that rules 'made respecting other debtors were not intended for those belonging to the Crown.' They also declared that such chamber rent was not deducted in other prisons.

This stand was probably dictated by the Customs, who were

The old Chelmsford Gaol, standing near the Stone Bridge on the London Road, was built in 1777 and demolished in 1859. After 1825 prisoners were housed in a newly-built gaol at Springfield. This painting dates from 1810.

evidently behind the petition. At any rate this was the beginning of a wrangle between the Customs and the county which rumbled on for a decade, though by the early 1820s the bone of contention had become 4½d a day, supposed to provide one and a half pounds of bread and a quart of beer. On proof of absolute poverty a supplementary allowance of 3d a day might be granted. These allowances were sent weekly by the Collector at Maldon to the officer in charge of smugglers using 'a person going to Chelmsford market to save the prisoners expense.'

Even discounting the dramatically pathetic phraseology of the petitions the county allowance was barely enough to support life. A seventy-year-old smuggler complained in 1819 that he had been 'unable to obtain any animal food since my confinement.' In 1825 eighteen foreign seamen petitioned that '4½d a day is inadequate to the supply of clean linen and other means of getting a sufficiency of bread exclusive of any attendant requisite comfort or the means of corresponding with their unfortunate families.'

The following month the visiting magistrates gave the debtors a choice between the county allowance of bread and beer or the 4½d. When they chose the latter, the county allowance was stopped and the gaoler was instructed to pay 4½d a day. (This, it will be noted, was the same figure that had been used to compute the cost of victualling a mariner in the packets eighty years before, though by 1809 it had risen to 1s 6d a day.)

Application was then made to the Customs for the supplementary 3d. The Customs solicitor responded with a characteristic display of confusion and prevarication. He asked for details and proof that 4½d was inadequate. The Maldon Comptroller patiently replied that the gaoler alone could answer that, and the gaoler in 1826 (when bread cost 4½d a loaf and beer 3d a pint) confirmed that '7½d is merely sufficient when in health, without any consideration of the cost of extra diet with which they are provided by the county at the direction of the surgeon when sick.'

The higgling continued for some years after this. The county magistrates took the view in 1825 that 'maintainance of these prisoners appears plainly intended to be imposed by law, as in justice it ought to be, upon the national and not upon the county purse. As 4½d a day is insufficient 7½d should be authorised [by the Board.]' The Honourable Commissioners adopted their usual attitude towards their creditors. They were not prepared to pay without the maximum difficulty and delay and then preferably only in part. As a result the Board slapped down the Clerk of the Peace in 1827 by observing that 'as the gaoler took on himself to give the allowance of 7½d a day without any sanction the request cannot be complied with.' They then imposed their own rate of 6d a day. The Board of Excise was even brusquer. When the county applied for an allowance for one of their prisoners the Supervisor merely called at the prison door and told the porter to tell the gaoler the petition was rejected.

Though an Act of Parliament gave powers in 1826 to grant 7½d a day the Customs were still paying 6d in 1836. William Taylor of Lymington (who had also been in Maidstone gaol) was refused an allowance in 1830 as he had 'friends in respectable circumstances.' The despairing gaoler observed, 'The magistrates had determined not to allow the smugglers any food and the Honourable Board of Customs had refused to allow Taylor any money. As gaoler I am bound to see a prisoner does not starve.'

One of the chief interests of the smugglers in prison must have been petitioning. References to petitions appear in the Harwich Collector's letters as early as the 1760s, but only in the early nineteenth century do they start to be quoted in detail by the Maldon Collector, providing most of the details of the offences as well as a picture of the unhappy lot of the offender.

The first petition, for the 3d a week supplementary subsistence allowance already mentioned, was undertaken immediately on arrival. It was usually approved on confirmation by the gaoler that a prisoner was destitute – often, I suspect, in the case of the smugglers a fiction in which the gaoler connived rather than face the task of extracting the money from the prisoner.

Then after about six months' confinement came the time for the first petitions for release. These pleas set out the misery of the prisoner's condition and the plight of his unfortunate family, and then went on to protest his innocence through total ignorance of the law, or alternatively to make confession of his guilt with sincere repentance and assurances that nothing of the sort could ever happen again.

These pleas were made nominally to the Treasury as creditor, which referred them to the Board of Customs, which referred them to the Collector, who referred them to the officer who had made the seizure, in which he often had a vested interest through seeking a reward. His response was to reiterate that he had smartly apprehended a notorious smuggler, and with that the first petition was usually rejected.

After nearly a year's imprisonment another petition was sent, this time signed by the Minister, churchwardens, merchants and inhabitants of the man's parish, influenced no doubt as much by a desire to rid the parish of 4s a week paid to the destitute family as by any sympathy or compassion. This was taken more seriously, and soon afterwards the Honourable Commissioners usually saw fit to release

their prisoner, provided they were satisfied they had squeezed the last
drop of information out of him.

One wonders who wrote all these petitions, for, while the majority
conform to a familiar style, each varies, in addition to including details
relevant to the case, so all were original compositions. Presumably it
was part of some lawyer's professional practice to visit the prison and
write them out.

Conditions changed in 1833, when an Act introduced hard labour as
a penalty, and from this time most smugglers were subjected to the
rigours of the treadmill (at Chelmsford thriftily geared to a pair of
millstones, so the operation made a profit!) or the other prison work-
shops. While the debtors had been committed for an indefinite period,
which usually turned out to be about a year, before the Customs
consented to release them, the convicts were given a fixed sentence,
usually of six months, with the Customs still retaining the power to
remit part of a sentence. Among several such sentences at this time
three Gravesend men found aboard the *Elizabeth* of London in 1837
near the Blyth with 7¼ lbs of cigars were sentenced to six months'
hard labour, and when the wife of one of them visited the gaol she
was 'refused all communication with her husband, though informed
his health was much injured from insufficient diet and labour at the
treadmill.'

Yet many of the sentences were still at the discretion of the Customs.
The Justices' subsistence account for 1836 lists fifteen smugglers, of
whom six had been imprisoned for 180 days, with the imprisonment
of the others ranging from 272 to 119 days. When Thomas Bacon,
former master of the notorious *Speedwell*, petitioned for release in
December 1838, after six months at Chelmsford, the Collector noted
'by your Honours' orders to be released after twelve months' confinement, which will be at June 14 next.' Under the new regime the
committal proceedings also became a little less of a formality. The
Magistrates began to be mentioned by name, and sometimes to take
the trouble to remand a prisoner for better evidence. Occasionally (as
in the case of Thomas Overall, presumably a member of a highly
respected Mersea family of oyster merchants, found in 1835 aboard a
boat in the Crouch with thirteen pounds of tobacco) they expressed
their disapproval at having to convict for so trivial an offence, but
they still felt powerless to refuse, or even to mitigate the penalty.

By 1840 two adjudicating magistrates actually joined in a petition
on behalf of a man found aboard the smack *Oyster* from Jersey, saying
there was 'no reason to suppose he had any knowledge when he
embarked that the vessel had any contraband aboard,' but they still

felt bound to convict him as a member of the crew, and could do no more than 'recommend him to the consideration of the Commissioners of HM Customs & Excise for a remission of the whole or part of the period for which he is now imprisoned.'

A common way to secure freedom was to buy it, usually after a haggle over the price. Few cases are to be found when the full £100 penalty was paid, but there are numerous examples of sums up to £50 being offered on behalf of men who a few months before had protested themselves penniless. Daniel London of Tollesbury, whose story appears in a later chapter, 'got friends to come forward and pay £50' and 'begs your Lordships to consider this and the loss of his vessel sufficient recompense,' while in 1818 a Foulness smuggler first tried £30, and when the Customs observed that he had an oyster laying and his own boat had to raise his bid to £50.

Escape does not often seem to have been contemplated by Englishmen, presumably because it would never have been safe for them to return home, but in 1774 the master of a craft seized by Cyprian Bridge managed it. He was Abraham Stagholt of Maldon, and his petition included the claim that he was 'inventor of the method of firing harpoons out of swivel guns now practised in the Greenland Fishery, for which he had a premium from the Society for the Encouragement of the Arts and Sciences.' Despite his talents he was 'not worth a shilling' – and despite that before he made his escape he offered £4 4s for his freedom, a bid the Customs refused.

For foreigners escape was more attractive, partly perhaps because they had no friends or relations at hand to buy them out, or to bring them any food or comforts while they were still inside, and partly because even during the wars it was not difficult to get a passage out of the country. In 1828 a Dutchman named Carolus Deseta secured his freedom 'by getting over the chevau-de-frise [iron spikes topping the wall] and then onto the roof of the debtors' side and into the street.' He had been captured with another Dutchman, William Deseta, who escaped at the time of their seizure, and an Englishman, William Phipps of Kirby-le-Soken, who was imprisoned despite his ingenious plea that he was 'a passenger and quite unaware' in the Ostend sloop *Joanna Maria*, caught sinking fifty-nine tubs of spirits and twenty of tobacco and snuff off the Maplin Sands. It will be observed that these Dutchmen were taken on the Essex coast, thus forfeiting the immunity enjoyed by foreign smugglers outside British territorial waters.

The alternative to the debtors' prison for a fit man was to be sent to Chatham to serve a spell in one of HM ships, or occasionally to remain as a mariner aboard the Revenue cutter which made the arrest. This form of impressment was carried out without even a formal approval by a magistrate, as the owner of the sloop *George*, mentioned in chapter twenty-three, protested in 1815, observing that his impressed captain 'is deprived of the most valuable heritage of Englishmen, that of being confronted face to face with his accuser who has been his ruin.'

While Revenue cutter commanders earned 'head money' for every smuggler impressed, the smugglers themselves received only half-pay, the balance going to the parishes supporting their wives if they were paupers. Perhaps for this reason, or perhaps to avoid more serious punishment, a smuggler occasionally chose to volunteer for the Navy as the best way out. John Miller enlisted in HMS *Barracouter* (sic) after being seized on board the Leigh peterboat *Endeavour* with ten casks of geneva and a cask of brandy. He was on remand to appear at Quarter Sessions, and jumped his bail. This suggests he was charged with something more than smuggling, perhaps violence in resisting arrest. William Pledger of Great Wakering, who was also aboard the *Endeavour*, was fined £100, which he paid – another unusual feature of this case. [2]

When a cutter loaded with brandy and tea was stranded at Wood-bridge Haven (Bawdsey) in 1739, in order to suppress evidence that would condemn a cargo the smugglers got the Master, John Reynolds, impressed aboard HMS *Boyne* at the Nore, where the Lieutenant refused to discharge him without orders from the Admiralty. The Collector asked the Board to apply for him to be transferred to one of the Revenue cutters 'till the tryall comes on, when the said Reynolds says he can be of service in informing the officers of the methods the smugglers take on this coast.' So much for loyalty among shipmates if they were also smugglers.

Poor John Pewter of Tollesbury was one of those impressed, only to find his troubles were not over when he was freed.

Till 1817 he owned the thirteen-ton smack *Hope* which – according to his account – he sold in that year to her skipper, William Cooper, for £40. Cooper had a new bottom put in her by Withey[3] at Mersea at a cost of £20, but had not paid his bill when he and the *Hope* were lost at sea, along with her papers including the bill of sale (if indeed there was one).

Meanwhile John Pewter was caught by the Gravesend Revenue cutter *Fortitude* aboard the smuggler *Mercurius*, of Flushing 'on the flat of the Knowl in five fathoms' (the Knoll Sand off the Colne estuary) and sent aboard HMS *Bulwark*. He was discharged from the *Blossom* sloop-of-war at Woolwich in Janurary 1824, to be confronted by the

Boadicea *as she appears today, sailing in 1955 Mersea Town Regatta. Built at Maldon in 1808, she has been rebuilt three times, once in the 1820s when owned by John Pewter, again in the late nineteenth century when her clinker planking was replaced by carvel, and finally by her present owner, Michael Frost, in the 1960s.*

debt on the *Hope*. Since he had no proof that he had sold her, he was committed to Chelmsford gaol, where he had the pleasure of meeting his brother Robert, held there on a £350 penalty arising out of another smuggling job carried out by the *Hope* before her loss – perhaps a visit to Boulogne mentioned in Chapter 25.

The Collector's response to his petition was to help him obtain the pay due to him from the Navy, and with the aid of this he re-established himself, for the following year he became the owner of the seventeen-year-old smack *Bodecia*, still in commission at West Mersea as the *Boadicea* – the only such link remaining with those distant days.

According to the oral tradition cherished by his descendants, [4] Pewter was a Preventive man when he first took a fancy to the *Bodecia* and was posted to St Helena before returning home to buy her. The documented story suggests, however, that this tradition became confused down the generations, and that John Pewter's acquaintance with the Preventive service was at the receiving end, with his introduction to naval service not of his own seeking.

14

Cut Up and Sold Up

The Fate of the Dagger: *Brandy Bargains.*

IN addition to the imprisonment of their masters and crews, and sometimes their owners, offending vessels were seized and often condemned – a loss much more serious than the capture of a cargo of contraband. As has already been shown, smugglers often tried to make a deal, by which they gave up their goods and kept their craft, and despite the repeated orders of the Board they often succeeded.

One of the quaintest ploys to avoid condemnation was tried at Maldon in 1767, when the smack *Success*, seized with a cargo of tobacco stalks, had her bottom removed, and the planks rebuilt as a 'luggage boat' – presumably in the belief that this could be sacrificed and the smack saved and rebuilt with a new bottom. The result of such ingenuity is not recorded, but a smack was sold at Maldon soon afterwards, and was I suspect the *Success*, with or without her bottom.

Once condemned, vessels could be sold, used by the Customs in its own service, or destroyed. Among craft the Customs took for their own use, Sainty's *Ruswarp* and Death's *Hebe* (both referred to in later chapters) were employed merely as stationary accommodation vessels, but the twenty-six-ton *Isis*, owned by William Willey of Brightlingsea (where she was built in 1798) was 'taken into the service of the Revenue and commanded by Capt William Dean' after her seizure in 1799.

Craft sold after seizure, providing a nice windfall for the Crown and for the seizing officer, are too numerous to specify; a summary of those so treated at the peak of the practice will be found elsewhere.[1] The seventeen-ton *Henry & Elizabeth* of Colchester (built at Wivenhoe in 1751) actually suffered this fate twice in two years, for she was seized in 1790 when owned by Robert Farrar of East Donyland and sold at Harwich to Joseph Cole of Rowhedge, from whom she was again seized and sold in 1801.

While a vessel could thus have several lives, perhaps the same did not apply to an owner; at any rate the reputation of Moses Gane, the East Donyland builder, may explain the fate of his newly-built *Liberty*, which when condemned at Harwich in 1787 was cut in pieces, but other vessels broken up, without any record of previous offences being alleged against their owners, included a ninety-two-ton brig in 1784 and the trading smack *Fisher* in 1797, both at Harwich, the eleven-ton *Boyman & Mary* of Maldon (built at Frindsbury in 1762) in 1791, the *John & Mary*, seized by Capt Phillips at Harwich in 1722, and the

Sawing up a condemned smuggler.

twenty-four-ton well-smack *Deary* at Colchester in 1733, while in 1756
a sloop from Helvoetsluys, caught near Maldon after a long chase by
the Colchester Custom House smack, with brandy, gin, tea and
muslins, was ordered to Leigh 'to be unloaded, her goods seized and
the vessel burned.'

Throughout most of the eighteenth century burning was the
favourite means of destruction, but towards the end of the century
cutting into pieces came into favour – perhaps because a few shillings
could be raised from the sale of the remains. The change was carried
out with the Customs' usual caution. In 1787 the Harwich Collector
had to give the reassurance that 'no smuggling vessels cut or saw'd
and afterwards put together and made fit for smuggling are registered
in Harwich.' (That this was not impossible is proved by the fact that
half-a-century later a Harwich smack was re-built out of the two
halves of a sawn-up smuggler, and known as *The Tobacco Box* to
commemorate it.) [2]

From 1811 onwards a record of all the craft cut up at Colchester and
Brightlingsea is to be found in a surviving list of Custom House sales.

The cutter *Fortuyn*, seized in 1819 and the smack *Bird*, seized in
1827, were sold intact for £15 and £35 respectively. The first recorded

examples of boats sold in three pieces were an unnamed vessel in 1826, and the *Friendship*, seized in October 1829, and sold in three parts in February 1830, the bow fetching 14s, the midships £1 and the stern 10s. With her gear she only made £10 10s, though a few days before her brandy had been sold in thirty-four lots for £105.

The following year there were two more such sales. The three-masted lugger *Dove*, seized in July 1830, was sold in pieces with fifty lots of brandy (£181), ten lots of white brandy (£49) and some geneva (£67), the sale totalling £312. The smack *Unity*, seized in February 1830, was sold in July with her gear, sails, gun and wildfowl gun for £14 13s, with her brandy going for £76 and thirty gallons of geneva for £46. In 1833 the smacks *Ann* and *Mary* were sold together, each in three pieces, for £21 14s 6d, along with seventy lots of brandy and gin seized in January and fetching £189.

There were two more such sales in 1835. One in February was an unidentified hull in three pieces, seized in October 1834 and sold with sixty-eight lots of boat gear for £39. The other, a stowboater, also unnamed, must have been James Cook's *Dagger*. Her spratting gear, including handfleets, baulks, wind rope and mingles[3] attracted the interest of the fishermen, the net alone fetching £7 10s and the stowboat anchor £2 10s. Thereafter no such destruction of seizures is recorded, though the smack *George and Mary* was sold intact in 1848 for £31.

It must have been a sickening spectacle to see these splendid smacks reduced to three heaps of firewood, knocked down for a few derisory shillings, followed by fishing gear, wildfowl guns, stove and cooking pots. The unhappy owner was not there to witness it but was brooding gloomily about it in the debtors' room at Chelmsford, but it must have made an impression on the other skippers, even if a surprising number failed to take heed of it. The picture is particularly poignant when one knows the background, as in the case of the *Dagger*, a forty-footer built at East Donyland in 1812.

James Cook, her owner and master, was spratting in the Swin in January, 1835, when he was hailed by the *Fanny* of Whitstable and invited to meet Daniel Rich in the Spitway the following morning. Now Daniel Rich, always known as Dick, was a known smuggler who had been in prison himself and already taken one accomplice there with him, as is recounted in Chapter 21. A native of Peldon, where he had had two years schooling, and so was able to read and write, he was at this time living at West Mersea, a married man with one child. All this Cook must have known, yet for £20 he agreed to put seventy-nine tubs under his sprats, run them into Brightlingsea and meet Rich at the Greyhound Inn, Wivenhoe, to settle up.

The story emerges, inevitably one would think, in Cook's petition from Chelmsford gaol where he was lodged along with his mate, William Bareham, at the time his smack was being cut up and sold up. There must have been some reunions of this Rowhedge family in that gaol, for in the same year there is a reference to William Cook facing a £100 penalty for smuggling twenty-nine half-ankers in his smack *Friends* and a petition by Samuel Cook on behalf of his seventeen-year-old son, David, whose two brothers had been lost two years before in the salvage of the *Marquis of Huntly*.[4]

As well as providing details of the sales described, the Colchester record throws light on the nature and extent of contraband dealt with by this particular Custom House throughout the nineteenth century.

For the first twenty years the sales were few in number and small in size, though there was a big seizure of German linen in 1813 and tobacco pipe clay was an unusual offer in 1811.

The early 1830s seem to have marked a peak, with many big sales of spirits besides those mentioned. In 1832, for example, thirty-seven lots of brandy were sold for £86 in January, fifty-two lots for over £100 in July and two other seizures for £120 in November. By the end of the 1830s sales were down to one a year, and a pre-Christmas sale of spirits established itself as an annual event.

Brandy in 1827 was fetching £1 13s for two gallons, with duty £1 12s 11d payable, and geneva £1 15s for two gallons (duty £1 14s 8d). These, along with silk handkerchiefs, were the chief seizures, with

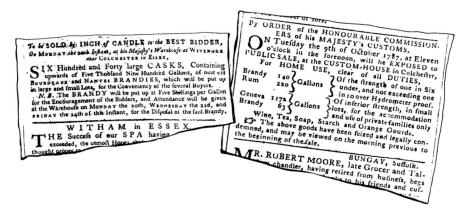

Advertisements in the Ipswich Journal *of 1743 and 1787. The Harwich Collector noted in 1767 that an advertisement in this paper and 'crying for two market days' cost five shillings.*

very little rum before the 1840s, when tea and tobacco also began to feature. Forty years before this, when 550 gallons of geneva were put up for sale at Maldon, it proved almost unsaleable due to being kept too long in small casks which gave it a bad colour and spoiled its flavour. Four hundred gallons went unsold, and the price of the rest was only five shillings a gallon.

Horses and carts were seized and sold in 1821 and 1856, and a donkey cart and harness in 1831 and 1833.

15

Seizing it Back

EVEN after they had lost their goods the smugglers did not always give up. The recapture of seizures was quite a regular occurrence.

Sometimes a raid was merely to recover a boat. A big forty-six-ton lugger, forty-six feet long, fitted with eight thwarts to row twelve oars, had been laid ashore outside the Custom House at Harwich in 1785 when thirty men, armed with bludgeons, were seen to cross from 'the two ferry houses on the Suffolk shore, viz Shotley and Colness' (on the opposite shore), and make off with her. In 1793 the Maldon Revenue men had put a boat in a field, ready to be cut up, with a hole knocked in her bottom, when she was recaptured and seen to be hoisted aboard a smuggling vessel off Bradwell, which was then put to sea. 'Next time' the Collector noted, 'I will take out a strake.'

Often, however, Customs warehouses were successfully robbed – an operation facilitated by the lack of security at some of these buildings. When a quantity of starch disappeared at Harwich in 1795 it was explained that probably a 'small person' had got into the warehouse and slipped the bolts of the windows. In the same year a robbery of cash was traced to a member of the crew of the *Walpole*, Alexander Kilgour, who unwisely kept a few gold coins in his pocket. He revealed to the Collector's clerk the place where he had buried the rest, and was sentenced at the Assizes to seven years' transportation. He seems to have escaped, and signed on in the armed cutter *Lurcher*, which unluckily for him came into Harwich where he was recognised and re-arrested.

The Burnham storehouse was broken into in 1835 and forty-seven bottles of geneva removed. They had been brought in by the smack *Rose in June* from the wreck of the Dunkirk schooner *Alliance* on the Barrow Sand. The master of the schooner asked for a certificate to exonerate him with the owners of the geneva, on which he had been told to pay salvage from the proceeds of a sale which now could not take place. The Customs procrastinated, advertising a £5 reward for information.

These were minor routine occurrences. A more spectacular venture is worth recounting in detail.

On 16 April 1748 the Colchester Collector reported: 'About two o'clock this morning two persons went to John Bloys (he being then in a granary on the town key) and inquired where the Custom House

132

was, pretending that a seizure of tea had been made and must be immediately lodged there or it would be rescued by the smugglers who were in pursuit of us . . .'

Bloys called the Collector's servant, who opened up the house, but both men were then threatened with pistols. 'Near thirty Smugglers with Blunderbusses and Pistols came into the courtyard threat'ning with dreadful Implications. The smugglers broke into the King's warehouse and took the tea seized by Robert Martin's cruiser near Woodbridge Haven. The King's Warehouse is very secure but the greatest security imaginable would not have prevented these desperate villains. William Lisle, Supervisor of Riding Officers, went after them. He heard they got to Hadleigh in Suffolk by six o'clock but what became of them afterwards they could not hear.'

Lisle was an exceptionally enterprising and interesting character. He must, I think, have seen the possibilities of making a lot of money, and set about building up his own organisation with all the vision and energy of a tradesman developing a business. He claimed that he himself rode a hundred miles a week, and secured an allowance to keep two horses, but he cannot have made all his captures single-handed. The Board evidently regarded him as exceptional, for in 1734 they made him a special allowance of £5 for each smuggler captured (soon afterwards raised to £12), out of which he had to pay all expenses and rewards to assistants. The Dragoons, who objected to turning out at night, received a half-share in his rewards, which they complained was not enough. In addition to his blood money he got his salary raised in 1740 to £70, with a bonus of £10 provided the King's share exceeded this sum.

Lisle specialised in multiple round-ups, often three men at a time. In April 1735 he arrested first one man, then three, then four more; in May he picked up one; in June three and then four; in July a trio; in September two single captures; in November ten men in six seizures; in December and January 1736 a double and a single in each month, with two more in February. Thus in one year nearly forty smugglers lost their liberty through his exertions, though several were released and were paid a few shillings a week subsistence to act as informers. And this level of activity went on year after year.

The smugglers returned his attentions, and in 1744 kidnapped him. He was ultimately released on giving a promise not to reveal names – an arrangement which may have been the start of collusion, for soon after this he fell under suspicion. The Harwich Collector reported that Captain Martin and his men believed he had a hand in the Colchester raid, or at least was aware of it. The Collector got into conversation with Lisle, who said the notorious Samuel Salmon of Thorpe was one of the gang, but had pretended to be sick. He also named Jonah Larret of Tendring, adding that he also did not go, but, said the Collector, 'we believe both were there.'

Lisle and the Harwich Collector were at loggerheads because the Collector wanted to arrest these suspects and Lisle wanted to keep them as King's evidence, producing a long list of smugglers whom Salmon was willing to incriminate. Thus when the Collector secured an affidavit from Larret that Salmon carried firearms he concealed it from Lisle, and after an affray in which the Handfleet boatmen were beaten up the Collector asked to be allowed to serve the writ, 'for if it goes to Colchester Mr Lisle will know of it and will (as we have reason to believe he did before) prevent it being served . . . Mr Lisle (for reasons best known to himself) has spread it about that it was another gang. He has lately acted a very inconsistent part.'

The Collector busied himself gathering information and opinions detrimental to Lisle, but after he had visited Ipswich for a long talk with Mr Sparrow (presumably the Collector there) he could not get agreement, Sparrow taking the view that Lisle's conduct was explicable and defensible.

All in all it is not easy to decide whether the Collector was in the right, or merely frustrated at being denied some useful rewards for convictions. But there must have been something in it, for in 1750 Lisle was suspended, the Collector being asked to return his Commission on pain of his bond being put into suit. (The Commission gave the officer his powers; the bond was his security for good behaviour.)

16

Birth of the Coastguard

Post-war Reforms: Business as Usual: Coast Blockade and Coastguard: The Preventive Waterguard: Cottages and Watch Vessels.

WAR against France did not, as might have been expected, interrupt or even diminish the smugglers' activities. It encouraged and increased them. For this there were various reasons.

The Continental ports were kept open to smugglers, who brought valuable information and equally precious supplies of English coinage. Duties were raised up to threefold and applied to an increasing range of imports to meet the cost of the armed forces, increasing the incentives and rewards of smuggling correspondingly. Revenue cutters and Dragoons had to be diverted to sterner duties. The cutters joined the Navy or were issued with Letters of Marque, and three of them fell into enemy hands, as has been described in Chapter 7.

The Government passed one Act after another, increasing penalties and rewards and introducing ever more complicated regulations – measures which were as ineffective as they were incomprehensible through lack of any means of enforcement. As a result, a decline in smuggling throughout the first half of the eighteenth century was reversed in the second half, with an all-time peak around 1800. And if any patriotic inhibitions were felt by those engaged in the smuggling trade over breaking these laws or undermining the national war effort, there is no evidence of them to be found.

Thus the restoration of peace in 1815 saw the Customs faced with an unprecedented challenge. They were not helped by the predictable disposition to economise by disarmament. The *Vixen* gun brig was sent round the East Coast dismantling signal stations which within a few years could have been found useful. The Board's inspector, noting in 1815 that the Burnham and Paglesham boats had not made any seizures in the past three years, observed 'They must be in each other's way.' The Paglesham boat was ordered to Shoebury, where a slipway was built in 1829.

Within a few years, however, it became clear that defences must be increased, not dismantled.

First assumptions were to rely on the time-honoured combination of Revenue cutters at sea and Riding Officers ashore, supported by Dragoons. Observing in 1815 that there were no troops nearer than Chelmsford, the Maldon Collector asked for detachments at Bradwell,

Southminster, Burnham and Foulness, extending this plea later the same year to the provision of Dragoons 'wherever there is a public house to accommodate them.'

This, however, was not the answer. New measures were needed against a new type of smuggling. Naval supremacy and military power had ended the old gallant system of the eighteenth century, when smugglers carried arms and fought their way. Speed had replaced guns as the smuggling vessel's first need, and, more important, clandestine sinking of contraband in rivers and creeks had largely replaced the open landing on shores and beaches. A new force was required to link the cruisers at sea and the Riding Officers ashore.

On the Kent and Sussex coasts, scene of the most intensive smuggling, the Coast Blockade, introduced between the Forelands in 1817 and extended as far as Seaford in 1818, attempted to provide a chain of posts within hail of each other. This system was not extended to Essex, and would in any case have been unsuitable for the creeks and estuaries of the area, though it would have been appropriate to the stretch of coast between Walton Naze and Colne Point.

The needs of marshland Essex were met as the result of an overdue re-organisation of the various Preventive forces, leading to the formation of the Coastguard. Up till 1822 the various agencies devised to combat the smuggler were never properly co-ordinated, and confusion became worse confounded by the strains of war and new arrangements to meet increased threats expected with the return of peace. As a result, the long-established Riding Officers continued to patrol their lengthy beats ashore, while afloat the command of craft large and small was absurdly divided. In addition to a number of Naval vessels devoted to protective duties, some Revenue cruisers in 1816 came under the orders of the Admiralty, while others remained under the control of the Customs or in a few cases the Excise. To add to the chaos, a Preventive Water Guard, now seen as the main answer to the new-style smuggler, had been established in 1809 under the control of the Customs, but was also re-organised in 1816 with its own Comptroller-General, Captain Hanchett, RN, who was later to be dismissed for selling his appointments, degraded of his Companionship of the Bath and stripped of his Commission. [1]

A Commission of 1822[2] observed, 'We do not find that any concert has been practically established between the several authorities, nor does it appear that any communications exist between the executive officers in the different services, even when employed on closely adjoining stations and acting almost in sight of each other.' An example of this friction in practice is to be found in a Customs' Order of 1817 that 'Captain Hanchett . . . is not to control the watch vessel at the

136

mouth of the Colne, which is solely under the control of the Tide Surveyor.'

The reforms put forward in 1822 aimed at 'an uniform system controlled by one authority. In this system the primary force will be that which is now called the Preventive Water Guard, although from the change in the nature of its duties since its first establishment the term "Coast Guard" would be a more appropriate distinction.' This was the beginning of the Coastguard service – a force of boatmen who were expected to patrol ashore when the weather precluded the use of their boats. While demobilised Naval officers and ratings were largely employed, the Coast Guard remained a civilian force under the control of the Customs for the first twenty-one years of its existence. The boatmen were employed not less than twenty miles from their homes, to avoid collusion, thus ending the 'local' tradition of the Revenue cutters, and incidentally introducing many new families into previously close-knit, inter-bred coastal communities.

Rationalisation was completed by the ending of the Coast Blockade, which while efficient was unduly expensive, and was also suspected of 'corrupt collusion between the blockade men and the smugglers,' and by transferring to the Customs such import duties as were still controlled by the Excise, ending the Excise presence afloat. The Coastguard reverted to the Admiralty in 1831 and became part of the Naval Reserve in 1845, by which time the 'uniform system' had largely brought the long war against the smuggler to a successful conclusion.

Around the Essex shores coastguard cottages were provided at some stations – still to be seen at many places including Walton, Leigh, West Mersea, Stansgate and Pin Mill on the Orwell – but most of the men were accommodated in stationary watch vessels guarding the main estuaries, with small cruisers on patrol, and boats at minor ports. The *Rattlesnake* was established in the Blackwater and the *Ruswarp* in the Crouch. Both are referred to in later chapters. The Colne seems to have had a small watch vessel. Harwich, protected by its Revenue cutters, had also long relied on a succession of watch vessels, including the *Trial*, which was described in 1815 as 'very small, of no service, but a useless expense.' She was a particularly unpopular station. Her Tide Waiter resigned in 1814 with the comment, 'I find myself uncomfortably situated as to be placed aboard the *Trial* watch vessel in danger of my life by being run down in the night,' and his successor protested a year or two later at having 'to keep watch day and night after being roll'd and tossed about in the *Trial*.'

The most interesting of all the watch vessels was Charles Darwin's *Beagle*, which ended her days at Paglesham lying in the middle of the river till the oyster company and local merchants petitioned in 1850 to have her laid ashore. At Bradwell (where an abandoned watchhouse had been re-commissioned in 1825) the coastguards were in 1833 put aboard the *Whitworth*, which lay afloat in the creek till at least 1838 when cottages were asked for as she could not accommodate the crew of eleven. She continued to be used, however, and later lay along the quay, but had apparently gone by 1862, as part of the evidence in a row over fishing rights in the creek in that year was that 'the WV *Whitworth* lay there for 21 years.' The first choice for Bradwell had been the *Chanticleer* but she was sent to the Crouch, a more important station with twenty-two men, to replace the *Whitworth* there. The *Chanticleer* was still in the Crouch in 1837 when the Burnham Oyster Company asked for her removal as they were 'unable to occupy a great portion of our best ground.' In fact they got £10 a year rent, probably what they were after, for in 1848 the watch vessel at Grays was also given notice to quit by the landowner with a similar result. There was also a watch vessel named *Dove* at Foulness in 1849.

17

Getting on with the Excise

Departmental Disagreements: 'Worth, Essex': Seizure of the Ophir: Squabbles aboard the Packets: Teething Troubles with the Coastguard: The Alien Officer Puts his Oar In.

IN addition to its internal fragmentation up to 1822, the Customs service also found its task complicated by its relations with other departments which were sometimes as quarrelsome as they should have been co-operative.

The Excise, which remained an independent service till 1909, was concerned primarily with duties on home commodities, as distinct from imports and exports (including the coastal trade) which were the responsibility of the Customs. Despite this, Excise duties were also levied on some imported goods up to the time of the general rationalisation of 1822; indeed, the Excise duty on tea and spirits was higher than the Customs duty. The Excise service at the end of the eighteenth century collected more Revenue than the Customs, and employed almost the same number of staff, including port officers to deal with import duties. There was no doubt a correspondence between the local officers and the Excise Board, but it has not survived. If it had, this story might have been different in content and colour, with another cast of players.

Though they had a force afloat, the Excise men's exploits were thus usually inland. In 1832 they seized a horse and cart carrying fourteen half-ankers at Kelvedon, a village on the main road between Colchester and Chelmsford. One man escaped from Maldon gaol; the other went to Chelmsford, where the prison doctor noted that he was 'in delicate health from hepatic disease through previous excess in ardent spirits'.

In the same year the Excise supervisor noticed a cart marked 'John Hooker, Worth, Essex'. There being no place of that name, he followed, cutting across some fields, and stopping a passer-by for help in making an arrest. One of the carters knocked him down, on which his faint-hearted helper made off. Three men also made their escape, taking the horses but leaving the cart, which again contained half-ankers. It transpired that it had come from Worthing, Sussex, and its new owner decided to make an economical job of repainting the address – a little folly which deservedly cost him dear, for he could not have found a surer way of attracting attention and arousing suspicion.

The Customs must have had some interest in these activities, for they are recorded in the Collector's letters. The Customs warehouse was also used for Excise seizures, which the Customs shipped to

139

London, including in 1787 a huge haul of tobacco from a pub at Hazeleigh. (The Collector, observing that pubs often sold tobacco, seemed in some doubt about the seizure.)

At sea, the Excise had its own fleet of Revenue cutters, acting independently in every sense of the word, till the reforms of 1822 transferred to the Customs responsibility for all imported goods. Bradwell was an Excise port to the extent that Excise sales of contraband were held in that remote little place. Excise cutters were also stationed at Colchester and Harwich, but whether regularly or intermittently it is difficult to tell.

Sometimes relations were friendly enough, even if not to the extent of being sensibly concerted. One day in 1799 Robert Howorth, the Bradwell Riding Officer, was on his way back from Maldon, where he had been to collect his quarter's pay. Nearing home he was told by a decoyman employed by the Rev Bate Dudley, the noted sporting parson of Bradwell, that there was a run on the Glebe Saltings. Howorth asked the Bradwell constable, Benjamin Lawrence, to muster all the hands he could, went home, loaded his guns and pistols, and with the constable's party of eleven men boarded a craft called the *Ophir* ashore on the saltings. Aboard he found 800 tubs of geneva and a man employed by Lieut Leckie, a naval half-pay officer in charge of the land signals at Bradwell. The man was in the cabin 'with a tub of Gin between his Leggs pouring it over into a half-pint bason'. Despite this Howorth engaged him, for he was a seaman and he said

Bradwell waterside in 1857, showing the coastguard watch vessel referred to in chapter 16.

with the wind north-east the *Ophir* was likely to float in the morning and drag her anchor. Howorth meanwhile put the King's mark on the *Ophir* and on her cargo, and in the morning got wagons and took 450 tubs up to Bate Dudley's house.

The usual squabble over rewards ensued. The Customs decided they had nothing to fear from Lieut Leckie, who had not been aboard himself, and anyway had no powers to seize, but a wrangle developed between Howorth and the other Riding Officers, John Pond, the supervisor, and Thomas Lackford, who 'with illiberal and abusive language' claimed a share for 'preventing embezzlement' and for transporting the cargo to Maldon.

The real threat, however, was from the Bradwell Revenue cutter *Fox,* for she was an Excise, not a Customs, cruiser. But in the end a relieved Collector noted there was 'no danger of any rescue of the vessel, or re-seizure of the prize by the *Fox* . . . as the chief mate of her came aboard and offered men to assist, which he (Howorth) declined.' According to Howorth's own account of the visit, the mate of the *Fox* 'gave me joy of my seizure, and told me if I had not been there on board he would have seized.'

The two services were often at odds in dealing with the North Sea packets. An order in 1754 'to behave decently and live in harmony with the officers of the Excise' was honoured more in the breach than the observance for the next half-century.

In 1755 Capt Dagnett of the *Walpole* boarded the *Prince of Wales* in the Sledway. Rummaging at sea was not allowed, so he came in with her. On arrival, Mr Price, the Excise Surveyor, came aboard, followed by Mr Matthews, the Inspector. After the passengers had left, Dagnett told two men to rummage, inviting Price to join them. They seized a few packets of tea which Price demanded, and Dagnett, observed the Collector, 'was weak enough to give in.'

Some of the troubles arose out of jealousy over the status of the various officers. On this occasion Dagnett complained that the master of a Revenue cutter, 'whom we esteem equal if not superior in station to the Tide Surveyor' should have the same liberty to rummage. Returning to the dispute the next year he insisted that the 'Commander of a sloop is generally looked upon as superior to a Tide Surveyor, and the Mate equal, but Mr Constable [the Excise Tide Surveyor] insists they are on a foot with his boatmen.'

Another cause of friction was the right of the Excise to make a first search of passengers. 'Mr Price', said the Collector, 'orders gentlemen to be examined as if their pockets were filled with brandy or tea. Though he has seized nothing from any passenger since he has been here, yet he persists. His boatmen are not the best behaved, being Gravesend watermen, and the worst sort of them, as no other would be with a man of Price's character. After they are gone the Customs are compelled to examine for prohibited goods that are not exciseable, and in that manner are gentlemen torn and pulled about.' He added that he 'would not be troubled if the Commissioners of Excise had sent an honest man here.'

The antagonism, however, ran deeper than personalities. The packet *Prince of Wales* was already under detention in 1797 when Capt Adams of the *Viper* Excise cutter insisted on rummaging her, despite the presence of Customs officers aboard. Challenged, Adams said he had placed four men aboard till he got further orders from his Board. A week later the Excise men were taken off, and the Customs were told to release the *Prince of Wales* on payment of 'a modest satisfaction'. No sooner was she free than she sailed for Yarmouth, where the packets were then stationed, only to be seized there again by Adams and the *Viper!*

Four years before this, in 1793, the *Amor Parentum* of Hamburg, bound to Bordeaux with wheat, was brought in by a smack and delivered to the Customs. While she had their Tidesmen aboard she was boarded by the Excise cutter 'by virtue of a Letter of Marque'. The High Court of Admiralty's ruling was that the *Amor Parentum* be sent to London, perhaps a way of taking her out of the hands of the quarrelling factions at Harwich.

As late as 1819, with the introduction of the watch vessels, the Excise laid claim to the *Rattlesnake's* seizures, 'she being considered a cruiser, notwithstanding being under the direction of the Comptroller of the Preventive Water Guard' – a notion promptly countered by the Customs with the ruling that the *Rattlesnake* and her tender were 'under the sole direction of the Comptroller General of the Water Guard'.

Though the reforms of 1822 ended the disputes with the Excise, the Coastguard which they introduced provided a fresh bone of contention.

In 1841 the Collector queried an order by the Inspecting Commander of the new force that all vessels should be accompanied by a coastguard from Bradwell to Maldon, which was 'never the practice since the establishment of the Coast Guard' and in the same year the Burnham Tide Surveyor declared himself 'much annoyed by the interference of the Coast Guard officers.'

Asked for details, he said he was overseeing the loading of oysters aboard the *Amity* and other smacks, whose masters had asked him what stores they were allowed. A man from the *Beagle* then came aboard and contradicted his instructions. On another occasion he had cleared a vessel named *Dolphyn* when Lieut Hussey, the Inspecting Commander, said he had information and would put a man aboard to watch. 'I think he exceeded his duty in waiting for my absence and going on board to persuade the glut Tide Surveyor to allow him to unbatten the hatches. Once a vessel is in my hands the Coast Guard have no right to go aboard and rummage.'

Such incidents, however, suggest no more than the friction inevitable between naval and civil forces. There seems to have been nothing comparable to the jealousy between Customs and Excise.

One further inter-departmental dispute which pre-occupied the harrassed Harwich Collector remains to be mentioned. This was a furious clash with the Alien Office, set up to oversee the movement of foreigners.

The Alien Service was at first operated quite amicably by the Collector and by an Alien Officer named Hake, who was appointed to oversee the packets while they were at Yarmouth, and who returned with them to Harwich in 1801. Then in 1805 a local shipping bigwig, Samuel Billingsley, secured the office of Principal Officer of the Customs for the Regulation of the Alien Act, setting up his own office and acting independently and in defiance of the Customs. In 1807 the Tide Surveyor protested that as soon as he boarded the *King George* packet, Mr Billingsley arrived and took ashore two passengers and two desks. The Alien Agent at Gravesend was threatening in 1808 to send the Revenue cutter *Ant,* 'usually employed on Alien Service at this port', round to Harwich. This seems to have been avoided, and in 1809, while Billingsley was in London, the Collector tried to step in and recover his powers. Billingsley, however, returned to resist him. 'He still withholds the use of a boat with four oars' protested the Collector.

18

Marshland Tub Sinkers

Policing the Saltings: Lieut Neame and the Rattlesnake: *Lawless Foulness:*
The Boatman's Tale.

THE change from runs on open beaches to clandestine sinking in rivers
and creeks increased activity in marshland Essex, which happily may
still be seen through the eyes of smugglers and Revenue men of the
period.

The Colne, winding its way up from Brightlingsea to Colchester,
past Wivenhoe and Rowhedge, has changed little since those days, and
its tributary creeks – the Pyefleet behind Mersea Island, its neighbour
the Geetings, and the little twisting channels leading to St. Osyth and
the tide mills at Alresford and Fingringhoe – hardly at all. The nobler
estuary of the Blackwater divides still round Osea and Northey islands,
with Thirslet Creek and Goldhanger on the north shore, Bradwell and
Stansgate on the south, till it suddenly narrows at Heybridge Basin to
reach Maldon by way of Colliers Reach. The saltings beside both these
estuaries are still tinted each summer by the shimmering sea lavender,
even though their acreage has probably decreased by half through tidal
erosion over the past two centuries. One may still sail up creeks to
Salcot and Tollesbury without a modern development in sight.
Though Mersea's yacht anchorage is as packed with moorings as its
roads are with houses, its creeks would be instantly recognisable to
the characters who people these pages. Bradwell today has an atomic
power station by the mouth of the creek, and a marina and sailing
school at the top of it, yet the old road winds still past the 'Green
Man' down to the little quay where the watch vessel *Whitworth* once
lay. Only at Burnham perhaps has the domination of yachting made
it difficult to recapture the atmosphere of earlier lustier times, but at
nearby Paglesham and the creeks around Foulness, little has changed.

Between Colne Point and Walton Naze a shore where cornfields ran
down to the beach, broken only by Martello Towers (numbering eight
by 1815, with batteries of up to five guns) and signal stations at
Jaywick, Eastwick and Little Holland[2], has been transformed by the
development of Clacton-on-Sea, Frinton and Walton, but between the
Blackwater and the Crouch the long low Tillingham shore is as lonely
as ever, with the beacon on the Buxey Sand gauntly presiding still
over the shallow Raysand Channel. Here there were countless quiet
corners, out of sight of the Riding Officers, where a smack could drop
a string of tubs, perhaps brought across from Flushing or Ostend, or

144

Recovering tubs.

perhaps trans-shipped from a foreign-going vessel out of sight of land and of the patrolling cruisers.

Most of this marshland smuggling paradise was within the port of Maldon, which at this time extended from Mersea to Gravesend. Smuggling here was continuous, but on a small scale. In 1807 the Collector reported that things had been quiet for the past few years, and 'no single vessel was engaged in illicit trade', meaning that there were no full-time professional smuggling craft.

Reports over the ensuing thirty years showed little more than periodical ups and downs in a continuing activity. In 1831 it was observed that 'smuggling in this port rather decreased in the years 1828 and 1829 but has a little increased the last year. No great run has taken place in the last three years, the method being either transhipment or sinking a string or two of tubs near the coast to be picked up by co-adjutors ashore. Tea and tobacco are only rarely smuggled and at any event in small quantities. Prices of smuggled goods here – Brandy 13s – 18s a gallon. Geneva 12s – 17s. Tobacco (shag) 1/6d to 2/6d a pound. Tea 4s – 12s a pound.'

The shore most used was the deserted stretch from St Peter's Chapel at Bradwell to Holliwell Point at the mouth of the Crouch, and the most favoured places included Tillingham Grange and Mersea Quarters. In 1807 there was a Preventive boat with four men under a Tide Surveyor at Maldon and one or two men under a sitter at Burnham. There were a Supervisor and Riding Oficer at Maldon and a Riding Oficer at Bradwell to cover a district extending from Mersea to Fambridge. The Collector suggested a Riding Officer at Tolleshunt D'Arcy, who was before long provided, and a decked boat at Burnham where, however, the Tide Surveyor had to continue content with his open lugsail boat, equipped with no better protection than a tilt, or canvas cover.

Mersea, where a couple of boatmen had been employed in 1760, was upgraded around 1819, when a six-oar galley was provided. (The Customs were too mean to build a new one, but ordered an eight-oar galley to be cut down from thirty feet to twenty feet 'and to be thrown out four or five inches in breadth.')[2] This followed a report in 1815 that the principal smuggling centres were West Mersea and the rivers adjacent, where 'smugglers come in with tubs, sink them and mix with the dredgers.' Most of them, the collector added, were Kentishmen, working in the daytime. Again he insisted (perhaps in self-defence) that little smuggling was being done, but (in September) 'it will increase as the nights get longer.' This time, in addition to the plea for troops and Dragoons already mentioned, he asked for boats to be stationed at Bradwell and Mersea.

Bradwell, in 1824, had, in addition to a signal station, 'an old watchhouse, still in existence but needs repair'. Tillingham, on the deserted marshes between the Blackwater and Crouch, had only a signal station till Coastguard cottages were built there in 1827.

This rough-and-ready disposition of scanty forces was revolutionised by the reforms of 1822 and the introduction of the new Preventive Water Guard. The watch vessel *Rattlesnake* was moored in the Blackwater, at first under the command of Thomas Dobbin, a former mate of the Harwich Revenue cutter *Active*. He was succeeded in 1818 by an energetic officer, Lieut Neame, RN, whose enterprise secured him promotion as one of the three Inspecting Commanders of the Water Guard in 1821. Under his control the *Rattlesnake* and her attendant cruiser *New Charter* conducted a vigorous war on the new-style smugglers, as did the *Richmond* which replaced the *Rattlesnake* in 1824. The *Enchantress* was also transferred from Leigh to the Blackwater in 1818, lying, I think, at Stansgate. Neame had a mate and nineteen mariners, three of them 'deputed'. He also had a force of boatmen, paid only £5 a year and 3s a day when employed, with their 'Sitters' paid £15 and 4s a day.

There was a similar set-up in the Crouch, based on the watch vessel *Ruswarp*.

The boatmen of the Preventive Water Guard were employed on shore patrols as well as afloat. A story of one of their exploits contrasts quaintly with the more heroic adventures of the earlier Revenue cutter crews. It took place at Foulness, which as one would expect was another favourite haunt of smugglers. It is an island which can be reached from the Crouch or the Roach rivers or at high water across the Maplins from the Thames estuary. It had a 'back entrance', the Haven Gore, navigable at high water, but at low water a-dry to provide a cart track, the Broomway, connecting the island to the mainland.

Because of its isolation it was clearly a lawless spot. When the Glasgow brig *Conqueror* was wrecked on the Maplins in 1849, bound from Bremen to Rio de Janeiro, with the loss of all her crew, 600 demijohns of spirits were missing. The Wivenhoe Lloyd's agent, J G Chamberlain, found much wood from the wreck at Foulness and suspected the spirits also finished up there. He accordingly asked the Customs for a 'strong force at the *Dove* watch vessel at 10 a.m. on Saturday to search the island.'

Perhaps he had been warned by a similar incident in 1840 when the Foulness shore was strewn with timber for three miles. It was guarded by the coastguards, but this did not deter a gang of 100 men, led by Gardner the Great Wakering postmaster, from attempting to collect it. The coastguards fired over their heads and dispersed them but they returned next day. Noting that on both days the two constables were absent, the Customs decided to prosecute Gardner and a man named Page. The solicitor chose to charge them with possessing an oar 'which I presume is foreign' (and so dutiable) but unluckily for him it proved to be from the sailing barge *Pratt,* bound from Rochester to London.

The seizure by the boatman took place rather earlier than this, in 1826. The narrator, Thomas Pugh, a Commissioned Boatman, clearly enjoyed telling his tale and made a good job of it.

The events took place at Newland Farm, owned by a Mr Finch, but as neither he nor his steward, Mr Wood, lived on the island it was managed by John Oliver as 'looker.'

One Thomas Hedgecock of Foulness had laid information, and a patrol set out on a Wednesday evening in October. Soon they saw Oliver running along the sea wall 'one marsh from the farmhouse', and from this point Pugh may tell his own story. He himself was 'Number Five' and 'Number Nine' was William Lay, a boatman.

'Number Nine says to him "Yorhoy", he says "Halloo". Number Nine says "You will see one of my people the back of me" and he says "What the hell care I for that?" About twenty minutes after came his brother down. Number Nine communicated with Number Five and told him "I saw two suspicious people." Number Five saw three suspicious people at half-past six going towards the farmhouse and returned at half-past seven that gave us suspicion to think there was smuggled goods about the farm. At nine o'clock came Anthony Burrows and Mark Abell and rapped in the old hobble which I did not know if they were after smuggled goods or stealing corn. Then they returned towards the barnyard.

'We went round the barnyard and pricked with our tucks. At ten o'clock we smelt liquor quite strong. Then we got off the straw and went the other side. Number Five pulling the straw about smelt liquor stronger. Number Five pulled the remainder out and found the concealment and put in his tucks and found there to be tubs. At eleven found the concealment. Then we stopped it up and watched it.'

Somewhat optimistically, one would think, they watched for several nights after this, and then visited Oliver's wife, who said her husband was out sowing corn, so they hired a wagon and took the tubs to the Commissioned Boatman's house.

Now the Customs hit their first snag. Hedgecock refused to testify and another suspected informer, Thomas Howgego Bennewith, was also so scared that he got the Preventive men to go with him to Oliver, saying, 'I have brought the officers down to satisfy you that I gave them no information about the tubs found in the Newland Farm, and if I had been so minded, damn your eyes, I could have done it when I saw you on the sands with the cart and the goods.' Oliver, looking greatly alarmed, replied, 'Thomas, I thought that had all been settled.' Later, however, Bennewith recovered his courage, doubtless in hope of reward, and made an affidavit that 'he gave information of the said tubs to William Lay, a boatman, and he considered the tubs were taken in consequence of the said information.'

Oliver was convicted in a mitigated penalty of £50 which he paid. In all, 187 casks were found and it was thought a gang of eleven was involved. The last mention of the case was an application by the Preventive men to be paid a moiety (in its old sense of a half) of Oliver's £50 instead of the usual one-eighth.

19

Tales from the Blackwater

'The Most Notorious Smuggler in Essex': Luggers and Galleys: The Tansleys of Mersea: The Londons of Tollesbury: The Naughty Nancy: The Cart that Vanished.

UP to the time of the introduction of the Preventive Water Guard the traditional smuggling luggers still plied their trade among the shoals and sandbanks of the Essex estuaries.

The lugger *Lord Collingwood* of Margate had the misfortune to get ashore on the Buxey Sand one December morning in 1813, and the still worse luck to be spotted there by the Revenue cutter *Hawk,* which was cruising in the Swin. As the *Hawk*'s six-oar boat approached, the crew of five left the lugger in their skiff, going over the top of the sand. The Revenue men had to go round the shoal, losing sight of the smugglers behind the sandbank, but they overhauled them off Bradwell Chapel, where the smugglers jumped overboard, only to find the mud too soft to walk in. They were hauled into the Revenue boat and in due course put aboard HMS *Reynard,* whose commander accepted two of them, rejecting the other three. Meanwhile the *Lord Collingwood* was towed into Harwich by the *Hawk* as soon as she refloated, with 283 half-ankers aboard.

Six years later on a February morning in 1820, after a thick fog lifted, another lugger was seen standing into Mersea Island. On touching the shore her crew ran away and escaped. The lugger, illegally built, smelled strongly of spirits. But though the Revenue men used their creepers they did not succeed in finding her tubs.

In 1832 Thomas Miles's long galley *Rover* was chased into the Black-water by the Bradwell coastguard crew. She was later found with her bow rammed into the saltings. A hundred and sixty small casks of spirits were discovered in a ditch nearby, and the footmarks in the mud showed that in addition to this unloading the crew had tried to relaunch her, but without success.

But by the 1820s most of the kegs were being slipped in by local smacks, occasionally making a voyage to 'the opposite side', but more often transhipping them from a foreign-going vessel to be dropped in some place where they could be picked up later in the course of dredging, perhaps with a grapnel replacing one of the oyster dredges. The oystermen would then claim the sunken trots of tubs were discovered accidentally, as no doubt they sometimes were, though the Customs were not easily convinced.

The sinking stones used to anchor the trots were often specially fabricated, with an iron strap and eye properly fixed round a suitable stone by a blacksmith. Surprisingly, there are few records of their discovery among the incriminating gear aboard smacks. Presumably they were easily jettisoned, as well as being impossible to explain away, so they were usually got rid of in time. While tubs were the most usual form of contraband sunk, the method was also used for dry goods, for in 1832 fifteen cases of cigars were crept up in the Wallet by Brightlingsea boatmen. 'This shows new methods are being used by the smugglers' observed the *Essex Standard*.

Sinking had, however, been regularly practised to some extent for a century. The packets often spilled some tubs overboard as they were entering Harwich harbour, for which reason the Revenue cutters met them at sea and put a man aboard, even though the rummage could not start till they were in harbour. In 1747 the *Walpole* had put a man aboard the *Dolphin* in this way. He reported that 'the pacquet people sank about twenty-nine large stone bottles at the mouth of the harbour before his face.' Three boats crept for them for forty hours but without success, as the crew had prevented the Revenue men from taking any shore marks. Two years before this the thrifty Board, knowing that hemp was cheaper than manilla, had issued an order to 'take care that tarred ropes, and not white lines, be used when they sweep for anchors and Bottles of Liquor'. Thirty years later, in 1774, the Burnham officers asked for 'a light galley for chasing and sweeping sunk goods' and three years after this the Maldon Tide Surveyor, pointing out that he had to go ten miles down the Blackwater in an open boat, whose arrival on the tide could easily be predicted by smugglers, requested the use of a decked vessel, a condemned smuggler named *Queen*. She was re-named *King's Fisher* and commissioned for a six-month trial, which proved successful, for she made four big seizures of tea, coffee, geneva, brandy and muslins, which were sold for £235 – a share for the King of £131 provided by a boat which had cost His Majesty nothing.

But it was not till the nineteenth century that sinking became the chief method of smuggling. The change may have been in two stages, for a report in 1804 refers to vessels coming in at night and 'sinking goods a few miles from the shore in deep water' for small boats to pick up. The later practice was to sink in sheltered estuaries and shallow creeks, or occasionally tubs would be sunk twice, once at sea and then again close to the port of landing.

There are countless references to the recovery of sunken tubs, from which it is only possible to quote a few of the most important or the most colourful.

Henry Stevens of Woodbridge sailed from Brightlingsea in the *Corsair* of Harwich in 1832. They trawled in the Whitaker and then went to the Sunk under pretence of taking a pilot out of a vessel. In fact they met the *Charles* of Hastings and took 600 half-ankers and some silks from her. They made for the Blackwater and sank the tubs in four fathoms off Stansgate, going on up to Maldon next day to sell their fish. The *Corsair* then sailed, but without Stevens, who to get his own back went to the Customs, telling them the tubs were the property of Gardner Hutton, a cabinet maker of Harwich, to whom they were to be delivered. The Customs could not find them, so maybe they were picked up again by the *Corsair* and reached Harwich after all.

Henry Wakeling of Tollesbury was oyster-dredging in 'the Rays'n' (the Ray Sand channel between the Blackwater and the Crouch) in his smack *Industry* with William Tansley of Mersea and his deaf, eighteen-year-old son, also William. Opposite the Tillingham signal station at low water he found forty-one tubs of foreign liquor, buoyed. He was picking these up with, he said, 'the motive of delivering the tubs over to His Majesty's disposal' when up came a boat from the *Rattlesnake*. The officer, without so much as asking what the dredgermen were doing, took the helm, sailed the *Industry* into Bradwell, found a magistrate and got the three men committed on suspicion.

Lieut Neame had no doubt about his success. 'I congratulate myself of taking the most notorious smuggler in Essex, which is William Tansley sen,' he boasted. He had noticed the *Industry* towing 'a boat much larger than she uses for Gunning or Dredging' and had cautioned his officer not to board her till she was getting under way, 'fearing the boat might be away under the sands, picking up tubs.'

William Tansley senior was seventy-two years old with a wife and seven children. He had been in trouble and had his furniture sold up as a result of an exploit with his former smack, the *Mayflower* of Mersea, a forty-footer built at Itchen Ferry in 1791 and overwhelmed off the Isle of Wight in 1831 with three hands – the most notable of Mersea smack losses. The *Industry* had also been chased and boarded a few months before the arrest in the Rays'n, but though she smelled of spirits and Henry Wakeling had 'three notorious smugglers' aboard there was not enough evidence for an arrest on that occasion.

From Chelmsford gaol the Tansleys started the dreary routine of petitioning, culminating with a massive appeal by the ministers, churchwardens, overseers and inhabitants of West Mersea. Henry

Wakeling also petitioned, referring to an 'open boat which could not have been to any foreign port' – a curiously flimsy-sounding defence.

After nearly twelve months' imprisonment William Tansley was discharged on a Customs detainer against him, but was still held on an Excise warrant for £250. How this was ultimately disposed of does not seem to be recorded. The *Industry* was sold in March 1820 by order of the Customs for £3 5s to Thomas Durden, the Maldon boat builder, who signed a bond of £30 'for proper use of the said boat's licence'. Unless the smack had been sold in pieces, the derisory price suggests a put-up job, perhaps with a view to her ultimate restoration to her previous owner.

The arrest of the Tansleys and Henry Wakeling was due to the vigilance of a Tollesbury member of the crew of the *Rattlesnake,* John London, whose father, Daniel London, was also in Chelmsford gaol, and who was prepared to go to the length of informing on his neighbours in his efforts to secure his release.

Daniel London had been dredging in the *George and Ann* in the Blackwater in November 1818, with his sons Daniel and William, when, in the Mill Hole, he caught hold of a warp to which he found attached a string of 160 tubs of geneva and brandy. He handed in 150 at Maldon Custom House, but next day received a visit at his home in Tollesbury from the Comptroller, who did not even trouble to search, but told him unless he handed over another nineteen half-ankers and a quarter-anker he would be committed. The Comptroller then resorted to the questionable tactic of promising that 'if he delivered them he should not be exposed but that it should be said they were entered.' The flustered London responded with, 'I have not twenty, only ten and a little one.'

These were duly produced, but London refused to name the smugglers. 'I do not know them but have agreed to give them half the sum I get from the Custom House,' he replied unconvincingly, adding for good luck, 'I think they came out of a vessel which is now taken.'

His son, William London, actually petitioned for a reward, saying that he did not see the tubs taken on board the *George and Ann,* but the Customs replied that they 'by no means consider him entitled to reward', for 'he forgets he made affidavit that his father and brother took the whole of the tubs aboard.' Moreover the Londons did not arrive at Maldon till the day after the incident, and it was again alleged that they had 'agreed to pay a moiety of the reward to the smugglers for which the said vessel has been condemned and sold.'

Daniel London, in gaol till he paid £150, told of 'a wife and nine children almost in a state of starvation', 'acknowledged he did wrong' and reported that he 'has friends to come forward and pay £50, which, with the loss of his vessel, he begs will be sufficient recompence.'

The 'little one' among London's tubs was quite a common feature. When Thomas Sturges went to prison in 1838 it was for having forty-one half-ankers and one half-cask in an open boat off Foulness, and Thomas Bacon's contraband in the same year (already mentioned) amounted to 149 half-ankers and three quarter-casks. This suggests that strings of tubs were made up complete with 'small change', to be used perhaps for payments to helpers, bribes or commission.

A regular Mersea smuggler was a smack called *Nancy*. A seven-tonner of this name was first registered at Maldon in 1802, but as the records refer variously to 'of Maldon', 'of Colchester', 'of London' and 'of Dover', it is possible there were in fact several craft of this name.

However that may be, a *Nancy* makes her first appearance when she was chased into Burnham river in 1809 by two Revenue cutters and seized by a boat from one of them, the *Repulse*. She was returning from Holland, but no tubs were found aboard, and it was considered they had probably been sunk. She had, however, 'fifty fathoms of small cordage with over 120 sinking stones fixed thereto.'

Her owner, Luke Nicholson of Wivenhoe, declared that this gear was aboard when he had recently bought her at a Colchester Custom House sale (suggesting this was not the first time she had been seized), but the Customs decided to arrest her and prosecute him. The *Nancy* was moored for safety in the canal basin at Heybridge, but though her hatches were nailed down she was broken into by the crew of a London barge and her cable was stolen. This led to a lively exchange, with the Customs threatening Nicholson with prosecution and Nicholson demanding compensation for his cable, which he valued at £40, though the Customs said it was worth about half that amount.

On the official level the Board's solicitor continued to defer a decision by requiring information as to why there was not a watchman on board, and why the cable was not stored ashore in a warehouse. On the unofficial level Nicholson evidently paid a number of friendly visits to the Maldon Collector, telling him he thought everything reasonable had been done to look after his property. In the end, after four months, the *Nancy* was released. Nicholson continued to demand that she should be returned 'in the same shape and style as when seized', but the Customs hardened their hearts and insisted she 'must be taken with all her faults.'

She was soon back in her old trade under new ownership, for she was again seized with contraband in 1814. Her then owner and master, John Firman, said he was out fishing when he picked up a job to pilot a collier up to Collier's Reach at Heybridge. He left his son in charge, but he too got a job, to pilot the *Nightingale* of Peterhead up to Heybridge Basin with wheat from Antwerp. So, declared Firman, it was quite a mystery to him how the goods got aboard.

Six years later, in March 1820, then owned by John Wyatt, the *Nancy* was caught unloading forty small kegs of spirits on Tillingham marshes. With Wyatt were James and Christopher Glading, who were released on payment of penalties of £15 each. Wyatt, in his gaol petition, asked for similar treatment, and when this was refused raised his offer to £25, which was accepted.

She was still at it in the time of Lieut Neame and the *Rattlesnake*. He reported that 'she is often absent from Mersea for weeks. The wind (I consider) smugglers sail from the opposite side, she arrives without any anchors or warps. When boarded she smells strongly of spirits. After laying at Mersea two or three days she sails for four or five days . . . on entering the river is found to have three or four small anchors and warps . . . for sinking tubs. Her crew consists of the same persons who sailed in the *Tilburina*.' (This name doubtless derived from the daughter of the Governor of Tilbury Fort who was the heroine of Sheridan's play *The Critic,* written not long before she was built at Rotherhithe in 1798. She was owned in 1825 by T Withey, the Mersea boat-builder.)

On one occasion the *Nancy* left Burnham river to cruise in the East Swin, 'assisting vessels in distress' (as the salvagers liked to call their trade), when she carried away her rudderhead and ran into Mersea. The *Rattlesnake*'s men found only half a pound of tobacco and half a pound of tea, with a bottle of spirits and water owned by one of the crew, James Nunn, who claimed he was ill. The tea and tobacco were promptly returned but Lieut Neame put the *Nancy* 'under stop,' declaring that the gin was not accounted for and that 'officers between this river and Orford Haven say this vessel is engaged in illicit practices.'

Four years after his arrest on Tillingham marshes John Wyatt was trying different tactics in the same place. He wrote to the Maldon Collector from the Cock at Tillingham in November 1824. 'While on the southernmost part of the Main in my canoe (*sic;* presumably a punt) I fell in and came up with a string of tubs of spirits of gin and brandy about seventy or eighty . . . have secured thirty-one . . . had no assistance or could have taken all. The rest drifted down the Raison . . . I have a great desire to make a legitimate entry. Shall I deliver to the *Richmond* or convey to Maldon? . . . Have no doubt I shall receive such reward as is due.'

The Comptroller noted, 'We are not aware if this is the same John

154

Wyatt against whom proceedings in March 1820 were ended on payment of £25 and costs.' Nor am I, but I should think it likely.

Up the Blackwater, halfway between Mersea and Maldon, Skinner's Wick is a little landing at the head of Thirslet Creek, below Osea Island. In living memory it was the home of Seabrook's sailing barges, and to this day – at any rate in winter when the speedboats and racing dinghies have gone and the brent geese take over – it looks ideal for smuggling, which it evidently was.

One night in March 1822 John Criswick, stationed at 'Salt Court' (Salcot), decided to take a walk down the lane leading from the farm to the decoy with two companions. No doubt someone had suggested this might be worth his while, and sure enough at half-past ten he found a man with a cart in the lane and another in a field on the other side of the hedge. After looking in the empty cart he asked the man what he was doing, receiving the reply 'Not anything,' on which the cart was driven away at high speed up the lane and the man behind the hedge made off with equal haste across the field.

Criswick had only to take a few steps to find three tubs of geneva in the hedge. At the same time he heard a crash and found the cart with a broken axle. Despite this they loaded the tubs into it and succeeded in getting it up to the house of Daniel Blythe, the Riding Officer at Tolleshunt D'Arcy, who put it in his yard for the night.

But when morning came the cart was gone! Blythe was given a grilling, but his Collector stood by him, observing that he had no help and nowhere else to put the cart, and that he was tired after a long day in Maldon. Suspicions of connivance were rejected; 'want of assistance and judgement were the cause.'

20

Heybridge and Two *Hebes*

The Collier and the Canal: Borrowing a Smack: A Skipper's Sacrifice.

AT the head of the estuary Maldon really became obsolete as an active Preventive station with the building of the Heybridge-Chelmsford canal in 1780, for most cargoes were then unloaded into lighters in Collier's Reach, two miles downstream, to be towed to Chelmsford, and even the Maldon trade was often lightered up the final reaches to the quay.

'Since the canal was built twenty years ago the legal quay has hardly been used' observed the Collector in 1814. 'Maldon is a dry harbour and the hours of attendance very insufficient.' (These office hours were for the Collector and Comptroller 10 am – 3 pm, and for the rest of the staff 9 am – 4 pm in winter and 8 am – 4 pm in summer.) The boat at the quay went down the river to meet ships as soon as they were sighted, but it was immobilised by lack of water fourteen hours out of the twenty-four.

As a result the Collector became concerned as to goings-on at Heybridge.

One day in September 1816 the *Joseph Mary* of Deptford and the yawl *Good Intent* of London handed in at Maldon seventeen casks which they said they had found sunk. But a Wivenhoe fisherman, R Stephenson, said he saw them pick up eighty half-ankers 'off Mersea shore' in fog. They told him they were going to enter them at Maldon Custom House, but Stephenson, no doubt scenting reward, followed them up river. At Heybridge he saw them unload sixty casks into an open boat. A boy went with them to receive fifteen guineas.

Things came to a head in 1818, when the collier *Duke of Wellington,* belonging to Parke, one of the local coal merchants, arrived in the Mill Bight and lay there for the night before going to unload through the official coal bushels under the supervision of the meters at the legal quay. The skipper, Robert Parke, sent the mate ashore to fetch one of the firm's lighters out of the canal, and this was loaded in the hours of darkness, with a few bricks on top of the coal as a flimsy camouflage and a pretext for some subsequent hard swearing by the mate that what he had unloaded was 2,000 bricks and 'six or seven bushels of coal left for ship's use.' John Payne, the rival coal merchant, not unexpectedly submitted angry protests, but he made the tactical error of including the Customs officers in his censure. The Customs found

themselves defending Parke in order to defend themselves and probably for this reason he escaped prosecution.

What was needed was a legal quay at the canal basin. The merchants
petitioned for it, and the Collector supported the petition, but the
Board do not seem to have allowed what was usually regarded as a
special privilege. A presence was, however, provided there, at first
in the thirty-eight foot smack *Hebe,* belonging to James Death of
Brightlingsea, where she had been built in 1813. She was seized in
January 1819. The *Rattlesnake*'s cruiser *New Charter* saw her hove-to
in the Blackwater, and noticed she had no boat astern. By the time
the Revenue men reached her she had her dredges overboard, but
unfortunately for her not on oyster ground. Moreover Death had only
one man with him, though there were coats, berths and blankets for
three. He declared that the missing boat had been left in Brightlingsea
for repairs, and explained that a couple of gallons of gin and a few
pounds of tobacco had been given him by a Dutch galliot he had
piloted. But oddly neither man could recall the name of the galliot,
their imagination going no further than remembering she had 'nearly
new sails, varnished and rosin'd sides and a caboose on deck'.

*Maldon lost most of its seaborne trade with the opening of the Heybridge-Chelmsford
canal in 1780, but coasting sloops such as this continued to use the quays below the
Fullbridge, and some sailing barges such as the* Rogue in Grain *lowered their masts
to pass under the bridge and reach Beeleigh Mill.*

157

A look round revealed the missing boat's towrope lying on deck, and the boat itself was later reported to have been seen on Mersea beach about the time of the arrest, near the house of the notorious Tansley, who was accordingly suspected of freighting the *Hebe*. But it then disappeared, hidden somewhere against seizure. Twelve fathoms of 'small line exactly the same that is used to sling sinkers and tubs' were found in the coal locker, the hold smelt strongly of spirits, and a timber-head had been cut from the lapboard quarter and the bulwarks cut in two places. This section, about four feet long, had been temporarily fastened with new nails 'only driven a few hours' in the opinion of the *New Charter*'s officer.

So in default of hard evidence, 'advantage was taken' of the spirits and tobacco aboard, 'together with six bottles of Dutch drops which he had in his pocket and which confirms to some extent he was unaware the spirits were more than is allowed by law', and James Death (described ambiguously as 'of fair character' by the Brightlingsea minister petitioning for his release) began his stay in Chelmsford. He offered £50 for the release of the *Hebe*, valued at £100, but Neame countered: 'From having spirits on board and the boat being away at the time there is no doubt she was employed in illegal practices.'

Now, as already mentioned, the Customs were concerned at their inability to keep an eye on Heybridge. The Comptroller casually suggested he had some property there that might make a Preventive station, but the Board were not falling for that, and ordered the *Hebe* to be used for a six-month trial. She was caulked and fitted with a galley, after which, in November, Death got her back on payment of his £50. She was re-licensed in 1820 and according to her register was lost off Guernsey about 1828.

A few years later the Customs had another *Hebe* on their hands. This was a London smack skippered by a Seasalter man named Jones. One afternoon in October 1826 she was lying hove-to in the Barrow Deep for no apparent reason when she attracted the suspicion of the *Maria*, the *Ruswarp*'s twenty-seven-ton cruising tender. When she made sail about four o'clock the *Maria* went after her and at six came alongside near the Mouse. As a string of tubs went over her side, the *Maria* hailed her and opened fire.

The *Hebe* stood away to the north-west into a fathom and a half where the *Maria* dared not follow but saw more tubs jettisoned. Going round the sand the *Maria* again gave chase, and at 7.30 near the Blacktail saw the *Hebe*'s boat leave her with five men in it.

Left alone aboard his smack, Jones began a vain, pathetic flight. He had no hope of escape, for even had he managed to slip over the top of the sands the *Hebe* had been recognised and arrest was inevitable. Still he sailed her as long as he could, giving his crew time to get clear away, with the *Maria* still chasing and firing, till at 8.30 a shot carried away the jib halyard, and thus disabled the *Hebe* was boarded half-a-mile above the Cant buoy.

The *Maria* picked up sixty tubs, but nothing incriminating was found aboard the *Hebe* beyond the wooden stock of a blue light and 'forty fathoms of line knotted to two other pieces of coils convenient for slinging, two ballast bags that could be used for slinging and a creep iron adapted for sweeping'.

This, however, was enough. Jones was committed to Chelmsford gaol on 2 November under the usual £100 penalty for having on board 103 gallons of brandy and seventy-two gallons of geneva in sixty-three illegal casks. After six months, petitions, first by himself and then by his wife supported by the vicar, churchwardens and merchants of Seasalter, were rejected and he had to make another appeal (presumably successful, for there the story ends) in October 1827 after nearly a year inside.

21

Crouch and Roach

Two Independent Tide Surveyors: Richard Miller's Misfortune: Thomas Patmore's Lost Licence.

THE Crouch and its tributary the Roach were a paradise for the latter-day smugglers, providing a labyrinth of creeks which would have been difficult to police even with forces much more formidable than the Customs were willing, or able, to provide.

The modern yachtman's Burnham-on-Crouch has largely extinguished the memories and traditions of the pre-railway Burnham, which had prosperous oyster fisheries and a vigorous commercial life. It did not, however, attain sufficient importance to have a Custom House of its own, but was left in charge of a Tide Surveyor. Till the arrival of the *Ruswarp* and the *Maria,* no decked cruiser was employed, despite many pleas that the rough Crouch estuary could not be properly patrolled by an open lug-sail boat, while Paglesham on the Roach, despite its notoriety as an eighteenth century home of smugglers, had only a four-oar galley which was not afloat till nearly high water. So inadequate were the forces of law and order that in 1817 Wiseman's, one of the leading oyster cultivators in the area, offered their services, waiving any participation in rewards for seizures. They even offered to give a security for a deputation to seize, so presumably the arrangement was worthwhile simply to police their grounds. The Maldon Collector liked the idea, for 'they with their father are very respectable', but it does not seem to have been approved.

The Burnham Tide Surveyors were remarkably lively characters. Between 1790 and 1819 this office was held by Charles Bull, who features continually and colourfully in the official correspondence of the time.

When the yacht *Flora* of London, owned by Major General Henniker of Southend, arrived at Burnham in 1807, Bull, who had been told she was smuggling, hailed her to come aboard. The skipper, J. Dove, said if he tried he would shoot him. He produced a musket, challenged Bull to show his Commission, and pushed him back into his boat. He then left, taking his keys. Bull put two men aboard the yacht and two days later Dove returned without his keys. The yacht's lockers and chest were, however, broken open – and found empty!

Despite this, magistrates at Maldon, Chelmsford and Rochford were soon afterwards asked for a warrant for Dove. All refused, saying a

Bench warrant would be required. This was apparently obtained, for a week later Dove was arrested for assaulting and obstructing Bull. The result is not recorded, but in 1814 a John Dove, pilot of the *William and Ann* of Antwerp, came ashore before the Customs could get their boat afloat, in defiance of the quarantine laws. There is no indication as to whether or not this was Bull's old adversary but the fuss over a technicality suggests there may have been an old score to settle.

Typical of the contrasting accounts given by opposing parties after a seizure was the case of the *Isis* of Leigh in 1802. Her owner, William Trayler, a Paglesham oyster dredgerman, sent a petition from prison, protesting that Charles Bull came aboard and asked for help in grappling for some casks. And then, instead of being paid for his service he had been seized!

Bull replied that the *Isis* passed so close to him he could see tubs on her deck. He pursued her and saw the tubs thrown overboard, after which the *Isis* hove to and was boarded. Bull found nothing aboard, but after three hours' grappling picked up sixty casks of geneva and two of brandy in two strings. He added a telling afterthought. If Trayler was so innocent why did he wait five weeks in prison before coming up with his story?

Not all of Bull's exploits were so correctly conducted. According to various scandalous accusations made against him, he found time to pilot coal brigs up the river 'twelve miles above the town' at a fee of fifteen shillings One cannot but feel that if he got these loaded colliers up to Battlesbridge he earned it. But finally some of his other private enterprises were his undoing. He looked after a gun brig called the *Ostend* for two years at 14s a week, and used the King's boat to ferry passengers and luggage ashore from visiting craft. He also claimed a monopoly in transporting people to the annual fair at Foulness, according to a disgruntled rival 'who have a boat to get his bread'. Having persuaded the Board that he needed an assistant he appointed his son and himself went off on an oyster voyage to Portsmouth.

Another information laid against him declared that 'Bull and the Customs boat were down river four miles below the town while one mile above a boat came from the other river over Crixsey Ferry causeway and did work their goods all safe. The smugglers can always buy Mr Bull in that manner.' (This short cut from the Roach at Paglesham into the Crouch at Creeksea, round the back of Wallasea Island, is no longer navigable.)

The Collector, declaring that Bull had in fact detected a man stealing oysters down the river while the run was made above the town, dismissed the information as 'a piece of spite'. This was ill-advised, for it finally became clear that Bull was guilty of some of the malpractices alleged against him, including looking after an empty collier for sixteen weeks on behalf of that extraordinary character Daniel Sutton, who claimed to be a Vice-Admiral of Essex,[1] and had appointed Bull as his local agent. This collier, the *Jane* of London, was 'detained by Mr Sutton but in which the Revenue had no interest.'

As a result of these misdemeanours the Bulls, father and son, were dismissed, their downfall also involving their superiors at Maldon, as has been mentioned in the Introduction.

Bull's successor as Tide Surveyor and Coast Waiter, George King, was an equally lively character. He had a busy and responsible job without the equipment he needed to do it. His twenty-three-foot lugsail boat, as he frequently pointed out, was really not man enough for knocking about down the exposed estuary in easterly winds – the weather the smugglers chose for a fast run. Present-day yachtsmen will know just what he meant, but the Honourable Commissioners were not yachtsmen.

His first 'crave' was 'one pistol each for my people and two cutlasses' for he found only one musket, and that unfit to use, with a useless spy-glass and no chest to keep his gear in. And for his four-oar galley he sought wash strakes, as 'the smugglers put to sea wind easterly'.

He had no watch-house, and though he successfully 'craved' one in 1819 he then had to put the begging process in train to secure 'fire and candle' for it. This watch-house also served as a boat store, and when in due course George King was in trouble because his paperwork was out-of-date and out of order the worm turned. He explained in no uncertain terms that he had no office, but the choice between a store full of oars and wet sails and a house full of young children, so all-in-all the Honourable Commissioners could think themselves lucky to get any paperwork at all.

King was in trouble again in 1838, and though the Collector found his books in order he was admonished and given three months' probation. He survived that, but died six months later in June 1839, to be succeeded by Alfred Busbridge, a relative no doubt of Egbert of Maldon, but not his son.

Thomas Patmore of Hullbridge on the Crouch was regarded as a particularly notorious character. One day in September 1823 he brought forty-four kegs of spirits into the Whitaker in his *Friends Goodwill* of Maldon. There he handed them over to one Richard Miller, another principal smuggler, whose open twelve-ton well boat was perhaps less conspicuous. Miller took the tubs into the river and sank them, where they were found next day by dredgermen, apparently by accident.

Miller in due course saw fit to return and set to work creeping. When he was told the tubs had already been lifted he was 'in great agitation', observing 'I never lost so many goods in my life.' This was only the start of his troubles, for the following February he was committed to gaol on a warrant amounting to £602, probably three times the value of the forty-four tubs, leaving a wife and ten children unsupported. The Customs were at first in doubt as to whether there was enough evidence to proceed against Patmore, but they evidently obtained an informer, for in April 1824 he too was petitioning for a gaol allowance.

In 1831 Patmore was in trouble again, this time through getting mixed up with Daniel Rich, who was later to be the ruin of James Cook and his *Dagger*. Rich came alongside in the Rays'n in his smack *Swallow* of Faversham. He transferred twenty-nine half-ankers into Patmore's well and told him to take them to the decoy in the Blackwater, where a party would be waiting.

Arriving off Goldhanger, he was directed where to land by John Gurton, a fisherman, who a few years before had sought the help of the Maldon Collector in getting his back pay on his release from HMS *Eugenie*, an action which suggests the Customs may also have had something to do with getting him into the Navy. With Gurton's help they rowed some of the tubs ashore at the decoy, while the rest were taken in the *Swallow*'s boat up Mersea Quarters, where they were met by Rich, who gave Patmore two sovereigns and told him to meet him at Wivenhoe the next Sunday for the balance of 12s 6d a tub, with 7s 6d for provisions – £12 in all.

But before he was paid Patmore was detected. He refused to produce the boat's licence, saying it had been given to a man at Milton, Kent, who was about to buy her, but it was found on Bradwell beach next day in a paper parcel, so he had evidently thrown it overboard.

This was apparently to protect Charles Paine, a Battlesbridge hoyman, who explained that he had taken the *Friends Goodwill* as security for a loan, but instead of taking a mortgage he was made owner and obliged to give a £53 bond for the licence. The Customs, noting that he was married to Patmore's daughter, took leave to doubt his ignorance and innocence and insisted on their £53, which he paid. Patmore himself went back to Chelmsford gaol, where the gaoler observed he had 'a small supply of provisions brought in by his friends but no money'.

Meanwhile Rich made a blunder. He was caught aboard 'a foreign vessel not being square rigged' with 228 gallons of brandy and 162 gallons of geneva, within eighteen leagues of the coast of Kent, and sent to Chelmsford by the Harwich collector. Lying in prison, with his *Friends Goodwill* lost, and still owed £12, Patmore came out with the full story, content that the *Swallow* be seized if he could gain some remission. Since both men were in the same gaol this is one of the many occasions when one wonders how they could get on together.

22

Trouble with Oysters

Are the Channel Islands Foreign?: Raids on Burnham.

MUCH of the Customs' work in the Crouch and Roach was concerned with oysters.

The principal Essex fisheries in 1824 were in the Colne, controlled by Colchester Corporation, and then worked by licensed dredgermen; the Blackwater, then claimed by Maldon Corporation down as far as the Knoll Sand; the Crouch, owned by the Mildmay Estate from the Ray beacon to Brandy Hole near Stow Maries, and Leigh swatchway, which was private property. There were also Wiseman's private layings in the Roach, already mentioned.

All the fisheries exported oysters, while the Crouch and Leigh, and to some extent the Colne, imported, chiefly from the Channel Islands. Because of the perishable nature of the cargoes both trades were troublesome. Duties on exports were abolished in 1812, but while this was doubtless welcome, it also resulted in the Burnham officer losing the right to search, so for every cargo a searcher had to be sent from Maldon. By 1819 the right of search was restored, for George King justified a 'crave' for a salary increase (from £80 to £100) on the grounds that he had had to search twenty-nine cargoes for Holland. In 1814 and 1815 sixteen cargoes were shipped to Holland and Ostend in Dutch vessels, and on at least one occasion the Paglesham merchants sent for the searcher and then refused to load till they got a fair wind, keeping him hanging about. No English vessels took part in this export trade.

An embargo on Dutch shipping in 1832, probably due to cholera, caused further difficulties. The *Jonge Frederik* and five men were detained in Woodrup Creek, Tollesbury, and in the following year the forty-four-ton schuyt *Maria Elizabeth,* with seven men, was stopped in the Crouch, with twenty-eight bottles of spirits and thirty-five parcels of tobacco – an excess over the four-and-a-half gallons and thirteen pounds of tobacco permitted by law. The Collector said such craft usually brought in small quantities for sale, but with the embargo it was thought fit to apply the letter of the law.

As a result Crush and Co, Burnham oyster merchants, reported that friends in Zierickzee wished to send a fishing boat for a cargo of oysters, but would she be molested? The Board ruled that the embargo did not include fishing boats, so the *Jonge Frederik* should be allowed to sail. Huffed, the Collector observed that a fishing boat exporting oysters was not fishing. If he had to release the schuyt could he retain the cargo!

The oyster trade from Jersey, carried on in the winter only, employed fifty-nine Maldon-registered smacks in the 1820s, making up to eight voyages a year, though most made only one or two. In 1823 over 84,000 bushels were imported in seventy voyages, employing 174 men.

The Channel Islands were a problem, since they were not a foreign country, but had throughout the eighteenth century been a 'smuggler's den'. Making up the rules as it went along, the Customs decided that 'such a voyage comes within the meaning of a foreign one although the oysters being British caught are not subject to duty.'

Alston's of Leigh observed in 1815 that there had been 'no great importation since 1792, except a few cargoes in 1802 and during the last year.' But with the post-war recovery of the trade they asked in 1820 that the coal meter should be given authority to discharge the smacks. The Customs granted a dispensation that oysters might be unloaded immediately on arrival, before the skipper went to the Custom House to make his declaration.

Needless to say the Customs were interested in more than oysters when the Jersey smacks came in. Peter Richmond, a member of a Burnham family later to become prominent in the barging world with the fine schooner barge *Lucy Richmond*, was staying at the Ship Inn, St Martin (presumably in the Isles of Scilly), in 1815 when he was robbed of his pocket book containing the precious licence for his smack, the fifty-four ton *Hope*. Six years later he made his first voyage as master, in command of the *Speedwell,* and was tempted into buying a dozen silk handkerchiefs. His father, Samuel Richmond, only secured the release of the *Speedwell* on payment of a £20 penalty, exacted despite a plea of poverty due to borrowing to buy the smack.

The Jersey trade continued to trouble the Customs up to the end of the present story, in the mid-nineteenth century. Twelve to fourteen smacks were working into Leigh from March to July in 1843, and in 1846 importing was extended to the Blackwater by the Tollesbury Oyster Company. Peter Richmond was once again detained in 1849, this time in Yarmouth (presumably Isle of Wight) in the *Amity* but for no worse offence than the lack of a licence. J Richmond Rome of Jersey (a name suggesting that the Richmonds' connection with the Channel Isles extended to inter-marriage) arrived at Burnham with the *Fearless* in 1848 and showed his stores, only to have a bottle of brandy and some tobacco later found in the smack's boat. The Collector accepted that two of his crew, who were drunk, were trying to take sea stock ashore.

The *Albion* of Brightlingsea was seized in 1846 with a few pounds of tobacco aboard, and her crew fined from £2 10s to five shillings.

Her owner paid the fines and got the smack released. The *Oyster* was in trouble in 1845 when her master, John Swain, was convicted in a mitigated penalty of £25, or in default six months' imprisonment. The owner, Laban Sweeting, applied for the release of the smack, declaring that he had warned the master against smuggling, but the Customs considered this warning referred only to that particular voyage, and was thus incriminating rather than exculpatory. Moreover, instead of assisting the prosecution he had hired a solicitor to defend Swain. In the end he was paid £75 – half the value of his forfeited smack.

Distinctions between native and foreign oysters gave continual trouble to the bureaucratic minds of the Customs. Two hundred bushels were sent from Burnham in 1832 in the *Active* of Dunkirk, but one hundred were returned through fear of the cholera, then rampant in England. The merchant could not persuade the Searcher they were not foreign, 'though wholly unlike any French oysters.'

The *Charlotte* of Leigh had had a comparable problem when, bound from Cancale with a cargo of Britannies, she had to put into Portsmouth for repairs. She laid her oysters there on the local layings, but inevitably some died and were replaced with English natives. The problem then was to get a refund of duty on the lost French imports and persuade the Customs that half the cargo was English.

The oyster trade also involved the Burnham Tide Surveyor, at that time Charles Bull, in one of the battles always liable to break out between Colne and Burnham oystermen.

One morning in March 1807 thirty or forty smacks from Wivenhoe and Rowhedge sailed up the Crouch and started to dredge in response to a signal from a vessel flying a flag at her masthead. Bull went off with the local merchants, accompanied by a constable, boarded the *Betsey* (J Willett of Rowhedge) and took off the master and two hands, leaving only a boy aboard. He also seized oysters from others.

The Colne smacksmen assembled aboard one of the other vessels, planning to rescue the prisoners, who were, however, taken before two magistrates and committed to gaol for felony. Bull was accused of endangering the *Betsey* by leaving only the boy in charge, but luckily for him Captain Bayley RN, in command of the Sea Fencibles, was present to testify that he acted 'in a very proper manner'.

This, it may be added, was by no means the end of the matter. The following January another raid occurred, leading to a fight and the commitment of seven Colne smacksmen to Chelmsford gaol. Still undeterred, the Colne men, this time from Brightlingsea, threatened to sail in and clean the oysters out. Despite an injunction secured by the Burnham oystermen, a fleet of thirty-five smacks duly sailed from

Brightlingsea smacks intercepted by the gun brig Turbulent *after a raid on the Burnham oyster fishery.*

Rowhedge, Wivenhoe and Brightlingsea just a week after the previous raid. They were expected, and their leaders were arrested. When the fleet made sail for home they found the Naval gunbrig *Turbulent* waiting to intercept them at the mouth of the river. Several men were seized for the Navy, including Abraham Lufkin who was in fact on lawful business and who secured £150 damages for wrongful arrest and detention.

23

Square-rigged Smugglers

Coasters join in: Robert Dodds and the Mary: *Half-ankers from Nieuport: The* George *in Trouble: A Big Haul from the* Charlotte: *The* Fortuna *and the* Neptune.

MOST of the smuggling yarns in these pages are concerned with cutters, luggers and galleys. Merchant vessels, whether coasting or deep-sea, do not feature so prominently.

This is because, particularly after the seizure and destruction of offending craft became almost automatic, it was not worth risking vessels of much size and value. The whole game was a calculated gamble, based on balancing the profits from success against the costs of failure. To commit anything more valuable than a smack, or perhaps a sailing barge, raised the stakes too high. Another reason was that a brig or brigantine was easily outsailed and caught by a Revenue cutter. That smuggling was essentially a fore-and-aft rigged trade is shown by the fact that the restrictions on the dimensions of craft, and the limitations of their permitted voyages, usually refer to vessels 'not being square rigged'.

But there were, needless to say, plenty of exceptions, specially in the early years before the prospect of detection, and of destruction after detection, became so high.

Most of the merchant vessels in trouble had merely a little contraband under their legal freight, such as the sloop *Charlotte* of London, found with tubs under her corn, on a voyage from Amsterdam in 1771. Other seizures were the incidental result of the innumerable wrecks off the Essex coast. The brig *Nepean* of Boston went on the West Rocks in 1772. Her cargo, salvaged under the direction of Capt Bridge in the *Argus,* was found to include sixteen ankers of rum, amounting to 559 gallons, despite the captain's declaration that he had nothing beyond ship's stores. Sometimes the salvagers were themselves tempted or pressed into smuggling. The *Sea Nymph* of Whitby struck Yarmouth sands in 1775, and her crew took to the boats. They were picked up and brought into Harwich by two cod smacks. In the well of one of these, Samuel Turner's *Neptune,* were found a half-anker of brandy and another of rum, with a parcel of silk and muslin handkerchiefs.

Of greater interest are the voyages planned with smuggling as their prime purpose. The 180-ton *Betsey* of London was found in Hole Haven in 1771 with charter papers from Amsterdam to the Canaries.

169

But the Customs insisted that her bills of lading had been fabricated in London, and that she had put letters ashore at Lowestoft asking for a vessel to take her cargo from her at Hole Haven. 'We never till now saw so artfull and daring an attempt as this' declared the Collector, perhaps intent on making sure of a useful reward, for the twenty-year-old *Betsey* 'had a great repair lately', and was worth £400.

Another ingenious dodge was employed by the *George* of Hull, which sailed from Hamburg for Lynn in 1769. Out in the wash she buried 150 half-ankers in the sands at Lynn Deeps; then she loaded timber in Lynn harbour and stowed the recovered casks under this after sailing. By the time she put in at Harwich Cyprian Bridge had been informed. He found only forty-two casks aboard, with two that had been started, so concluded that she had disposed of 106 on her passage from Lynn. The *George* was condemned and burned, Bridge getting his reward at the rate of ten shillings a ton. Another craft burned at the same time, and yielding the same reward, was the cutter *James and Polly*, which had unloaded eighty half-ankers at Cromer, and delivered 150 more to 'the Riders of the Norfolk coast'. She was bound for Sizewell Gap to unload the remainder when she was picked up by the *Argus*.

Colliers off Flamborough Head, an aquatint from R. Dodd's North Country Shipping, 1797. *The cutter may well be a Revenue cruiser keeping an eye on them, as she flies a long pennant and has a boat alongside.*

The *George's* disposals may well have been to other shipping, for not all the smugglers ran their goods ashore. When a fleet of thirty loaded colliers from Sunderland and Newcastle put into Harwich in April 1763, they reported being visited by 'ten sail of loaded smuggling cutters . . . The said cutters cruise between Spurn, Cromer and Flamborough Head, chiefly around the latter. They regard not in the least any Custom House smacks or Admiralty cutters.' These copers also catered for fishermen. The cutter *Good Intent* of Rochester was seized in 1768 after boarding several smacks and offering to sell them half-ankers. She had often been chased but never before caught by the *Walpole*. On this occasion Thomas Williams of Happisburgh was found to have £46 in gold and silver 'in a leather bag and worsted purse between his thighs.'

When the brig *Constant Friends* of Wells was found to have 40lbs of tea and thirty gallons of spirits aboard in 1765 her master declared that they had been taken aboard unknown to him from the sixty-ton brig *Norfolk*, also of Wells, bound from Rotterdam to Woodbridge with barley. A further ten pounds of tea and twenty-eight gallons of spirits were found aboard the *Norfolk*, which was allowed to proceed to Woodbridge, with two Revenue men aboard, so that her barley cargo could be saved, after which her owner, Mr Hall, sacked her captain, who was on his first voyage, and asked to be allowed to pay two-thirds of her value (£106) to redeem her. The fate of the *Constant Friends* is not revealed.

Some of the smugglers' ideas were more ingenuous than ingenious. When the brig *Mary and Jane*, bound from Danzic to Barcelona with wheat, put into Harwich, the master told the Revenue men in the cabin 'not to open the hatch that led to the run of the vessel, for that he had several barrels of gunpowder'. Responding to this obvious invitation, the rummagers found the first cask did indeed contain twenty pounds of gunpowder, but the next three were half-ankers of geneva, which were seized along with two pounds of tea and four pounds of coffee. The Revenue men left nine gallons of geneva and nine gallons of brandy aboard, along with the tea and coffee, despite which the captain bitterly complained that they 'took the greatest part of my stock for so long a voyage. I give my ship's company some mixed with water every day.' (The idea of foremast hands swigging gin and brandy daily seems improbable. But the accounts for Capt Munnings' farm in 1837 include the item 'one gallon of gin for the cattle, 11s', so all things are possible!)

In the later smuggling era, with the dice at last loaded against the smuggler, ventures in merchantmen usually involved vessels used without the owner's consent or craft that had deteriorated till they were expendable.

The most notorious Essex exploit in the former category was that of twenty-seven-year-old Robert Dodds of Wivenhoe and the Newcastle collier brig *Mary* in 1832. She sailed from Stockton with a coal cargo, and off Flamborough Head her young skipper revealed his plan to his crew. At first he tried to make out it was conceived on that occasion, but in fact it had been hatched earlier at a meeting in the Swan inn at Stratford St Mary, between Dodds and an Ipswich man named Phillips, who had a house at Bramford, another in London which he used as his smuggling headquarters, and another at Blakeney, Norfolk, where he went under the name of Barry. Also present were a Nacton farmer named Taylor, a Brightlingsea man named Bloomfield (a notable smuggling family), William Powell of Wivenhoe, a farmer, and Joseph Woods, mate of the *Mary*.

The agreement, made between Dodds, Phillips and Taylor, was that the *Mary* should rendezvous off Nieuport, Belgium, with a cutter (also named *Mary*, twenty-eight tons, registered at Colchester or Ipswich and owned by Phillips and his brother, a Nieuport merchant) and load spirits from her. When they reached the Belgian coast, however, the wind was too strong north-west for trans-shipment at sea, so they entered Nieuport harbour where they saw the cutter *Mary* also loading a cargo. They buried their tubs under their coal, filled main and fore tops with tobacco, and sailed for their destination, the Burnham river, where two vans were to be ready at Fambridge to take Phillips's share to London.

At Fambridge[1] things began to go wrong. The Coastguards' suspicions were aroused by 'a dreadful smell below'. Keeping watch, Lieut Hussey, chief officer of the Coast Guard, observed a great deal of nocturnal coming and going between the brig and the shore. Finally, when the crew were ashore, he boarded, removed part of the cargo and discovered the half-ankers and the tobacco in the tops. The crew disappeared, leaving only two apprentices aged fifteen and twelve aboard. After a remand by the magistrates they were discharged by the Customs.

Thomas Moulton was picked up, but claimed only to have been the pilot from Harwich, so he too was discharged. The Colchester Tide Waiter then declared that he was a notorious smuggler, already planning a fresh venture with the *Pearl* of Ipswich, and had in fact been aboard from the time the *Mary* left Stockton, including being present at Nieuport when the spirits were loaded. Moulton said he had denied this 'for fear of a beating', but the problem then arose that as he had been discharged he could not be arrested again for the same offence.

The Customs thought he had only been taken before one magistrate and that this might invalidate his discharge, but whether this pretext was tried is not revealed.

The mate, Joseph Woods, despite his presence at the planning meeting, seems to have refused to participate, returning home from Nieuport in a steamer. Whether the other members of the crew, Joseph Herring and William Bloomfield (brother of the plotter at the Stratford Swan), both of Wivenhoe, were prosecuted is not revealed.

Dodds himself made a swashbuckling exit. 'Come to Wivenhoe', he wrote to the Colchester Tide Surveyor. 'You will find me at the Times with Father and Friends.' The thought of a man throwing a party in a pub before facing his fate is a curiously moving one. The Tide Surveyor accepted the invitation. Dodds was convicted at Maldon Town Hall and sent to the Navy for five years. He made a full disclosure (the basis of this story) aboard HMS *Ocean* at Sheerness. The petition on his behalf was a striking one, for it was signed by Lord Western, the distinguished Whig statesman and former M.P. for Maldon, on behalf of 'certainly all the respectable inhabitants of Wivenhoe' – who numbered just over one hundred and thirty! 'Mr Brummell of Wivenhoe is anxious to obtain some relief' the petition stated. I hope young Dodds survived his impressment and returned to the community which clearly thought so highly of him.

The *Mary* herself was taken round to Maldon, where she pulled the moorings out of Payne's coal quay. This damage, along with pilotage, creeping up anchors, help in moving, warehousing, printing and advertising, bottles, corks and cooperage, brought the costs of the case to £51, but as the seizure was valued at over £5,000 it was still a profitable day's work.

Her owners, George Dixon and Robert Bell, of Stockton, petitioned for her return, pleading that they were unconcerned in the smuggling and unaware of it, but the Customs hardened their hearts and sold her to J Levy of Rochester who registered her in London. It is usually possible, reading between the lines, to detect reasons for doubting such protestations of innocence, but on this occasion it seems extraordinary that the owners were penalised while no attempt, apparently, was made to trace Phillips and his accomplices.

As an example of a worn-out trading vessel being risked, the story of the sloop *George* of London may be quoted.

She was seen and boarded three hundred yards off Orford beach in 1816 with a cargo of butter and cheese. Ashore were a number of people, which looked suspicious, so the boarding party inquired about some bales. The mate declared he did not know what they contained,

173

but when they were opened it was found to be silk handkerchiefs and crapes, at which point the mate admitted he had been told not to enter them 'on the slate or in the log book'.

The *George* was taken to Harwich by the Revenue cutter *Surly,* and it was found that aboard were two notorious smugglers, Richard alias Robert Wilson, and Dan Delany, a hawker from Chelmsford. One of the crew said that after sailing from London they had been twelve days weather-bound in the Brill (the river Brielle in Holland), after which they had again sailed for London. Coming on deck at night he had commented that two lights ahead did not look like the Sunk, and was told they had had to haul up for Orford Ness. But, as Captain Deane, commander of the Revenue cutter *Hawk* observed, they had a fair wind for London.

The passengers were confined aboard for some time in Harwich, and the skipper, Robert Boyce, and his mate were sent aboard a naval ship, provoking the protest from their owner quoted in an earlier chapter.

So far this is a routine example of a traditional run onto an open beach in broad daylight. The interest is in the owner's case. James Elder, of Horsleydown, gave a touching account of his misfortunes. His vessel had been driven ashore in the Brill and lost one third of her cargo by plunder. He had suffered further loss from the delay for repairs because of its perishable nature. To which Captain Deane replied that the *George* was a small, old, decayed sloop, only recently purchased by Elder for £40. Her sails and gear were rubbish and the reason she got ashore was that she unshipped her rudder. On this occasion one feels less sympathy for the owners.

The humble sailing barge, coming to dominate the coastal trade from the beginning of the nineteenth century, was one type of craft cheap enough to be risked in a smuggling venture and eminently suitable. The Maldon Collector in his report for 1839 observed 'barges by their easy draught and frequently at the head of creeks are suspected of creeping up goods on their passages'. He may have had in mind the seizure of the London barge *Alfred* off Birchington in 1828, claiming to be bound from Arundel with a cargo of wooden hoops. But when an obstruction beneath her coamings was cut away it was found to conceal 1,045 tubs of gin and brandy. Twenty years after this one of the biggest of all seizures in the last years of traditional smuggling was the capture in 1849 by the Revenue cutter *Vigilant* of the barge *Charlotte* in Sea Reach, loaded with no less than 14,402 lbs of tobacco. She was given away by a boy aboard who bore the same name as a member of the *Vigilant*'s crew. The rewards for this great haul amounted to

£431 for the cutter's master, £86 each for the gunner, bosun, carpenter and steward, £30 each for five mariners and £21 each for seven boys, with a bonus of £6 'head money' for the impressment of the barge skipper into the Navy.

Some years before this the sailing barge *Fortuna*, loaded with chalk and rubbish, was used to sweep up sixty-two half-ankers and two quarter kegs of spirits sunk in the Swin. With them under the chalk she arrived at Burnham where the discovery was made. She had four men aboard (in itself, one would think, enough to arouse suspicion). Two of them, James Howard of Rochford and Benjamin Saunders of Fambridge, were convicted as fit for the Navy; the two others, George Preston of Dell Quay, Chichester, and George Knight of Eastwood, Essex, went to Chelmsford, where Preston was suspected as the man who knocked down the Excise supervisor when he attempted to arrest J Hooker's wagon a few months before, as described in Chapter 17. The Supervisor visited the prison but could not identify him.

While under arrest the men handed in a letter to be posted to John Flight, butcher, Whitstable. It was, of course, opened, and found to contain the words 'It was an information . . . We have lost the things and ourselves.' Yet as usual no effort seems to have been made to arrest Flight.

The owner of the *Fortuna*, William Goodchild, a Poplar barge builder, set about trying to recover his property, valued with her boat at £140, but he got short shrift. While he claimed he had merely hired the barge to Howard at £50 a year, the Customs said Saunders was a notorious smuggler and Goodchild must have known all about it, for he had been much involved with Howard, who had once owned two barges and had transferred the *Fortuna* to Goodchild 'by way of liquidation'.

A few months after this the Maldon barge *Neptune* was seized at Rochford with 105 tubs of spirits, and her skipper and mate, John and David Hansell, went to Maidstone gaol. She was owned by Dixons, the big Essex millers, who being highly respectable got her back on payment of costs. Under a more law-abiding skipper she had been regularly employed by the Maldon Collector to transport contraband from his Custom House to London.

175

The Marquis's Yacht Builder

Phillip Sainty and the Ruswarp: *A Partner's Betrayal.*

ONE of the most interesting of all the Essex smugglers was Philip Sainty, builder of the Marquis of Anglesey's famous yacht *Pearl*, whose success did much to establish Colneside as a rival of the Medina and Haslar creek in the esteem of the yachtsmen of the day.

For a century and a half the story has been told at Wivenhoe and Rowhedge of how Sainty was in gaol for smuggling when the Marquis, who had lost a leg at Waterloo, wanted his yacht, and had to get him released to build her, along with a relative in Maidstone gaol for the same offence. This tradition[1] is now strikingly confirmed – and a new picture emerges of the plight Sainty was in before he received the patronage that was to transform his life.

It was in April 1815 that he sailed to Ostend in a vessel curiously named *Ruswarp* with his brother-in-law John Pullen, his son-in-law John Pullen junior and Alfred Sainty. After lying there about a month they loaded 170 casks of spirits to the order of James Forster of the Colchester Arms public house, who paid them 10s per cask. They unloaded these at the Prince Regent public house at Woolwich, fifty casks going to James Warr, a butcher at Billingsgate, and the rest being kept by the landlord of the Prince Regent.

Sainty then returned to Bruges and on 4 June loaded a further 176 casks under the same arrangement.

A third freight of 182 casks was loaded on 26 June, also at Bruges. This time the destination was the Stour, where thirty casks were unloaded at Stutton for Samuel Baker, a Manningtree carrier, who paid in gold, and the remainder at Cattawade Bridge, above Manningtree, the upper navigable limit of the Stour for craft with fixed masts.

A final freight of 140 casks was loaded at Ostend on 8 August and delivered two days later at The Devil's House on the Thames. These casks were unshipped into a horse ferry belonging to John Avinger, who kept eighty of them, the remaining forty going to a tea and coffee wholesaler named Marsden of Charles Street, opposite the London Hospital.

At this point Sainty decided he had had enough, and refused to make another run for Forster, who turned King's evidence to save his own skin. Information was laid in May 1816, and the *Ruswarp* was seized by the Colchester Tide Surveyor. Sainty and John Pullen senior were committed to Chelmsford gaol on 14 August faced with a penalty of no less than £4,426 – treble value on 1,476 gallons of geneva – with £100 for illegally having it aboard in small casks. A year later Sainty was one of half-a-dozen Crown debtors transferred to the Fleet Prison (at any rate approval for the move was given in September 1817, due to the insecurity of Chelmsford) and he was not released till the end of 1818.

Just what part the Marquis of Anglesey played in securing his freedom is not clear. John Pullen senior was not mentioned in the gaol transfer of 1817 so may have been released earlier. His son, John Pullen junior, was committed to Maidstone gaol, presumably because he was picked up in Kent. He was liberated in November 1818. A letter from the Maldon Collector confirms that he was 'the person alluded to in the enclosed letter from the Marquis of Anglesea (sic)', but alas the enclosure was not copied, and the Rochester Collector's letters do not go back to this date to provide any confirmation from Maidstone. Samuel Baker, the Manningtree carrier, was also picked up on Forster's information and found himself in the Fleet under a penalty of £780, three times the value of 260 gallons.

As for the *Ruswarp*, the Customs used her for a Preventive boat, first at the Isle of Grain (in October 1817) and later nearer home in the Crouch, thus doing the Tide Surveyor out of his reward, which the Customs told him was only payable on sale. The last we hear of her was when she was laid ashore at Burnham for a refit by Durden, the Maldon shipwright, who caulked her without blocking her up off the ground. The Burnham merchants (perhaps jealous at seeing the job go to Maldon) protested to the Board that the job could not be done properly with the caulkers having no space to swing their mallets. The Board told them to mind their own business.[2]

Throughout these stories a question which constantly arises is why men so freely risked their boats and their liberty in smuggling. The answer in Sainty's case (and it doubtless applies to many others) is that he was in desperate financial straits, and had twice been bankrupt. The first occasion, of which there are no details, was around 1800. The second was immediately before his smuggling escapades, for he was examined before the General Session of the Peace under the recently passed Act for the Relief of Debtors in July 1814, at which time he was still in Chelmsford gaol as a common debtor.

Sainty stated that he had bought the *Ruswarp* from Robert Guy, a Chelmsford corn factor, in November 1811 'under an agreement which I have not been able to comply with and the vessel has been delivered up to Mr Guy and made over to Mr Mark Lay by him. I use her by permission of Mr Lay, paying him interest for her value. She is now in the care of the dockman in the Surrey canal.'

Sainty went on to say that he formerly owned a small fishing boat called the *Essex* of about twenty tons. 'She was taken by the French five years since and carried into Holland. I do not know where she is and I am not entitled to any other ship or vessel.'

So when the Customs helped themselves to the *Ruswarp* the loss, in fact, fell on Robert Guy, though Sainty had contrived to remain her registered owner — an apparent illegality perpetrated perhaps with a view to saving anyone else from involvement in her misdeeds. There is no suggestion that Guy was in any way implicated, but it seems unlikely that Mark Lay, who bears a good Rowhedge name, was unaware of what she was up to. Whether any of them got her back after her spell of duty as a watch vessel in the Crouch is not revealed.

Could Sainty have found a law-abiding way to mend his fortunes? His previous efforts had not been encouraging, though he must have had some reputation as a builder to cause the Marquis of Anglesey to go to such trouble to secure his services. Perhaps, however, there was a bit of smuggling in the Sainty blood, for Philip's brother, Robert, was also a full-time smuggler down Channel with the lugger *Wolverine*, trading from Newhaven till she was ultimately caught by two Revenue cutters off Beachy Head and had to be run ashore at Worthing and set on fire.[3]

According to the Colneside tradition it was this brother who was also released from Maidstone gaol by the Marquis of Anglesey, whereas the story now emerging shows it was Philip's son-in-law — unless the Marquis's efforts extended to securing the freedom of the whole family.

25

A Busy Week at Boulogne

*Fishermen Informers: Poacher and Gamekeeper: A Customs Collector's
Speculation: Gaolbirds' Tales.*

SAINTY'S exploits are only one of many examples of the extraordinary failure to watch the ports where contraband was loaded, with little or no attempt at concealment. This is how the amateur yachtsman-smuggler is caught today. He stows his bottles and boxes with great care and cunning under the cabin sole, but he is wasting his time, because the shopkeeper has made his report before he has even banked his francs or guilders. At his home port the usually friendly Customs officer glances at a list and starts his rummage.

Why this obvious method was seldom employed in the heyday of smuggling defies explanation – or perhaps leaves as the only possible explanation the Customs' lack of enthusiasm to stamp out completely the trade on which they depended. Certainly before the time of the telegraph it would not always have been easy to transmit a warning from a foreign port so that it was received before the smugglers' cargo arrived, but even so the opportunities for spying are clearly shown in the experience of two Dover fishermen, William Dangerfield and Henry Trigg, who in October 1816 sailed to try their luck on a newly discovered oyster ground on the Ridge, between Dover and Boulogne.

Their luck was out, for weather forced them into Boulogne, where they lay for eleven or twelve days watching the smugglers being freighted. An old gun brig lay along the quay, and tubs were loaded into her for easy trans-shipment into vessels as they came alongside. There was no attempt at secrecy. Brandy casks were marked B, spirits of brandy SB, spirits of geneva SG and the geneva casks were not marked. But you could also tell by the smell, for many of the casks were so leaky they had to be coopered on the quay.

The fishermen watched thirty half-ankers loaded into the smack *Hope* of Maldon, 120 into the lugger *Juno* of Hastings and 200 into the lugger *Ann* of Rye. They also went aboard the cutter *Isis* of Rye, where they saw at least one hundred and tasted one of them.

On the evening of the 19th the decked lugger *Bee* of Folkestone came in, and next day loaded 546 casks, sailing two days later with the *Isis*. On the 24th two luggers arrived, the *Union* of Hastings and the *Lord Nelson* of Hove (with the name of her owner, Richard Hammond, painted on her stern), each loading at least 200 tubs. They sailed next day, but had to put back because of the weather. It then

Smugglers loading at Boulogne from an old gun brig.

became finer and the fishermen started dredging, seeing the *Union* and *Lord Nelson* sail again.

Despite having fraternised with the crews, who told them the number of tubs going to each craft, and even drinking their gin, the Dover men now proceeded to pass all this information to the Customs. The local Collectors were told to report. Hastings said they had two luggers named *Juno*. No *Isis* cutter was registered at Rye, but there were three smacks of that name with fixed bowsprits – a further example of the confusion caused by the Customs' attempt to define a cutter. The lugger *Ann* was known at Rye, and so were the luggers *New Union* and *Lord Nelson* at Hove 'built agreeable to the Act and not licensed'. As for the *Hope*, Maldon reported they had two; Peter Richmond's fifty-ton cutter at Burnham, licensed 'for fishing, piloting, wrecking and mercantile trade', and John Pewter's little Tollesbury oyster dredger which, as mentioned in Chapter 13 was in trouble at this time – perhaps for this exploit.

What happened to them and what reward the Dover men obtained is not revealed. But it is an interesting little picture of the day-to-day illegal exports from Boulogne and of the way betrayal by informing was accepted practice.

On the one recorded occasion when a spy was employed at Flushing, he was posted there, not officially by the Board, but as a private venture of the Harwich Collector, presumably in the hope of making a profit out of his rewards – an expectation which was not fulfilled.

The individual chosen was James Glading, an Ipswich man, and a typically shady character in this shadowy underworld, smuggler or informer as suited him. Two years before his arrest in the *Nancy* (already described), he had been detained in November 1815 aboard the lugger *Bee* of Ostend, along with Henry Gooding and John Gouden, the Dutch master, with 106 tubs aboard.

This was a job done in company with the Harwich smack *Providence* (J L Rainbird), which loaded 100 tubs, both cargoes supplied by a Flushing merchant named Browning to the order of Banks, father and son, of Harwich.

The two craft sailed from Flushing for 'Bardsea' (Bawdsey) in Suffolk, the wind south-west, the *Bee* in tow of the *Providence* till 10 a.m. next morning when they parted company 'within three leagues of the Sunk light vessel.' The *Providence* got into Harwich undetected, but after three hours the *Bee* was taken by the Revenue cutter *Hawk*. Glading was lodged in Harwich prison, where Rainbird visited him with the news that the *Providence*'s tubs had been first sunk in the harbour and then successfully worked ashore, sixty of them going to Banks junior and twenty to a Mr Chisnell at Dovercourt.

Glading then concocted a story that he was just an innocent passenger aboard the *Bee*, unable to afford the packet boat fare, but the Harwich Collector observed this was unlikely as in that case there would have been only one man aboard to work the *Bee*, and he was duly committed to Chelmsford. After he had cooled his heels there for a year the Maldon Collector visited him, and he told the story already narrated, adding a plea for a reward. 'If I had about £50 to get a small vessel I could render the Revenue good service,' he wistfully observed.

Instead he had to pay £20 to regain his freedom, which was short-lived, for as already recorded he was soon in trouble with the *Nancy* and a few years after that in November, 1827, he was caught yet again in the Barrow Deep with twenty half-ankers of geneva from Gravelines in the *Bishop Blaize* of Ipswich.

On this occasion he barefacedly declared he had done nothing to injure the Revenue since 1800, but had been employed in 1825 by Mr Woods, the Collector at Harwich, to go to Ostend and Flushing. Then he had suffered a severe rupture and had been 'out for many nights in Ipswich river endeavouring to find smuggling from the butter vessels belonging to that port [a trade recalled in the name of Butterman's

Bay below Pin Mill]. Distress drove me to Gravelines, but my intention was . . . if I had landed what I had it would have been more for the good of the service of Revenue than hurt, for I should have proceeded to Mr Cook (the Tide Surveyor) immediately and should then have proceeded to Faversham to recognise two vessels which took in a cargo of contraband.' He added that he knew one of the men aboard but 'could not see the vessels' names as they were daubed over with mud at Gravelines.'

The Collector confirmed that Glading was 'employed (at my expence) at Flushing in 1825 and though information there was not attended with success . . . he would again exert himself for the benefit of the Revenue.' Apart from the way the Collector apparently employed his own agent privately at Flushing, it is surprising that he selected such a doubtful character, and inexplicable that he failed to mention Glading's record, of which he must have been aware. But neither his blind eye nor Glading's perjury availed him much. He paid a third visit to Chelmsford and the *Bishop Blaize* was condemned to be destroyed.

The chain of information started by Glading was continued by Rainbird of the *Providence* who, despite the success of his own venture, was compromised by Glading's information, and who sought to obtain his release by contributing his own collection of tit-bits.

He told how he had seen a boat called the *Sophia,* belonging to the barrack master at Landguard Fort, pick up a string of fifty-six tubs with her anchor as she was getting under way. He later saw ropes and anchors aboard her and six tubs on the beach, which were stolen by soldiers. One of the crew of the governor's boat confirmed that he was employed working the fifty-six tubs from the *Sophia*.

Rainbird added that he could prove that a vessel called the *Michael and Mary* of Orford, avoiding arrest at Harwich by claiming to be Dutch, in fact belonged to William Kemp who lived on Orford beach.

He further reported that the *Good Intent* of Harwich, Edward Lewis owner, John Lewis master, then detained in Southwold, had loaded 200 casks in Flushing the previous March, sailing in his company and landing them on the Suffolk shore. The *Good Intent* was a thirty-two foot carvel-built cutter seized by the Revenue cutter *Viper* in 1815 and bought by Edward Lewis, a member of a notable family of Harwich salvagers.[1]

After naming the clench-built cutter *Lottery*, of about sixty tons, working regularly on the Suffolk and Norfolk coasts under Dutch colours, though she was believed to be English, he added that the Brightlingsea smack *Industry* (W Bloomfield) was a constant smuggler and had also loaded 100 tubs with him in Flushing in March, landing them safely at Brightlingsea.

The *Lottery* and *Industry* both went on the wanted list, and Lieut Neame noted that he expected to seize the *Industry* shortly. But before he could do so she disappeared from Brightlingsea on 21 January, 1818. Whether she and Bloomfield got clean away is not revealed; certainly neither of them seems to reappear in these records.

26

Free Trade Finds Favour

Smuggling in Decline: Smack Yachts Suspected: A Field of Tobacco.

SMUGGLING, already almost obsolete on the open coasts, declined in the creeks and estuaries in the 1830s, and by the 1840s what had been a regular business was reduced to occasional sporadic ventures.

This is commonly attributed to the general acceptance of Free Trade. Certainly a general dislike of Preventive duties was being shown in the 1840s by Parliamentary Committees of Enquiry into the Revenue, but the decline anticipated this political trend, which in any case did not extend to the spirits, tobacco or (to a major degree) tea which were the smugglers' staples.

Other causes must therefore be sought, including the increase in legal distilleries in England and Scotland.[1] But the principal reason for the decline was probably the increased efficiency of the Preventive Water Guard and the Coastguard, and the treatment of offenders as convicts instead of debtors.

Certainly the reports of the Coastguard era generally make quieter reading. The Chief Officer at Bradwell recorded nil returns for smuggling from 1839 to 1851, with a steady coastal trade increasing from fifty-seven arrivals and sixty-four departures in 1840 to ninety vessels inward and one hundred and sixteen outward in 1851. These included about seven colliers a year. The little quay must have been quite busy, as only one or two vessels went elsewhere – to Stansgate, Ramsey Stone or Mayland creek.

Maldon reported in 1839 that smuggling had been decreasing over the last three years with no great run. What was done was by 'poor persons who carry on their business by retail'. Spirits 'from Ostend and places east and west of it' were the chief item, with little tobacco. Over the three years there had been nineteen seizures by the Coastguard – two horses and carts and four open boats – leading to four prosecutions and six convictions and two seizures by the Customs.

As this report shows, open boats were now generally used, presumably because it had become too risky to employ a smack. Thomas Bacon's capture in a boat by himself off the Crouch in 1838 has been mentioned. Joseph Chapman and John Mace of Blackwall were likewise caught in Sea Reach in a boat containing sixty-four boxes and four packets of 'segars' (the universal spelling at the time) in 1840. As late as 1851 the cruiser *Despatch* brought in eight half-anker casks of gin and brandy found sunk off Chapel Point, Bradwell, but such a find in the Blackwater was by then a rarity, though in 1859 Lieut Carr RN, Inspecting Lieutenant of the Blackwater Division of the Coastguard, was putting out a warning that 'the smack *Eclipse* of Colchester has sailed from Mersea for Ostend for the purpose of bringing up a cargo of tobacco'.

This sort of rumour was now commonplace, to an extent suggesting that perhaps the lack of factual evidence encouraged the fabrication of fiction, if only for something to report to the Honourable Board. In August 1836 the Collector learned 'from a private source' that the schooner *Agenoria* of Portsmouth was to run spirits from Cherbourg to Mersea, or if unable to land there to try the Crouch. No more was heard of it. Two years later, in January 1838, reports of a run at Goldhanger boiled down to the fact that there were 'several strangers about on Xmas Day'.

There was also much excitement over a sixteen ton 'yacht', *Lady of the Lock*, owned by Edward Kilworth. She sailed from Paglesham in 1839 with a cargo of potatoes, put fourteen sacks ashore at Burnham and sailed to collect contraband for the Thames or Medway in the opinion of Lieut Carr, who declared that a former owner named Rolphe, who had been convicted and sent to the Navy, was aboard as her master. Later he decided that Rolphe was 'over channel' fixing a cargo. Then it transpired that Kilworth had gone bankrupt and sold the *Lady of the Lock* to Samuel Watts of Shoebury. The Customs'

The Hole Haven coastguard station on Canvey Island at the end of the nineteenth century, with its naval atmosphere and paraphernalia, a far cry from the nocturnal patrols, afloat and afoot, of the earlier Preventive Waterguard.

solicitor ruled she could be detained for sailing without the change of ownership being recorded in her licence. It all fizzled out when Watts applied for the new licence, explaining he had taken the yacht for debt and wished to sell her at Leigh. One suspects Lieut Carr was a bit of a gossip, and not the only one at this time.

Such seizures as were made were now principally in the Crouch and the Thames Estuary.

Early in 1843 ninety-eight tubs were crept up near the Blyth beacon off Leigh, and sixty-five more were seized a mile above Thames Haven docks. During this period the Newcastle brig *Coquet* brought up at the head of Sea Reach in darkness and calm. Her anchor 'rode' and she drove close in shore 'just above the place where the large sign is placed for the collier dock at Shelhaven'. On the next tide she tried to get away, but could not move, so she anchored again to await daylight, by which time there was half a gale from the south-west and she had to take the steam tug *Lion* to get off the lee shore. Round the anchor fluke they found a new three-and-a-half-inch rope attached to a string of green-painted tubs. When they cut this the tubs sank, except for one which floated up on the flood tide.

A few old style incidents were still reported from Leigh, where the Collector observed in 1837 that over fifty shrimpers were at work daily, providing such opportunities for getting into mischief that he wanted their permitted fishing area reduced. He also observed that 'they do not confine themselves to that section of the Smuggling Act with respect to their being painted black.'

Charles Cotgrove, of a good Leigh family, found himself in Chelms-ford gaol in 1849 after the discovery of wine, spirits and cigars aboard the *Spray*. She had been built three years before by a London yachtsman named Martin 'to assist an industrious fisherman' – a foretaste of that Leigh classic *Gotty and the Guv'nor*. Martin said they had picked up the contraband at sea where 'it had probably floated out of a wreck' and that it was 'seized before they were given a chance to declare it'. His petition for the release of the *Spray*, worth £250, was granted, 'but we do not think fit to direct the release of the party', perhaps because 'the party' (Cotgrove) had imprudently threatened to throw the coastguard overboard.

Three years later there was trouble over another smack yacht *Spray*, possibly the same vessel, but this seems unlikely, as she had been registered at Maldon since 1843 and was employed in the Jersey oyster trade in the winter and fitted out as a yacht in summer. She entered the Swale in Kent in June 1852 on passage from Gravesend to Faver-sham and refused to heave-to when told to. The Commissioned

Boatman fired a blank and went aboard, on which she lowered her flag and hoisted a Royal Yacht Club burgee, claiming this denied the right to search. The action was a typical example of the arrogance of the Victorian yachtsman, but the Collector was determined to find a villain. He refused to believe that the owner, Richard Solly junior of Mundon, who was also secretary of the Tollesbury Oyster Company, was entitled to fly a Royal Yacht Club ensign (it transpired he was a member of the Royal Thames Yacht Club), and declared, 'As I know *personally* many of the largest landed proprietors are the chiefest supporters of smuggling I submit such conduct may be noticed.'

The use of smacks for summer yachting was now coming into favour, for another, the fifteen-ton *Medora* of Maldon, was under suspicion in 1845, having been sold by W Hygate to R T Craneis, 'who has been seen in the company of suspected characters,' and who had appointed as her master John Death of Brightlingsea, another suspect. The *Medora* was also reported in 1846, along with the *Rebecca* of Colchester, for leaving with dredges on board 'within the period prohibited by the Articles of the Fishery Convention' – a fragment of oyster cultivation history now forgotten.

These incidents were casual and haphazard, and no longer seemed part of any pattern of regular activity, but as one comes to the end of the story one cannot but be surprised at the continuing inability of mariners to keep their fingers off 'hot' goods, even after so many decades of making an example of those arousing the slightest suspicion.

The forty-eight-ton Goole sloop *Eleanor* came into the Blackwater in March 1846 in ballast, having taken wheat to Boulogne. When she was boarded by the cruiser *Despatch* there was a tub on her hatches. The skipper said he had thought it would make a good anchor buoy, so he had grabbed it with a boat hook. Fortunately in this occasion the Customs observed he was very young, very ignorant and very innocent.

A more bizarre example occurred three years later, when shipping discovered a floating 'field' of unmanufactured tobacco, presumably from a wreck. The stuff was valueless but everyone had to have a go. The Maldon barge *Hopewell* picked up thirty pounds and took it into the Crouch. The Revenue cutter *Despatch* found the Faversham barge *Isabella* with three pounds aboard and 500 pounds in her boat astern. She then went after James Harris's Rowhedge smack *Benevolence*, having to fire at her to bring her to. She had 150 pounds, and the *Despatch* herself later picked up two tons.

The *Benevolence* at the time was chartered by the Wivenhoe Lloyd's agent to take an anchor to the brig *Hebe* at Sheerness, and had the brig's captain aboard. The smack's skipper went to Chelmsford gaol for six months, with her detention leaving the *Hebe* at risk for lack of an anchor. The *Isabella*, which had helped the *Despatch* clear up the tobacco field, was restored to her owner, John Shrubsall, who wrote a friendly letter of thanks, adding that he would be more grateful still if he could have her boat back as well, though he had failed to license it, as it 'belonged to Stephen Taylor of Sittingbourne that builded my vessel'.

The tobacco itself was a great nuisance. Two tons were put in a Customs boathouse and turned over as often as possible. But 'the stench was unbearable' and it got so heated that 'we fear it may ignite and destroy our premises'.

27

The Traders' Revolt:

Retrenchment: Merchants Kick at the Pricks: Challenge by the Rogue-in-Grain: *The End of old Enmities.*

THE decline in smuggling permitted a reduction in many of the Preventive forces. The cruising tenders were sold off – the *Onyx* in 1837 for £93; the *Fanny*, which had been built for the Coastguard service at Shadwell in 1826, to J Woolvet in 1839 for £22; and the Bradwell tender *Seagull* for £80 to one of the Banyard family – a deal complicated by the fact that her ballast bore the Queen's mark. The Essex smack fleets thus made good two of the losses the smuggling war had inflicted on them.

Some of the Coastguard stations also closed. The men from Shoebury, including the former crew of the *Onyx*, were moved to Leigh in 1844, leaving fourteen cottages, built in 1827, on the hands of the Honourable Board, who could not get rid of them till luckily for them the Board of Ordnance decided in 1847 to use the site for the artillery range which still exists there.

The mounted guards at Bradwell and at Rochford had gone by 1846, when rumours of a tobacco run in Steeple Creek in the Blackwater brought the comment 'there is now no inland guard for the south side of the river. If a boat succeeded in entering the river, which is not very difficult if the cruiser is away, or of a dark night, there is nothing to prevent a landing either in Steeple Creek or Mayland Creek.'

Rochford was a small station which has not found much mention in these pages. It tended to be alternately manned and then neglected according to whether there had been trouble in the area. Its chief character in the later years was the Principal Coast Officer, George Ventris, who was frequently drunk. His superiors stuck by him even when in 1845 his response to people knocking on his door was to fire his shotgun through it, wounding two of his visitors.

Meanwhile trade in general, and coastal trade in particular, increased as smuggling declined. Merchants, faced with new competition from the railways, continually demanded better facilities and fewer restrictions, which were, it seems, actually tightened up at a time when relaxation was clearly needed. In 1842 Coates, the Chelmsford timber merchants, sought approval to deposit imports from Quebec in the Heybridge canal, and John Smith of Burnham 'finding his business fast increasing' asked for a bonding yard at his premises. Sadd's of

The coastguard era. Above: The watch vessel Kangaroo, *placed at Burnham off the site of the present Royal Corinthian Yacht Club in 1872, and broken up about 1890 when houses were built in Silver Road. Below: The watch vessel at Stansgate in the Blackwater.*

Maldon, encouraged by the new railway to Witham, also opened a bonded timber warehouse in 1845.

As well as wanting new places for unloading and storage, the merchants were annoyed by the restrictive hours at the sites they had. Piggot & Son, who had the busy watermill at Langford, with its own branch connection to the canal, wanted to bond wheat in their granaries in 1848, and complained in 1842 that they 'had to wait to work out foreign cakes, wheat etc other than between eight and four o'clock'. Apparently they got no response, for two years later they joined the other merchants in a protest against 'recent rules by which (contrary to established customs of fifty years) we are allowed to work on ships from foreign ports only from eight to four'. Their request was to work from six to six in summer and from sunrise to sunset in winter.

The needs of the coastal trade were equally pressing, harassed as it was by a multiplicity of coastwise duties and restrictions.

At Maldon the issue came to a head in a clash with Henry Ward, owner of the great Beeleigh mill, at the head of the tidal estuary, just above the Custom House. Beeleigh was 'newly built' in 1807 when Arthur Young visited it and described in his *General View of Agriculture in Essex* how 'all the barges come under the mill for loading and all the machinery and contrivances for abridging labour appear to be disposed to much perfection'.[1] It was purchased in 1834 by Joseph Ward, of Merton Mill, Surrey, who a few years later built a sailing barge to serve it, amusingly named *Rogue in Grain*. In 1842 Joseph Ward made over the mill to his two sons, Henry and Charles, who in 1845 added a steam engine to drive five pairs of stones additional to twelve pairs driven by two water wheels. This magnificent mill was destroyed by a fire in 1879, though the beam engine and its boiler were saved, and survive there to this day.

Beeleigh was thus a natural champion of the new mercantile enterprise in defying the obsolete regulations the Customs had to enforce. The challenge came when the *Rogue in Grain* arrived on a Sunday in October, 1850. The skipper took the hatches off and started unloading. The Custom House was of course closed, with no-one to issue authority to discharge cargo, but this did not prevent the Collector sending two men to stop the operation, after which he sat down to pen a demand that an example should be made of Henry Ward. Defying Divine commandment by breaking the Sabbath was bad enough, but nothing to flaunting the yet more sacred provisions of the Act.

Ward's London shipping agent, John Norman, fired a broadside. 'The officers at Maldon Custom House from a mistaken zeal . . . and too strictly adhering to the letter of the law will I am convinced destroy the coasting trade of that port and certainly that of Messrs Ward's tidal mill at Beeleigh, within sight of the Custom House, unless directed by your Honourable Board rather to extend than contract the facilities for free trade when competition with rail conveyance is so injurious to our water carriage . . . To and from Rochester barges obtain but one clearance for every six months' sake. From Gravesend to Westminster vessels unload at all times and places . . . Messrs Ward & Sons have received notice from the Collector that for the future they are not to load nor unload any wheat, flour or merchandise arriving coastwise but in accordance to the Act . . . Confining the working times to those specified in the Act would in effect annihilate this portion of their business . . . When the tides are taking off it is often absolutely necessary to lighten the vessel for to prevent a detention for the next ten days.'

The Collector replied that he was 'now aware by what authority Mr Norman took upon himself to call our conduct into question. The coasting trade is very considerable and all have opportunities for communication with foreign vessels at sea.' The Board threatened to prosecute the skipper, telling him to pay £3 within three days or proceedings would be started for a penalty of £20. Ward's paid the £3 and then set about trying to get it refunded, and in December 1850 proceedings against the *Rogue in Grain* were waived, though not before the Collector had brought a new charge against Norman of 'persuading the masters of coasting vessels belonging to this port that they are not required to keep a log book', and had made two final attempts to squeeze ten shillings out of Ward, 'who treats your Honours' orders with silent contempt'.

The following year Norman took up the cudgels again on behalf of another leading miller, William Taylor Meeson, who as well as being a big farmer, chalk merchant and barge-owner, had the Battlesbridge tide mill at the head of the Crouch. His complaint was that he often loaded a small part-cargo at Wallasea in the Burnham Customs district before clearing his main freight, loaded at Rochford. This meant he had to clear twice, once at Burnham and once at Rochford. 'This is the second time this agent has taken on himself to call into question the proceedings of the officers at this port. We allude to Mr Ward's case' observed the Collector. The Customs solicitor ruled there 'were no grounds the law should be dispensed with' and the Board ruled that Meeson's request 'cannot be complied with'.

Other barge owners and skippers showed their impatience by taking the law into their own hands. James Vandervoord, who had been a hoyman for twenty years and so certainly knew what he was doing, sailed in his *Minerva* without clearing in 1839. James Murrell loaded oil cake in the *Unity* and sailed for London in 1850. The Collector urged that an example be made of such lawlessness, and the *Unity* was actually rummaged in the vain hope of finding some other irregularity.

John Howard loaded manure in his *Lapwing* at Wakering and sailed without a 'transire' or clearance permit, becoming liable to a £50 penalty. 'He takes no notice of our Commission,' complained the Collector, 'but began loading a cargo of hay for London. The latter will not require coastal documents but is subject to light dues etc. The mate of the *Lapwing* thinks so long as he gives in his half-yearly returns it is quite sufficient.' The following year (1852) James Phillips of Bradwell, owner of a little six-ton sloop, complained at having to clear every quarter of corn he took up to Maldon, though both places were in the same port.

At last the tide had turned – or perhaps it would be truer to say the Canutes in the Custom House could no longer stand against it. Their long domination of the national economy, involving a despotic control over merchants and mariners, was at an end. As the nineteenth century gave way to the twentieth, the Customs & Excise, finally united after a century's bickering, were to face a new war against a new breed of smuggler, exploiting the craving for drugs or the despair of West Indian immigrants, as well as pouncing on an occasional bungling amateur yachtsman or cruise passenger motivated by a supposedly romantic tradition as much as by the hope of some quick swindled savings. They were to find new powers in the exaction of Purchase Tax and VAT, not to mention duties on those old milch-cows, spirits and tobacco, at a level reminiscent of the duties that had formerly proved unbearable and unworkable. But from now on it was to be the Inland Revenue's turn to assume the role of public enemy number one in the eyes of commerce and its customers.

A story which opens with a chapter of drama and violence closed in an anti-climax of petty bureaucratic peccadiloes. It was, we have seen, far from the romance which has been dreamed up by subsequent sentimentalists. But it remains a story not without its interest and attraction, its humour and pathos, its dignity and absurdity, above all as a wonderfully vivid illustration of the way human beings will behave and react in the face of economic and social pressures. Since human nature does not change, it thus contains its lessons, which are not confined to one brief period or one small corner of the coast of England.

The Workings of a Customs Outport

The Collector and the Comptroller were the chief officers, jointly signing letters. Originally the Comptroller was the senior, but over the centuries the order of precedence came to be reversed, leaving the Collector in charge, with the Comptroller providing an independent check and a dual responsibility as a safeguard against error or corruption.

The Landing Surveyor, the next senior rank, supervised the Landing Waiters in examining imported goods.

The Tide Surveyor supervised the Tide Waiters, or Tidesmen, in boarding and rummaging.

The Coast Waiter was responsible for collection of duties in the coasting trade.

The Riding Officers, under their Superintendent, were employed on patrols ashore.

The Coal Meter measured and weighed coal for the charging of Customs duty.

The Water Guard (developed as the Preventive Waterguard in 1809) comprised craft of two kinds.

Revenue cutters (usually referred to as cruisers, sloops or smacks) were under commanders (who sometimes had an interest in them as contractors), and mates (who in practice were often in command in the absence ashore of the Commander-Contractor). The crew included a few Deputed Mariners, who had deputed powers to board suspected vessels and make seizures.

Boats, both pulling and sailing, were under a Sitter, who controlled established Boatmen (who were on the strength) and Glut Boatmen (who were casually employed).

With the development in 1822 of the Preventive Waterguard into the Coastguard, stationary Watch Vessels with cruising tenders took over many of the Waterguard duties. Boat controls became increasingly important, with Commissioned Boatmen in charge. The boatmen were also required to patrol on foot, taking over some of the responsibilities of the Riding Officers, who were renamed The Mounted Guard.

A Cocket (derived from the Latin *quo quietus est*) and a Transire (also Latin) were clearance documents.

An anker was a measure of spirits, roughly seven-and-a-half gallons; the more convenient and usual half-anker, or tub, held three-and-a-half to four gallons.

Creepers were grapnels, and creeping was the process of towing such grapnels over the sea bed to secure sunken contraband.

The Revenue officer's hanger was a short sword; his tuck was a long, skewer-like blade. ·

An owler (a term obsolete by the time of 'the smugglers' century') was an export wool smuggler.

Letters of Marque were a Government commission issued to a privately owned vessel (privateer) to wage war on enemy ships.

Chief Boatman's Jacket
1829

Chief Officer's Hat
1829

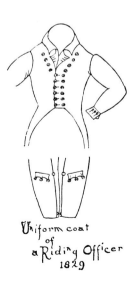

Uniform coat of a Riding Officer
1829

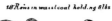

18 Rows in waistcoat holding 8 lbs

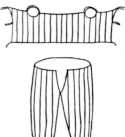

Drawers stuffed with 18 lbs of Tea

METHODS OF SMUGGLING TEA.—II.

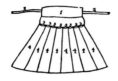

1 Collar   2 Tiers
3 Mouths of Pockets   4 Pockets of Tea

METHODS OF SMUGGLING TEA.—I.

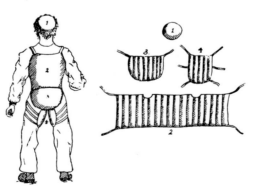

METHODS OF SMUGGLING TEA.—III.

1, Cotton bag to fit crown of hat ; 2, Cotton stays or waistcoat ; 3, Bustle for lower part of back ; 4, Thigh pieces. N.B.—The whole contained 30 lbs of tea.

Footnotes

CHAPTER 1

1. An undated cutting pasted in the diary of William Goodwin, a landowner of Earl Soham, Suffolk. At Ardleigh Chaplin was referred to as 'Robert.' Thus the reference may not be to the same smuggler, but contemporary reports were not particular as to such details; for example William Sextroh, also referred to in Chapter 2, appears as Sextro and Sestroy, and is sometimes called a Frenchman and sometimes a Dutchman. I also suspect that 'Isaac Siggers' was in fact the Isaac Seggers who died in 1858 aged 85, and that 'Farley Spratlin', Isaac Dagnett's brother-in-law, was a member of the Harwich Sprackling family.

2. *Ipswich Journal*, 24 July 1869.

3. *Napoleon at St. Helena*, by Barry O'Meara, quoted by Shore: *Smuggling Days and Smuggling Ways.*

4. Reproduced in *Once Upon a Tide.*

5. *Life and Behaviour of John Skinner, executed 29 August 1746 for the Murder of Daniel Brett, 23 May 1744, London.* A copy is in Colchester Public Library.

6. Fine Rolls Ed III (quoted by Brown: *History of Bradwell on Sea*), and Calendar of Charter Rolls, 8 April, 1361 (E.R.O.)

CHAPTER 2

1. John Dowsett, 'of Burnham, mariner' also in 1767 sold the thirty-six-ton smack *William and Mary* of Burnham to Thomas Cutter of Colchester for £49. The original conveyance turned up in 1955 during the demolition of a house at Tollesbury, in a cupboard where it had presumably lain for nearly 200 years. It suggests that Dowsett may also have had a legitimate oyster business.

2. A.F.J. Brown: *Essex People, 1750–1900.*

3. See Chapter 9, footnote 4.

CHAPTER 3

1. E.N. Mason: 'Capt Matthew Martin', *Essex Review,* vol XI.

2. According to Mr J. Bensusan Butt, who identifies it as No. 3, High Street, on the corner of Darkhouse Lane, last used as the shipyard office.

3. His opposite number on the South Coast, Warren Lisle is described in 'The Great Anti-Smuggler,' by Graham Smith, *Dorset County Magazine,* 1982. I have not traced any connection with William Lisle, the Colchester Riding Officer mentioned in Chapter 15.

4. The story of the *Repulses* is complicated by a journal kept by William Sandford, a Wivenhoe oyster merchant, recording that one of them was lost with Capt. Stacey, her commander, and all her crew of twenty-seven on 18 February, 1807. This was however the day on which the Yarmouth cutter *Hunter* was lost at Winterton with her commander, Capt. T. Jay, and all her crew. It seems likely that the report of this tragedy reached Wivenhoe in garbled form and it was wrongly believed the local cutter had been lost. The diary is quoted by John Leather in *The Northseamen.*

5. Thomas Phillips was Mayor in 1722 and 1727, and his son, also Thomas, was Master of the sloop *Gloucester*, which brought in a load of Holland duck ordered by His Worship, leaving the Customs in doubt as to whether it had paid duty in London. Another of the clan, William Phillips, a shipwright, charged £24 for work done to the Revenue cutter *Walpole.* Considering this excessive, the Honourable Board deducted £9. Phillips refused to accept the £15 offered and threatened to arrest the Collector. The Board's order not to employ him again was met with the reply that there was no other builder. Yet another member of the family was a Harwich pilot, frequently employed in the Royal yachts. On one occasion, bringing

over George II from the Continent, bad weather made Phillips anxious to land anywhere, and he proposed running to a Scottish port. 'No', replied the Hanoverian King 'I would sooner land in Hell.' The pilot's son, Lieut. Baker Phillips, RN, found himself in 1745 in command of the 44-gun *Anglesea* after her captain was killed in an engagement with the more powerful French warship *L'Apollon*. He proved unequal to the challenge, surrendered his ship, was court-martialled, sentenced to death, and, despite a recommendation to mercy, shot aboard the *Princess Royal* at Spithead.

6. John Clements, shipwright, bought a tenement at St. Clement's, Ipswich (adjacent to the river) in 1709. In a petition of 1716 he is described as a 'foreigner'. He was probably a Harwich man, as in 1731 a James Clements was Mayor there. In 1729 he sold out to Edmund Goodea, who can be claimed as the founder of the great Ipswich shipbuilding industry.

The *Walpole* was given a false keel in 1751, when the labour was charged by the tide. The keel itself cost £2 10s, wages and blocks 10s, staples, spikes and stirrups 35s 8d, and 'Four tides' work, four men at 3s 6d per tide, £2 16s.

7. A Thomas Fidget alias White Eyes is also mentioned among the associates of Will Laud in Cobbold's *History of Margaret Catchpole*. Three years later, in 1755, according to the *Ipswich Journal* and *Bath Advertiser* of 6 December, 'on Tuesday night an outlaw'd smuggler, known by the Name of Young White Eyes, who lately returned from France, where he had been several years, was surprised by a party of Dragoons at a little alehouse near Benacre in Suffolk and taken after a smart engagement, in which he was so terribly wounded that it is thought he cannot recover. There was £500 Reward for apprehending him.' So perhaps John Mill's murderer escaped justice, or perhaps the name passed to a son or junior relative – a common tradition in Essex and Suffolk.

CHAPTER 4

1. Capt. Bridge's sterling qualities did not include the ability to keep a mate. John

Hobday left him after six months, and his successor, James Mason, resigned 'after some difference between him and his Commander' two years later. Two years after this (in 1774) he dismissed his second mate, J. Lewis, who became master of a vessel in the corn trade, the *Garrick*, which brought in new oyster bushels – evidence that the Harwich oyster fishery was then vigorous enough to justify official measures.

The Bridge family of Harwich descended, according to the Essex historian Morant, from John Bridge, who was Lord Mayor of London in 1520 and who settled at West Ham. Around 1580 a Thomas Bridge, alderman of Harwich and churchwarden of St. Nicholas', married a girl named Sara, and their son was the first to be christened Cyprian. Another member of the family was created Lord Chandos by Queen Mary in 1544 (the earlier Peerage of that name having become extinct), and William Bridge, captain of the Royal yacht *Mary*, who was buried at Harwich in 1743, bore the Chandos arms, which are carved on his tombstone.

During the Civil War certain residents were appointed to oversee ecclesiastical areas; the name of Cyprian Bridge (spelled Ciprian) appears in the Essex list for 1648, living at Tendring or Great Oakley, near Harwich. His grandson, also Cyprian, born 1690, lived at Dovercourt, and was grandfather of the commander of the Revenue cutters *Walpole* and *Argus*, who was born in 1738 and died in 1814.

It is not easy to distinguish him from another Cyprian Bridge, who had a doubtful reputation. He was enrolled as a Tidesman and Boatman in the Handfleet Water boat in 1741, and three years later, along with his mates, was in trouble because only seventy-four half-ankers out of a seizure of eighty-one reached the Harwich warehouse. Bridge was one of those found guilty, and, said the Collector, 'We believe very justly, for he is certainly the most idle, lazy, drunken fellow that ever we have had in the port.' Despite this he was employed as a mariner aboard the *Walpole* in 1749, when he was charged with embezzling geneva, but evidently cleared, as soon afterwards he was giving evidence concerning a theft of money by her mates, and signing a plea on behalf of her crew when she was in dispute with the *Princess Mary* over seizure rewards. He was still a Boatman in 1765 and a Tidesman Boatman in 1770.

Can this have been the father of the Commander of the *Argus,* who makes his first appearance as a cabin boy in the packet *Prince of Wales* in 1754 (when he could have been 16)? A passenger gave him half-a-crown to take a parcel ashore, and, finding it contained needlework, the boy wrapped it round his thighs in the most professional smuggling way, but was nevertheless detected. He went to the inn to report his failure to the passenger, who to his credit gave him the half-crown! He was appointed to the command of the *Walpole* in 1770. Yet he was already of sufficient importance to have had his portrait painted by Sir Joshua Reynolds in 1759 (if this date given in Sir Cyprian Bridge's *Recollections,* mentioned below, is to be trusted). He became one of the City Fathers of Harwich, and when he died in 1814, aged 76, he was memorialised as 'Father of the Corporation'.

He married a daughter of Lieut. Baker Phillips RN and had a numerous family, including four sons who had distinguished Army careers. In addition to these, the eldest son, Cyprian, entered the Navy and after serving with Lord Rodney in 1782 was lost at sea in one of the prize ships. Another son, Baker Phillips Bridge, also a midshipman in the Navy, was drowned in a yachting accident. A third son, Walter Sickleprice Bridge, also served in the Navy, which he left during the 'long peace' (1783–1793) to became a merchant, settling on the Continent.

A fourth son, Thomas (1772–1858) joined the East India Company as a midshipman, but then followed his father in the Harwich packet service. An account of his gallantry in getting the mails through to Cuxhaven in the *Prince of Orange* in 1798 will be found in *Once Upon a Tide.* The reminiscences of his grandson, *Some Recollections,* by Admiral Sir Cyprian Bridge, also mention that he received two gold medals from the Senate and the Admiralty of Hamburg, and add that 'at a later period' he was sent on a special mission to take despatches through enemy-occupied Holland into Germany. After being captured by the French he escaped and reached a British man-of-war

at Heligoland. He died in 1858, aged 85, 'for many years Senior Captain of HM Packets.'

His son, Thomas Finch Hobday Bridge (born 1818) was unable to follow the sea, due to bad eyesight, and entered the Church, becoming Chaplain to Admiral Sir Thomas Cochrane, Governor of Newfoundland, and ultimately Archdeacon before dying of cholera in 1856, refusing to leave his flock during an epidemic.

His son returned to the Naval tradition and achieved much distinction as Admiral Sir Cyprian Bridge (1839–1924). While commanding the Hong Kong station just before the Russo-Japanese war he horrified the Admiralty by predicting not only the war but the Russian victory.

Another member of the family, Sir Nigel Cyprian Bridge, was appointed a Lord Justice of Appeal in 1980, taking as his title Baron Bridge of Harwich. His brother, Very Rev. Anthony Cyprian Bridge, is Dean of Guildford Cathedral.

The journal of a Major Cyprian Bridge of the 58th (Rutlandshire Regiment), dealing with the Maori wars in New Zealand in the 1840, was published in 1879 as *To Face the Daring Maoris* by Michael Bartop.

2. A mainsail for the *Bee* in 1775 used 310 yards of Hollands duck at 2s 6d a yard, total cost £38 15s. Her running rigging was: jib halyards and runners 32 fathoms 4-inch rope; jib tack, 14 fathoms 6-inch; main halyard 24 fathoms 3½-inch; gaff halyard 24 fathoms 3½-inch; tackle falls, a 'quoil' of 3½-inch; jib sheets 14 fathoms 3½-inch. This would make sense to a modern 'old gaffer' with the exception of the huge jib tack. Presumably the jib was tacked down by a heavy rope led through a bowsprit sheave to the windlass – an arrangement which would also explain why the jib halyards were heavier than those for the mainsail.

J Wigner quoted in 1827 for the following suit of sails for the *Maria.* Main: 199 yards bleached Number 0 Double Coker canvas at 2s 4d, £23 4s 4d. Foresail: 38 yards ditto £4 8s 8d. Jib: 64 yards Number 1A Single Coker canvas, grass bleached, £6 8s. Gaff topsail: 56 yards Number 4 best Coker grass bleached £5 2s 8d. The Board pointed out that as the *Maria* was only 27 tons she could not have Number 0 Double

Coker canvas which was only for large cutters. Yet in July 1829 Wigner again quoted for Double Coker canvas, 'same sort as the present ones are made, with not so close-made canvas'

CHAPTER 6

1. A.F.J. Brown: *Essex People, 1750–1900*

2. Being a condemned smuggler, this *Rose in June* was not, I think, the same vessel as a cruiser of that name which in 1791 failed to make any seizures while employed between Orford and the South Foreland, for the reason that 'most smugglers are laid up on account of the great advance on spirits in France.' This most beautiful of names was popular for smacks at this period. A *Rose in June* of thirteen tons was sold at Brightlingsea in 1837 and a larger Maldon cutter of thirty-four tons at Burnham in 1840. Other characterful names, in addition to those mentioned in the text, include *Dark Lanthorn, Mince Pie, Green Lettuce, Wig Box, Gold Watch, Night Rambler, Ink Bottle, Pestle and Mortar, Mo and Mary, Rhino, Tub,* and *Jew.*

CHAPTER 9

1. Seizures of craft, for an infringement of a licence as often as for participation, real or suspected, in smuggling, reached a peak at the end of the eighteenth century and the beginning of the nineteenth. The following details are in addition to seizures mentioned in the text. Many were not mentioned in the Collector's letters but are from the vessel's register, where they are noted, sometimes in red ink, like endorsements on a driving licence. In some cases the two sources supply different details; where this occurs both are quoted. Capt George Munnings and the *Repulse* reaped this harvest: 1785, the 33-ton *Essex,* owned by James Root of Brightlingsea; 1787, the 27-ft smack *Gnat,* owned by William Harlow of Wivenhoe; 1790, the 36-ft. sloop *Fearnot,* owned by B. Fairhead of Wivenhoe (built at Southampton 1785); 1793, the 39-ft. cutter *Friendship,* owned by Evangelist Bloomfield of Wivenhoe (built at Dover,

1785 or at Brightlingsea, 1791); 1794 the *Hazard* of Harwich, and the 41-ton square-stern smack *Ox,* owned by Thomas Jessop (built by Cole at E. Donyland, 1793); 1800, the 14-ton *John & Sarah,* owned by J. Bunn of Brightlingsea (built at Wivenhoe 1765), and the 22-ton *Neptune,* owned by Isaiah Bloomfield (built at E. Donyland 1770, or Wivenhoe 1765), both off Walton Naze in April, and the 27-ft. yawl *Friends* (owned and built by J. Cole, East Donyland, 1799.) See also Chapter 14, footnote 1.

2. See *The Salvagers.*

3. Probably the snow *Sunbury* of Liverpool, 327 tons, built in New Brunswick in 1826. According to *Lloyd's Register* for 1835 she was then owned by E. Hall, W. Hinde Master, and on a voyage from Liverpool to Quebec. The same Register also includes a *Sunbury* of Yarmouth, 108 tons, J. Abbott Master, but without details of ownership, rig or building date.

4. George Munnings's christian names suggest an inter-marriage between his family and that of John Huske (1724–1773), MP of Maldon, 1763–1773, but of that there is no evidence. He must, however, have been related to Benjamin Agnis Munnings and Robert Sayer Munnings, merchants of Wivenhoe, who in 1800 bought a foreign dogger which had been a war prize, and registered her at Colchester as the *Thornton.* Five years later George Munnings became part owner with Robert in the *Fox,* a Dutch schuyt also picked up among the fortunes of war. Robert also owned another war prize, the 75-ton schooner *Nile* of Colchester which was lost off Flamborough Head in 1799. He then in 1800 bought the former Burnham smack *Neptune* (built there in 1797 and owned by William Richmond) after she had been seized and condemned for smuggling. Benjamin was in 1791 owner and master of the *Sally,* a 67-ton ex-Dutch galliot, registered at Colchester in 1796. In 1781 a warrant was issued to prosecute a Charles Munnings following the seizure of contraband at his house, but whether he was any connection is not revealed.

5. See also E. E. Wilde: *Ingatestone and the Essex Great Road*

6. The Vice-Admiralty of Essex, referred to in connection with those two nineteenth century scallywags, Daniel Sutton and Charles Bull, was an ancient office having its origins in the 'Admirals' appointed in the thirteenth century with particular responsibilities for 'piracy' – a misleading description of civil disputes and actions to restore wrecked ships and their cargoes. An 'Admiral' tried a case over the alleged obstruction of a navigable creek near Colchester in 1346, and in 1442 the Duke of Exeter as Lord Admiral appointed a Lieutenant or Commissary for Norfolk, Suffolk and Essex.

The system of Courts was established in the time of Henry VIII. In 1606 the Earl of Suffolk granted powers to hold Admiralty courts in certain manors in Essex, and to appoint a Vice-Admiral and Commissary for that purpose. Since the prime concern of the Admirals was to collect dues and perquisites under their patents, they were the enemy of private salvagers, while mariners faced with shipwreck, it was said, 'had rather trust God with their souls than the Admirals with their goods'. In the seventeenth century, however, private salvagers established the right to sue against Admirals and owners.

After County Lieutenants were established in the 16th century it became the custom for the two offices to be held by the same man, the last Lord Lieutenant of Essex to hold the title of Vice-Admiral being Lord Dacre, who resigned in 1869. The fourth Earl of Rochester, whose awkwardness deprived the Handfleet Water officers of their watch-house in 1754, had his seat at St Osyth Priory, but his estate extended to Thorpe-le-Soken. He had been appointed Vice-Admiral of the coast of Essex in 1729 at the age of 20, twenty-seven years before he was constituted Lord Lieutenant of the County in 1756. Thus the two appointments had not at this time fully coalesced.

In 1761 some salvaged casks of oil were brought into Harwich by a cutter belonging to one John Hines, whom Lord Rochford had appointed as his deputy as Vice-Admiral. Hines (who was presumably the troublesome Deputy Postmaster referred to in Chapter 11) refused to deliver up the salvage, and Lord Rochford complained of a breach of privilege. The Collector observed that 'by his taking powers to take into his custody goods from stranded ships, here is a wide door left open for great frauds . . .' He asked for instructions 'in case anything of this nature (in respect to the Vice-Admiralty of the County) should happen in future, which is very likely to happen'.

The Letters Patent conferring the title of Vice-Admiral granted powers over seas, creeks and rivers 'below first bridges', covering 'suits, crimes, offences and misdemeanours' and 'traitors, pirates and manslayers', down to the more mundane duty 'to reform nets too close and other unlawful engines and instruments for the catching of fishes'.

By the 1820s, and the exploits of Daniel Sutton, it was the custom for the Vice-Admiral to assign all these rights and duties to the Clerk of the Peace, who appointed agents for the outports. But in practice about the only surviving responsibility by this time was some disposal of salvage, and this was trivial enough. The Southend agent, Robert Jemson, only disposed of six anchors and one small boat between April 1844 and May 1845. A sale there in 1847 realised £75, of which the Vice-Admiralty received £25 after payment of £25 to salvors and various other expenses.

Nevertheless, there seem still to have been sufficient perks to make the agencies attractive, for in 1848 the father of the Burnham Landing and Tide Surveyor (Elias Lawrence) wrote to the Clerk of the Peace asking for his son's appointment 'instead of an agent appointed by the Vice-Admiral'. This shows that a Customs officer was allowed to accept an agency, but it is also perplexing, for the Clerk of the Peace was, effectively, the Vice-Admiral. The explanation is probably to be found in Jemson's Southend accounts, for he credited the nett proceeds of his sale to 'the Deputy Vice-Admiral'. It would thus seem that some individuals, including Hines and Sutton, worked themselves into the system, taking this title as intermediaries between the Clerk of the Peace and the outport agents, though the powers which entitled Sutton to detain the collier *Jane* at Burnham remain obscure.

It was, in any case, of no concern to Lawrence, for the answer to his father's application was that under the Wreck and

Salvage Act Vice-Admirals were no longer 'to interfere in wrecks'. Thus, after the English fashion, a long tradition finally flickered and was snuffed out.

CHAPTER 10

1. Joyce: *History of the Post Office* (1893).

2. See *Once Upon a Tide*

3. For details of the cod smacks see *The Codbangers*.

CHAPTER 11

1. A Harwich report on the salt duties shows that in 1730 there were 'only two offices belonging to this port, the one at Manningtree which refines Rock, and the other at New Mill which Boile it from the Salt Water'.

2. The Maldon Collector and Comptroller applied for exemption from Militia service in 1803. The Deputy Lieutenants rejected their application, but exempted their boat-men as seafaring men.

3. The Debneys were a notorious smuggling family at Sizewell. For an account of Robert Debney's suffocation in a smug-glers' hide in 1778, and other stories of him, his brother 'Nosey' Debney and their gang, see Chandler: *Smuggling at Sizewell Gap* and Thompson: *Smugglers of the Suffolk Coast.*

CHAPTER 13

1. White: *History, Gazetteer and Directory of the County of Essex,* 1848 and 1863.

2. The 'head money' rewards earned by Revenue cutters for men sent to the Navy are referred to in Chapter 8; the issue of protection certificates for the *Courier* and the use of the *Repulse* for pressing in Chapter 9.
The impressment system also affected the Revenue service in several other ways. The Navy grumbled about the protection certificates issued by the Harwich Collector, saying they were sometimes taken by deserters from the *Walpole.* But Capt Dagnett replied that he had impressed twenty men in three nights, and that aboard the *Walpole* dismissal meant summary transfer to the nearest man-of-war, often in the cutter's own boat. As a result desertions tended to occur when the cutters were at Deptford for a re-fit.

Embargoes on sailing were imposed (e.g. in July 1779 and September 1798) to 'freeze' shipping for the benefit of the press gangs. When after one or more days ships were allowed to sail again, officers had to ensure they carried no more men than necessary. It is not clear whether the limitation on crews referred to in Chapter 12 was for this purpose or to prevent smuggling craft outmanning the Revenue cutter crews. An 'embargo warrant' was served in 1739 on the *Diamond,* berthed at Colchester, requiring her to provide a seaman for the Navy.

Foreigners seem to have been impressed, as well as imprisoned, if caught within territorial waters, despite their protests. When Thomas Holman was picked up by the *Walpole* in 1760 after landing six gallons of geneva near Aldeburgh from a boat called *L'Amatie,* and sent to a sloop of war, his father produced an ingenious defence. He said his son was a native of the United Provinces and resident at Flushing where he had a Sea Brief from the States. He had been at sea off Flushing looking for a ship to pilot when *L'Amatie* was forced by a gale on to the English coast. The Collector said he was an old offender and 'as to the Burger Briefs (as they call them) the Smugglers lend them to one another and make use of them occasionally to protect them from being impressed into HM Sea Service'. While the press gang did not have freedom to raid the prisons, Lieut Firth of the impress service at Wivenhoe was in 1782 allowed to recruit three smugglers who were pris-oners in Chelmsford Goal – presumably by their choice.

3. Thomas Withey was at West Mersea between 1809 and 1836, building at least eleven vessels, including the fifty-six-ton smack *Essex* in 1831. He owned two of the smacks he built, *Harriot* (19 tons) and *Nancy* (21 tons). Most of his craft were carvel built, though his last smack, the

seven-ton *March* in 1831, was clinker planked.

4. See *Once Upon a Tide.*

CHAPTER 14

1. Seizures by Capt. Munnings and the *Repulse* are set out in a footnote to Chapter 9.

In addition to these the Gravesend cutter *Ant*, under her mate John Dozell, in 1794 seized the 39-ton *Juno* owned by James Root of Brightlingsea (built at Brightlingsea 1791).

Seizures by Excise cutters (probably those at Bradwell) included: 1783, the 30-ft *Mayflower* of West Mersea, skipper-owner Lionel Jessop, who was also ship's carpenter for Philip Sainty (built at Gravesend, 1761), seized by 'the officer of the Bradwell Excise cutter'; 1786, the 35-ton cutter *Mary Bush*, owned by Thomas Warford of East Donyland (built at Burnham 1784), seized by Capt Henvill of the *Lily*; 1791, the 11-ton *Endeavour*, owned by Charles Vine of Maldon, and sold at Bradwell, and the 14-ton square-stern yawl *Rambler*, owned by W. Hatch of Paglesham (built at Margate 1780), both seized by Robert Adams of the *Wasp*; 1797, the 12-ton *Hope* of Maldon, 'formerly a French privateer,' seized by the *Viper*.

Unspecified seizures include: 1787, the *Bowl* of Maldon, owned by R. Farrance of Burnham (built at Maldon 1767); 1790, the 28-ft *Friends Goodwill*, owned by Ambrose Death of Brightlingsea (built at Gravesend, 1750), the eight-ton *Fly*, based at Burnham, where she had just been rebuilt, and the 11-ton *Happy Return*, based at Paglesham (built at Gravesend, 1762); 1791, the 11-ton *Bee* of Maldon (registered at Sandwich 1794), and the 16-ton *Leigh Roads* (built at Southend, 1777); 1792, the *Lapwing*, owned at Burnham by her builder in 1787, William Bayley, but condemned and sold in London; 1793, the 14-ton *Dove* of Maldon (built at Burnham, 1788); 1800, the 13-ton yawl *Achilles* of Maldon (built at Margate 1791), sold to William Parrish of Wivenhoe, and the 21-ton *Tryal* of Colchester, rebuilt at Rowhedge in 1795 and 'sold to a person at Orford'; 1803, the

12-ton yawl *Good Intent*, owned by John Pittuck of Wivenhoe (built at Southwold, 1786); 1805, the 7-ton *Nancy* of Maldon, converted from open boat into yawl by J. Basson, 1802.

During the same period Colchester craft lost to the enemy included the 29-ton smack *Swallow*, owned by J. Rivers of Clacton (built at Burnham, 1777), taken in 1793, 'master returned the May following'; the 113-ton brigantine *Endeavour* (built at Hull, 1790), taken by the enemy and sunk according to the testimony of John Death master, and Joseph Blyth, mariner, 'the other part of the crew being confined in prison in France'; the 26-ton smack *Betsey* (built at Queenborough, 1788), taken in 1793, her master (Edward Leverick of Brightlingsea) returned in 1795; the 16-ton smack *Active* of Brightlingsea (built there, 1794), taken in 1798, 'master returned same month'; the 40-ton sloop *Francis*, owned by Josiah Bloomfield of Wivenhoe (built at Whitby, 1771), taken in 1795, her master, Evangelist Bloomfield (whose smack *Friendship* had been seized by the *Repulse* in 1793) returned the same year; the 50-ton sloop *Vine* (built near Leeds, 1792), taken in 1800.

Harwich vessels destroyed by the enemy included *Shadwell* and *Friends Adventure*, both in 1786, and *John and Susannah* in 1791. The *Shadwell* had been seized in 1773 with brandy and geneva from Dunkirk.

2. This was John Lewis's *Queen*, see *The Salvagers*

3. See *The Stowboaters.*

4. See *The Salvagers.*

CHAPTER 16

1. Shore: *Smuggling Days and Smuggling Ways*, quoting from the *Mutiny at Spithead and the Nore*.

2. Twelfth Report of the Lords Commissioners of the Treasury (1822).

CHAPTER 18

1. Walker: 'Martello Towers and the

Defence of N.E. Essex in the Napoleonic War', *Essex Review,* vol. X/VII.

2. Though Essex shipwrights built a number of boats for the Customs, when Durden of Maldon in 1820 quoted £27 for a twenty-seven foot, four-oar, copper-fastened boat, the Maldon Collector recommended getting a quotation from Deal, observing the 'Shipwrights here are unable to build boats for the Preventive service at the prices charged in Kent, where it is their sole employ.' Customs boats in the eighteenth century were rigged with spritsail and jib. Lug sails are not mentioned till the nineteenth century. A six-oar galley needed two pairs of eighteen-foot oars, and two pairs of seventeen feet.

CHAPTER 19

1. A manufactory of tobacco and snuff was established at Tollesbury in 1769 by two Londoners, Richard White and Samuel Gibbard. They received their tobacco stalks both overland and coastwise from Rochester, to the annoyance of the Maldon Collector, for each clearance involved an officer in a nine – mile walk. Whether its remoteness was the reason for choosing Tollesbury is not clear, nor is it known how long the venture lasted.

CHAPTER 21

1. See Chapter 9, footnote 4.

CHAPTER 22

1. See *The Big Barges.*

CHAPTER 23

1. A century and a half later, in 1984, the same landing place at North Fambridge (which cannot have changed much in the meantime) was chosen for one of the biggest drug-smuggling runs ever attempted. The schooner yacht *Robert Gordon* was seized with four and a half tons of cannabis resin, worth £10.8m, the largest seizure of its kind in Western Europe. Five men were gaoled for terms of up to ten years.

CHAPTER 24

1. Recorded in The *Nautical Magazine,* 1902.

2. The reminiscences of a Customs Officer stationed at Colchester include this story (quoted by John Leather in *The Northseamen*), but refer to Sainty's partner-turned-informer as Brown, a whipmaker by trade who took a public house in Barrack Street. The Colchester Arms was in fact in Magdalen Street. It would seem that this officer's memory was faulty, for which reason one need not take too seriously his statement that Sainty's *Ruswarp* had false sides, nor one or two other picturesque details.

3. See *Last Stronghold of Sail.*

CHAPTER 25

1. See *The Salvagers.*

CHAPTER 26

1. Bawtree and Savill's Colchester Distillery, converted from an oil and corn mill in 1812, produced over 40,000 gallons of gin annually.

CHAPTER 27

1. See *Some Essex Water Mills.*

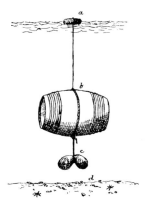

As well as being sunk, tubs were sometimes set adrift at the mouth of a river or creek at low water, and allowed to find their own way to some point where a watcher was on the lookout for them.

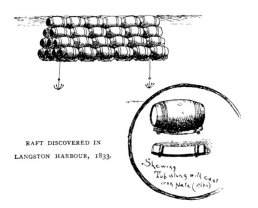

RAFT DISCOVERED IN
LANGSTON HARBOUR, 1833.

Shewing
Tub slung with cast
iron Nate (olby)

Not content with drifting single tubs on the tide, smugglers in Langston Harbour in 1833 constructed this raft of 63 tubs. It drew seven feet of water, and was fitted with two small grapnels, perhaps to pick up a sweepline set for the purpose.

205

Index of Ships' Names

Rc indicates Revenue cutter (including tenders and vessels temporarily commissioned); Sm indicates smack; lr indicates lugger; sb indicates sailing barge; wv indicates watch vessel.

Index of Personal Names

Adams, Capt, 142
Anderson, J., 60
Anglesey, Marquis of, 12, 176

Bacon family, 112, 123
Baggott, T., 45, 88
Baker, S., 176
Ballanger, A., 118
Banks, W. S., 112
Bareham, W., 130
Batten, Capt J., 51, 63, 70
Bayley, G., 112
Bennewith, T. H., 148
Bentley, J., 49
Billingsley, S., 143
Bloomfield family, 85, 172, 182
Blythe D., 155
Bones, C., 109
Boyce, R., 174
Brand, J., 85
Brett, D., 21
Brett, R., 31
Bridge family, 12, 52, 53, 54, 56, 169, 170, 198
Brockman, W., 73
Brotherton, E., 32, 107
Bugg, W., 9
Bull, A., 81
Bull, C., 160 et seq
Bury, J., 43
Busbridge, E., 10

Cackett, B., 114
Caley, Capt., 53–4
Carbold, E., 117
Carr, Lieut, RN, 185
Catchpole, E., 72
Chaplin, R., 16
Clement, Capt, 44
Clements, J., 44, 118
Coates, 189
Cock, H., 58
Cole, D., 112
Coleman, J., 90
Collis, T., 65
Constable, G., 12
Cook family, 111, 129
Cotgrove, C., 186
Cottee, J., 111
Cowing, C., 106
Criswick, J., 155
Cross, T., 20
Crowder, W., 55
Crush & Co., 165

Dagnett, I., 49 et seq, 51–3, 77, 91, 141
Davies G. & H.P., 7, 54, 70, 88, 119
Deane, Capt J., 92, 174

Deane, W., 71
Death, J., 157, 187
Debney, R., 106
Dekker, I., 47 et seq
Dines, I., 26, 27
Disborough, A., 34
Dobbins, T., 146
Dodds, R., 172–3
Dove, J., 160
Dowsett family, 25, 26, 59, 60
Doyley, H., 24, 27
Dudley, Rev. B., 140
Duke, E., 101
Durden, T., 152, 177

Eastee, R., 91
Ellingford, S., 111
Emberson, 25, 26

Fidgett, T., 47
Fitch, I., 22
Forster, J., 176
Freeman, S., 49
Frost, J., 61
Frost, M., 12

Gane, M., 127
Gilham, T., 73
Glading, J. & C., 154, 181
Goodwin, W., 113
Gunthorpe, Capt M., 79
Gurr, J., 8
Gurton, J., 163
Guy, R., 177

Haggis, J. B., 96
Haggis, W., 60, 63
Hallum, J., 27
Hammond, Capt T., 93
Hanchett, Capt RN, 136
Harlow, J., 69
Harriott, J., 26
Hart, Capt E., 56 et seq, 62
Hart, S. G., 111
Harvey, Capt D., 37, 77
Harvey, J. Martin, 37
Heard, J., 109
Henniker, Maj-Gen, 160
Hiblett, J., 52
Hinde, M., 103
Hines, R. & J., 102
Hitchcock, J., 72
Hobday, J., 53
Holdee, J., 105
Holland, Lord, 15
Hopkins, M., 69
Howorth, R., 140
Hudson, Capt, 33

Index of Subjects and Places

Villages are in Essex unless otherwise indicated.

The sinking stones were always bent on, and kept on deck till just before slipping.